The TV Almanac

The TV Almanac

Louis Phillips & Burnham Holmes

Macmillan·USA

MACMILLAN
A Prentice Hall Macmillan Company
15 Columbus Circle
New York, NY 10023

Library of Congress Cataloging-in-Publication Data

Phillips, Louis.
     The TV almanac / Louis Phillips and Burnham Holmes.
          p.   cm.
     Includes bibliographical references and index.
     ISBN 0-671-88798-X :
     1. Television programs—United States—Miscellanea.   I.
Holmes,
     Burnham, 1942–   .   II. Title.
     PN1992.9.P45   1994
     791.45—dc20   94-14094
                                                            CIP

Designed by Richard Oriolo

Manufactured in the United States of America

10 9 8 7 6 5 4 3 2 1

For Nelson, Dana, and Alex Breen (LP)
and for Frank Ashe, Joel Pliner, and Ken, who
have joined me in front of the set (BH)

George: What do you think of television?

Gracie: I think it's wonderful—I hardly ever watch radio anymore.

—*The George Burns and Gracie Allen Show*

"This instrument can teach, it can illuminate; yes, it can even inspire. But it can do so only to the extent that humans are determined to use it to those ends. Otherwise, it is merely lights and wires in a box."

—*Edward R. Murrow, broadcaster*

Acknowledgments

A book of this nature (whatever nature it is) requires the help of numerous individuals. The authors would like to extend their deep appreciation to Ivy Fischer-Stone, to Casey Schulberg and Mark Musicus of RHI Entertainment, to Kirk Browning, to Nelson Breen, to Lenny Gibson for his insights into the future of television, to Hugo Jimenez and the School of Visual Arts Writing Center, to Jonathan Sternberg and Beth Bressan of CBS, Inc., and most of all, to our around-the-clock editor Deirdre Mullane for making sense of it all.

Contents

Opening Lines of Classic TV Shows

"Good e-e-evening."

—*Alfred Hitchcock Presents*

"Hello, I'm Mr. Ed."

—*Mister Ed*

"And now here he is, the one, the only . . . GROUCHO!"

—*You Bet Your Life*

"Can two divorced men share an apartment without driving each other crazy?"

—*The Odd Couple*

"Ladies and gentlemen, the story you are about to see is true. Only the names have been changed to protect the innocent."

—*Dragnet*

"Extraordinary crimes against the people and the state have to be avenged by agents extraordinary. Two such people are John Steed, top professional, and Emma Peel, talented amateur . . . otherwise known as . . . The Avengers."

—*The Avengers*

"Space. The final frontier. These are the voyages of the Starship *Enterprise*. Its five-year mission, to explore strange new worlds. To seek out new life and new civilizations. To boldly go where no man has gone before."

—*Star Trek*

"The happy gang of Buster Brown is on the air.
The happy gang of Buster Brown is on the air.
We'll laugh and frolic and sing and play,
C'mon, you buddies, and shout 'Hurray!'
Buster Brown is on the air."
(sung to the tune of "Mademoiselle from Armentieres")

—*Buster Brown's Gang*

"Space Academy, U.S.A., in the world beyond tomorrow. Here the space cadets train for duty on distant planets. In roaring rockets they blast through the millions of miles from Earth to far-flung stars and brave the dangers of cosmic frontiers, protecting the liberties of the planets, safeguarding the cause of universal peace in the age of the conquest of space."

—*Tom Corbett, Space Cadet*

"Sunset Strip is a body of county territory entirely surrounded by the city of Los Angeles, a mile and a half of relentlessly contemporary architecture housing restaurants, bistros, Hollywood agents, and shops where the sell is as soft as a snowflake and just as cold."

—*77 Sunset Strip*

"Here we are,
Back with you again.
Yes, by gun, and yes, by golly,
Kukla, Fran and dear old Ollie."

—*Kukla, Fran & Ollie*

ANNOUNCER: [*Sounds of Morse code signals over Wagner's* Flying Dutchman] P-O-S-T . . . P-O-S-T . . . the cereals you like the most! The cereals made by Post . . . take you to the secret mountain retreat of . . . *Captain Video! Master of Space! Hero of Science! Captain of the Video Rangers!* Op-

erating from his secret mountain headquarters on the planet Earth, Captain Video rallies men of good will and leads them against the forces of evil everywhere! As he rockets from planet to planet, let us follow the champion of justice, truth and freedom throughout the universe! Stand by for . . . *Captain Video . . . and his Video Rangers!*
—*Captain Video and His Video Rangers*

"Faster than a speeding bullet! More powerful than a locomotive! Able to leap tall buildings at a single bound. . . . Superman . . . strange visitor from another planet who came to Earth with powers and abilities far beyond those of mortal men! Superman, who can change the course of mighty rivers, bend steel in his bare hands, and who—disguised as Clark Kent, mild-mannered reporter for a great metropolitan newspaper—fights a never-ending battle for truth, justice, and the American way!"
—*Superman*

"There is nothing wrong with your television set. Do not attempt to adjust the picture. We are controlling transmission. We will control the horizontal, we will control the vertical. For the next hour, sit quietly and we will control all you see and hear. You are about to experience the awe and mystery that leads you from the inner mind to . . . *The Outer Limits.*"
—*The Outer Limits*

"There is a fifth dimension beyond that which is known to man. It is a dimension as vast as space and as timeless as infinity. It is the middle ground between light and shadow, between science and superstition, and it lies between the pit of man's fears and the summit of his knowledge. This is the dimension of imagination. It is an area we call *The Twilight Zone.*"
—*The Twilight Zone*

Inside Television

Viewing Habits

The Number of TV Sets

More TVs were sold in the United States in a shorter period of time than was any previous invention. In 1946, there were a scant 7,000 seven-inch TV sets plugged in around the United States. As the screen size grew, so did the audience. In 1947, the total number of TV sets had increased to 178,000; 1 year later, it was up to 975,000. In 1949, there were 3 million TV sets; and in 1950, more than 15 million sets were casting their eerie glow. By 1992, there were more than 92 million homes with sets. Approximately 60 million homes had 2 or more sets; and less than 2 million homes had only black-and-white sets. Amazingly, more than 56 million homes with TV also had cable. The rise of TV was not confined to the U.S. In 1992, there were 900 million TV sets worldwide.

Before the introduction of television, 63% of Americans were asleep by midnight.

4

The Average Number of Hours Spent Watching TV

In 1991, the average household spent 6 hours and 56 minutes watching television each day. (In February, the average was 7 hours and 30 minutes; in July, it was 6 hours and 26 minutes.)

Hours Watched? Well, It Depends on Age and Sex

According to the Nielsen Media Research from 1992, children aged 2 to 5 watch an average of slightly more than 26 hours a week; children 6 to 11 years average slightly more than 21 hours. Teenagers watch around 22 hours, with boys watching somewhat more TV than girls. This gap increases for 18- to 24-year-olds, with men averaging about 23 hours and women, almost 19 hours. But older women watch more TV.

Women aged 25 to 54 watch an average of 32 hours a week; men in the same bracket watch 28 hours. Women 55 and older spend an average of 43.5 hours in front of the boob tube; their male counterparts, slightly less than 40 hours.

"By the time the average American child reaches the age of 5, he or she will have spent more than 4,000 hours in front of the TV. Absorbing the good, the bad, and the frightening."

—*advertisement for public television, 1993*

The 36 Highest-rated Television Shows of All Time

*O*n February 28, 1983, the final episode of *M*A*S*H* was watched by more viewers than any other television episode in history. Approximately 50,150,000 households tuned in. Here is a list of the 35 top-rated shows of all time.

All-Time Top Television Programs

Rank	Program	Telecast Date	Network	Rating (%)	Households (in thousands)
1.	*M*A*S*H* (last episode)	2/28/83	CBS	60.2	50,150
2.	*Dallas* ("Who Shot J. R.?")	11/21/80	CBS	53.3	41,470
3.	*Roots* (Part 8)	1/30/77	ABC	51.1	36,380
4.	Super Bowl XVI	1/24/82	CBS	49.1	40,020
5.	Super Bowl XVII	1/30/83	NBC	48.6	40,480
6.	Winter Olympics '94	2/23/94	CBS	48.5	45,690
7.	*Gone With the Wind* (Part 1)	11/7/76	NBC	47.7	33,960
8.	Super Bowl XX	1/26/86	NBC	48.3	41,490
9.	*Gone With the Wind* (Part 2)	11/8/76	NBC	47.4	33,750

Rank	Program	Telecast Date	Network	Rating (%)	Households (in thousands)
10.	Super Bowl XII	1/15/78	CBS	47.2	34,410
11.	Super Bowl XIII	1/21/79	NBC	47.1	35,090
12.	Bob Hope Christmas Show	1/15/70	NBC	46.6	27,260
13.	Super Bowl XVIII	1/22/84	CBS	46.4	38,800
14.	Super Bowl XIX	1/20/85	ABC	46.4	39,390
15.	Super Bowl XIV	1/20/80	CBS	46.3	35,330
16.	ABC Theater (*The Day After*)	11/20/83	ABC	46.0	38,550
17.	*Roots* (Part 6)	1/28/77	ABC	45.9	32,680
18.	*The Fugitive*	8/29/67	ABC	45.9	25,700
19.	Super Bowl XXI	1/25/87	CBS	45.8	40,030
20.	*Roots* (Part 5)	1/27/77	ABC	45.7	32,540
21.	*Cheers* (last episode)	5/20/93	NBC	45.5	42,360
22.	*The Ed Sullivan Show*	2/9/64	CBS	45.3	23,240
23.	Super Bowl XXVII	1/31/93	NBC	45.1	41,990
24.	Bob Hope Christmas Show	1/14/71	NBC	45.0	27,050
25.	*Roots* (Part 3)	1/25/77	ABC	44.8	31,900
26.	Super Bowl XI	1/9/77	NBC	44.4	31,610

Rank	Program	Telecast Date	Network	Rating (%)	Households (in thousands)
27.	Super Bowl XV	1/25/81	NBC	44.4	34,540
28.	Super Bowl VI	1/6/72	CBS	44.2	27,450
29.	*Roots* (Part 2)	1/24/77	ABC	44.1	31,400
30.	*Beverly Hillbillies*	1/8/64	CBS	44.0	22,570
31.	*Roots* (Part 4)	1/26/77	ABC	43.8	31,190
32.	*The Ed Sullivan Show*	2/16/64	CBS	43.8	22,445
33.	Super Bowl XXIII	1/22/89	NBC	43.5	39,320
34.	Academy Awards	4/7/70	ABC	43.4	25,390
35.	*Thorn Birds* (Part 3)	3/29/83	ABC	43.2	35,990
36.	*Thorn Birds* (Part 4)	3/30/83	ABC	43.1	35,900

A. C. Nielsen estimates through May 20, 1993.

The Ratings

Arthur C. Nielsen began a rating system known as the Nielsen Television Index (NTI) in the 1950s. Today, *the Nielsens* are synonymous with *ratings*, although the Arbitron ratings are almost as important. These numbers determine whether or not a network or cable show will succeed or go off the air and how much an advertiser will have to pay to run a commercial.

Of course, not every viewer is consulted to get these numbers. Only a sampling, 4,000 households, is used based on the demographics of the U.S. Census and the 200 designated market areas that have the most influence in the United States. The viewers who are selected to participate in the studies use diaries or household meters to keep track of the shows they watch.

What is important to advertisers and networks is the size of the audience. This audience size, expressed as a rating, is the percentage of the population that watched a particular TV show. For example, a rating of 25 indicates that 25 percent of the actual population living in a particular market saw a show.

$$\text{Rating} = \frac{\text{Households turned to a particular channel}}{\text{Total number of TV households}}$$

The highest-rated TV program of all time is still the last episode of *M*A*S*H* shown on February 25, 1983 (60.2).

However, as the households using television vary from hour to hour during the day, and day to day during the week, many advertisers and networks prefer to use an indicator known as an audience share. Because a show cannot be watched if a television set is off, a share is an indication of how many people watched a particular show out of all the sets that were turned on.

The houses using television and the share can be shown by these formulas:

$$\text{HUT} = \frac{\text{Households using television}}{\text{Total number of TV households}}$$

$$\text{Share} = \frac{\text{Households turned to a particular channel}}{\text{Households using television}}$$

"Nielsen Media Research may soon install special TV meters in homes of Nielsen families that will recognize each member by his or her facial characteristics; the company expects this new technology to help it better understand exactly who watches each TV show and whether they stick around for the commercials."

—Erik Larson, *"Attention Shoppers: Don't Look Now But You Are Being Tailed,"* Smithsonian, *January 1993, 72.*

Larger numbers than ratings, shares are useful to advertisers because the numbers indicate how they are doing compared with other advertisers.

Seven Rules for Programmers

1. In any given time period, the success of a show depends solely on its competition.

2. More than three-quarters of new programming will fail.

3. Never reschedule a whole night.

4. Never schedule one comedy by itself.

5. Never start feature movies at the beginning of the evening, because so many of them do not appeal to younger people.

6. Try to protect a new program by scheduling it between established shows.

7. Remember, the position a program is assigned is far more important than the content of the program itself.

These rules were formulated by Michael Dann, the former head of programming at CBS in the 1970s

Bucking a Trend

Most programs that succeed on television—from *I Love Lucy* to *Cheers*—have had short names. Nonetheless, the following shows, all with six or more words in their names, proved to be exceptions:

The Adventures of Wild Bill Hickok (syndicated 1951–58)
Buck Rogers in the 25th Century (NBC 1979–81)
The Double Life of Henry Phyfe (ABC 1966)

Kay Kyser's Kollege of Musical Knowledge (NBC 1949–54)

That Was the Week That Was (NBC 1964–65)

TV Jargon

Like most industries, television has given rise to a lexicon of its own. Here are some current terms used in the industry, many of which have crossed over into the mainstream.

Bimodal appeal—programmer's lingo for a show that appeals to several audiences, like older people and children.

Channel surfing—with the introduction of the remote control, viewers have shown little patience and now frequently switch channels back and forth between shows.

Cradle to grave—a show with appeal across all age groups, not surprisingly a rarity.

Double-pumping—broadcasting the same show twice in the span of a few days.

Hammock hit—a show achieves this status by being placed between two other highly rated shows. Its prospects would probably be lessened if it were on its own.

HDTV—high-definition television presents a much sharper picture than what is now commonly viewed in the United States. Instead of the 525 scan lines, there are more than twice as many (1,125 in Japan). Although the technology has been around since the mid-1970s, Europe and the United States have resisted it because it was all patented by Japan. Manufacturers in the United States are trying to devise HDTV with existing equipment.

HUTs and PUTs—the number of homes using television and people using television is used to gauge ratings.

Insult television—in this new brand of talk show, hostile hosts grill their guests before a jeering audience. The best at this game are Morton Downey Jr. and Geraldo Rivera.

Satellite hit—a show that survives by its association with a bona fide hit.

Sound bite—television newscasters have come to depend increasingly on the 20-second-or-less quotation that "defines" a particular issue or event. Needless to say, in this emphasis on style over substance all the nuances are lost.

Stunting—broadcasting a show in a better time slot than the one it will regularly have, usually in an attempt to introduce it to a new audience and boost ratings.

Tabloid television—like the tabloids in the supermarket, these shows focus on scandals involving celebrities and stories chockablock with shock values. Like their print counterparts, they often pay for their guests' revelations. Some leading practitioners are *A Current Affair, Hard Copy*, and *Inside Edition*.

Tent pole—a show in an evening lineup that anchors the programs before and after it.

Traction—a certain staying power among the same viewers week after week, necessary for a show's survival.

VCR—when the videocassette recorder was first introduced, there were two systems: Sony's Betamax and Matsushita's VHS. The VHS system won out, and is now practically standard equipment in American homes

Virtual reality—in this interactive world, a person enters a simulated real-time animated situation, usually by donning a helmet and glove connected to a computer. The computer images appear "real" in this three-dimensional environment and the viewer interacts with them.

A Brief TV History

Hugo Gernsback and the Invention of Television

Each year science fiction writers eagerly await the announcement of the Hugo Awards. These awards, presented to the top writers in the field of "speculative fiction," are named in honor of Hugo Gernsback, who is sometimes burdened with the weighty epithet of the Father of Science Fiction. Whatever his limitations were as a writer and editor, there is no doubt that the field of science fiction would indeed be quite different if he had never lived. The world of television might have been different too.

Born in Luxemberg in 1884, Gernsback emigrated to the United States about 20 years later, and by 1908, he began publishing *Modern Electrics*, a magazine that displayed a lively interest in the future of electronic marvels. High on the list of Gernsback's many interests was the possibility of transmitting pictures through the air or through telephone/telegraph wires. In the December 1909 issue of *Modern Electrics*, for example, the lead article was titled "Television and the Telephot." Written by Gernsback himself, the article explored the principles of television and examined the difficulties involved in creating a practical transmission device:

> The principle of television may be briefly stated thus: A simple instrument should be invented which should reproduce objects placed in front of a similar instrument (called Telephot) at the other end of the line. In simple language, it should be possible to connect two mirrors electrically, so that one would show whatever object is placed before the other one and vice-versa. . . . In the Telephot it should be possible to see the party at at the other end while that party should see you, both through the medium of your Telephot.

Almost 20 years later, Gernsback boasted in the pages of yet another of his magazines—*Radio News*—that he deserved credit for coining the word *television*: "The word 'television' was first coined by myself in an article entitled 'Television and the Telephot,' which appeared in the 1909 issue of *Modern Electrics*."

Not all historians of television agree with Gernsback's contention. In his book *4,000 Years of Television*, Richard Hubbell states that "apparently the first person to coin the word tele-vision from Latin and Greek, was a Frenchman named Peryski. In preparing some material listed in the 'ANNEXES, Congres Internationale d'Electricité' for August 18–25, 1900, Peryski seems to have given birth to the French word *television* in its modern connotaton."

Whether or not Gernsback coined the word *television*, it cannot be denied that through his various publications he encouraged inventors of all abilities throughout the United States to give serious attention to the creation of television and the telephot. In addition, Gernsback's early science fiction novel *Ralph 124C 41+* (originally published in *Modern Electrics*, 1911–12) contains vivid scenes that prophesy the worldwide use of television. These scenes, among the first of their kind in American fiction, may well have inspired numerous ideas in books published decades later, books such as the ever-popular *Tom Swift and His Television Detector* (1933).

In *Ralph 124C 41+*, the hero with a name and a number is an inhabitant of New York City in A.D. 2660. In the course of many adventures, Ralph entertains a number of dinner guests in his distinguished home by showing them his Tele-Theater. When the guests are seated, facing a shallow stage, a young woman named Alice expresses interest in seeing the French comic opera *La Normande*. The opera is being presented that evening by an opera company that is four miles away, but Alice no sooner expresses her wish, then the hero leaps into action:

> He walked over to a large switchboard from which hung numerous cords and plugs. He inserted one of the plugs into a hole labelled 'National Opera.' He then manipulated several levers and switches and seated himself again with his guests.
>
> In a moment, a gong sounded, and the lights were gradually dimmed. Immediately afterward, the orchestra began the overture.
>
> A great number of loud-speaking telephones were arranged near the stage, and the acoustics were so good that it was hard to realize that the music originated four miles away at the National Opera House.
>
> When the overture was over, the curtain rose on the first act. Directly behind it several hundred especially constructed telephots were arranged in such a manner as to fill out the entire space of the shallow stage. . . . The illusion was so perfect in all respects that it was extremely hard to imagine that the actors on the telephot stage were not real flesh and blood.

A Television Chronology

This chronology outlines the rise of television with some highlights along the way. For more information on individual programs and actors, see the following chapters, "The Shows" and "A TV Who's Who."

1897 K. F. Braun introduces the cathode-ray tube, a crossroad invention toward modern-day television.

1907 The word *television* is used in an article in *Scientific American*.

1908 A. A. Campbell, a Scottish electrical engineer, outlines the basis for modern television. Three years later, addressing the Rontgen Society in London, he suggests the use of cathode tubes for the transmission of pictures. Unfortunately, his ideas are too far ahead of the technology of the day. They will be put into practice many years later.

1925 Using mechanical-disk scanning, C. Francis Jenkins transmits an image of President Harding from Washington, D.C., to Philadelphia. On June 13, Jenkins demonstrates television to Curtis Wilbur, the Secretary of the Navy. Moving images are transmitted from a Navy radio station to a 10" × 8" screen four miles away. Some historians credit Jenkins with creating the world's first working television system.

1926 RCA forms the National Broadcasting Company. (NBC is broken down into the Red and Blue networks; the Blue becomes ABC in 1943.)

1927 Columbia Broadcasting System (CBS) is formed.

1928 John Logie Baird transmits a TV image from England to the U.S. The first TV station in the U.S. is WRNY in Coatsville, NY. *The Queen's Messenger* is televised over WGY in Schenectady, NY. General Electric develops a TV set with a 3" × 4" screen. The first TV sets for sale are $75 from the Daven Corporation of Newark, N.J.

1929 Bell Telephone Laboratories experiments with color television.

1931 There are 9,000 TV sets in New York City; 30,000 in the rest of the U.S.

1936 The British Broadcasting Corporation (BBC) begins the world's first regular television service. The programs are on the air three times a day, for a total of three hours. The 10" × 12" pictures are received on sets which amateurs build for themselves.

1937 In the United States, eleven stations are licensed to transmit television images experimentally. The first televised production of Sherlock Holmes is aired from Radio City Music Hall. The dramatization of *The Three Garridebs* starred Louis Hector as the Master and William Podmare as Dr. Watson. *The New York Times* TV critic wrote that "While the televised version of *The Three Garridebs,* as such, offers no serious challenge to the contemporary stage or screen, considering television's present state of development, the demonstration revealed how a skillful television producer may make use of the best of two mediums, how viewers may witness the realism of flesh-and-blood setting allied with the more spectacular scenic effects achieved by the screen."

Television engineers coin the term *televisionphobia* to explain complaints they receive from viewers. Some viewers believe that television is "watching them." One young woman insists that a certain television Tom peeks at her whenever she takes a bath. One man accused a friend of using television to try to steal patent ideas.

1938 The Empire State television station transmitter is now on the air for five hours a week. Georg Valensi of France patents a method for televising pictures in color.

1939 RCA exhibits a demonstration of commercial television at the World's Fair in New York.

"The problem with television is that the people must sit and keep their eyes glued on a screen; the average American family hasn't time for it. Therefore, the showmen are convinced that for this reason, if for no other, television will never be a serious competitor of broadcasting." *The New York Times*, March 19, 1939

1940 CBS demonstrates color TV in New York City. The Democratic and Republican political conventions are telecast. Two cultural breakthroughs on television, the first Broadway play, *When We Are Married,* and the first hour of opera performed by members of the Metropolitan Opera are televised.

1941 WNBT (later WNBC) begins commercial broadcasting in New York City. The first sponsored quiz show on NBC made its appearance, *Uncle Jim's Question Bee.* On May 9, an audience of slightly more than 1,400 persons at the New Yorker Theater watched a wide screen showing of the Billy Soos–Ken Overlin championship boxing match as televised from Madison Square Garden. The fight provided the occasion for the first public showing of large-screen theater television.

NBC issues the first television rate card for advertisers. A full hour of television time in the evening will cost sponsors $120. Daytime telecasts are priced at $60 an hour. An hour of programming on Saturday and Sunday will cost $90.

R. W. Stewart, writing for *The New York Times* for July 13, 1941, wrote: "It may be just the novelty, but to this reporter the high spots of television entertainment since it relinquished its amateur standing for profit have been the commercials."

1942 The war delays the dissemination of television. The manufacture of TV sets is curtailed. There is some telecasting—in New York City, Albany, Chicago, and Los Angeles—but stations are on the air for about four hours per week. The majority of telecasts are aimed at furthering the war effort and devote themselves to educating the public about first aid, civilian defense, and war emergency matters.

1943   Because of World War II, no additional television sets are manufactured or sold.

1944   On April 10, the NBC movie *Patrolling the Ether* is televised. The movie, dramatizing how the FCC tracks down illegal radio transmitters, is the first world premiere of a movie on television. On May 25, Eddie Cantor and Nora Martin sing the duet, "We're Having a Baby, My Baby and Me," but the song is considered too suggestive and so the sound is cut off. This is the first incident of on-the-air network censorship.

On Saturdays in 1944, there are no programs telecast on any of the four major networks. On Sundays, the Dumont Network televises two shows—*Thrills and Chills,* and Irwin Shane's *Television Workshop.*

1945   The Federal Communications Commission (FCC) sets aside 13 channels for commercial TV. By the end of the year, the FCC will have more than 130 applications for commercial broadcast licenses. RCA develops the Image Orthicon Tube, which has a light sensitivity of at least 100 times greater than prewar camera tubes.

"Electronic eyes perfected by wartime research," writes RCA president, Brigadier General David Sarnoff, "have given long-range radiovision to mankind. The electron tube, which extended man's range of hearing around the world, now enables him to see distant events and people far beyond the range of the human eye."

1946   For many television historians, this year marks the birth of television soap opera with the debut of *War Bride* on station WRGB in Schenectady and *Faraway Hill. War Bride,* presented in 13 installments, concerned the return of a soldier and the new woman in his life. *Faraway Hill,* broadcast in New York and Washington (and hence the first nationally televised soap opera) ran for 12 weeks. Gillette pays $125,000 for the TV rights to the Joe Louis–Billy Conn fight. An estimated 100,000 to 300,000 viewers watched more than 5,000 sets in a three-city hook-up (Philadelphia, Washington, and New York.) Milton Berle begins a weekly series.

1947   At the start of the year there are about 10,000 TV sets in the U.S. (most in taverns, bars, and public meeting areas). By the end of 1947, between 175,000 and 200,000 sets are manufactured. There are 16 television stations operating in 11 metropolitan areas: New York, Schenectady, Philadelphia, Baltimore, Washington, Chicago, St. Louis, Milwaukee, Los Angeles, Detroit, and Cleveland. The FCC approves licenses for 55 more stations.

   The opening session of Congress is televised for the first time—with the Dumont, NBC, and CBS networks teaming up for the telecast.

   One of the first practical reproductions of television for a film was accomplished by Frank Capra in his movie *State of the Union* for scenes showing Spencer Tracy, as the presidential candidate, making a fireside chat via television. (Of course, in earlier film history there had been a TV screen monitoring Charlie Chaplin as a factory worker in *Modern Times.*)

1948   *Barney Blake, Police Reporter* makes its debut on NBC. It becomes the first regularly scheduled mystery series. NBC also presents the *Gillette Calvacade of Sports.* It remains on the air for fourteen years, the longest continuous boxing show in television history. CBS presents *Ford Theatre,* a dramatic anthology of hour-long dramatic plays. The next year it will become a regular series starring such actors and actresses as Lilli Palmer, Frederic March, and Hume Cronyn.

If you lived in St. Louis in May, 1948, you could have seen the following programs on Monday night on KSD-TV:

8 P.M.—*Union Electric Tele-quiz Calls* (an old fashioned charade prize party in the modern manner, starring Harry Gibbs and Dottye Bennett)

8:30—Film Short

8:40—Bob Ingham's Sports Interview Show

8:50—Film Short

9:00—Russ David's 'Teen Bar'

9:15—Film Short

9:30—News and Views

9:40—Sign off

1949 There are one million television receivers in use throughout the U.S. In June, *Captain Video and His Video Rangers,* one of the more popular of the early television shows for children, is telecast for the first time. The first Emmy Award is presented. (*See Emmy Awards.*)

1950 Saturday morning programming for children begins.

The Charles Alldredge Public Relations firm asks questions in 400 Washington, D.C. homes about television viewing habits. Mr. Alldredge concluded that "Television is keeping families together." His poll revealed that husbands spent 42.8 percent more of their leisure time at home than they had before; wives spent 39.7 percent more time at home; and children 41.3 percent more time.

1951 CBS transmits its first program in color. CBS also asks its 2,500 employees to sign loyalty oaths and brings the popular radio show *Amos 'n' Andy* to television. Walter White, leader of the NAACP, sees the television series as an insult to black Americans. The Manhattan hearings of the Senate Crime Investigation Committee are telecast. *Videodix* reports that 69.7 percent of New York City's television sets are tuned into the show. Mobster leader Frank Costello refuses to allow his face shown on camera, and so the camera crew concentrates on Costello's nervous hand gestures.

The FCC proposes to set aside some 70 channels for educational programming. For a Christmas Day special, Coca-Cola sponsors *One Hour In Wonderland,* and so Mickey Mouse, Donald Duck, and Pluto appear on national television. Another Christmas Day treat was *Amahl and the Night Visitors,* one of the few operas ever commissioned for television. It became a Yuletide tradition for the next fifteen years.

Pope Pius XII designates the Archangel Gabriel as the patron saint of the Radio and Television industries.

1952   The FCC lifts its "freeze" on the construction of new television stations (the moratorium on new stations had been in effect since 1948). There are an estimated 21 million TV sets in America with 108 stations in operation. The number of available frequencies is increased from 12 to 82. Bishop Fulton J. Sheen appears on the Dumont Television Network with his show *Life Is Worth Living.* Even though the bishop is opposite Milton Berle on NBC, *Life Is Worth Living* attracts a large audience. Later, in a witty speech, Bishop Sheen will attribute the success of his show to his four writers—Matthew, Mark, Luke, and John.

1953   *TV Guide* begins publishing. Hallmark Hall of Fame presents a production of *Hamlet.* More persons watch the play at home than had ever seen it on the stage in the 350 years since it had been written.

1954 This year is a turning point for the television industry because it marks the first time that TV's gross income is greater than that of radio. All in all, television grossed $593 million for the year.

1955 About 7.4 million TV sets were sold in the U.S. of which about 40,000 to 50,000 are color. By the following year, color programs will be available every night of the week. The World Series is telecast in color, but *Variety* is not impressed. Its critic writes, "NBC-TV's colorcast of the World Series games between the Yankees and Dodgers this year made it look as if the annual classic was played in Kentucky, rather than New York, if viewers went by the hue of the outfield grass. It was a deep blue. Video addicts may have forgotten but the grass in both Yankee Stadium and Ebbets Field is of the green variety." Seven out of ten Americans say that they are satisfied with the content of television shows.

1956 There are 42.2 million TV sets in the U.S. The motion picture version of *Richard III*, starring Laurence Olivier, is colorcast at the same time the movie is released in motion picture theaters. Bell Telephone Co. publicizes "televisionfone" in which both parties to a phone conversation can see each other.

1957 *Douglas Edward with the News* is videotaped for the West Coast. Using videotape, rather than doing shows live, becomes commonplace. The NBC Opera Company presents a 2½ hour colorcast of Prokofiev's opera *War and Peace*. When Rodgers and Hammerstein's musical *Cinderella* is telecast, it attracts the largest audience (up to that time) in the history of entertainment. On *Queen For a Day*, MC Jack Bailey is knifed in the leg with a fingernail file by a woman angered over the fact that she was not a winner. In Bartlesville, Oklahoma, a theater chain experiments with pay television. Thirty movies are offered for a special monthly fee of $9.50. Nearly 500 subscribers sign up for this early forerunner of HBO.

"The Nielsen Television Index of January 2, 1957, showed that the Western was the most popular program category on the air, 'regardless of program length,' carrying a Nielsen AA rating of 27.1. The top half-dozen program types were, in order: Western drama, situation comedy, variety (30 minutes), general drama, suspense drama, and variety (60 minutes)."

1958 There are about 49.8 million TV sets in use throughout the U.S. Congress pressures the FCC to delay authorization of pay TV. CBS's Playhouse 90 presents an original television play by David Karp, *The Plot to Kill Stalin,* starring Melvyn Douglas. The Soviet Union officially denounces the production and then Moscow orders the closing of the CBS Moscow news bureau. NBC unveils its early morning *Continental Classroom.* The program presents lectures on academic subjects, and viewers in some areas of the country are able to earn college credits. Texts for the courses are in great demand.

1959 There are more television and radio sets in the U.S. than there are people. The famous "kitchen debates" between Soviet Premier Nikita Khrushchev and American Vice President Richard M. Nixon is telecast at the U.S. fair in Moscow. The heavyweight title fight between Ingemar Johansson and Floyd Patterson proved to be one of the more successful theater-TV events. The TelePrompter Corporation reported an estimated gross of $1.5 million for the film-TV-radio rights to the event.

A letter in the London *Daily Mail* went:

"Three of my children went to approved schools (reform schools) for minor offenses. Another was beginning to go the same way until I got a TV.

"The boy became good as gold. He started to go to church after watching services on television and would not go out even when we wanted him to. Since the set went back because of nonpayments he has reverted to his old ways."

1960 Television changes the future of political campaigning by presenting the John F. Kennedy and Richard M. Nixon debates, watched by some 68 to 78 million viewers. NBC drops Steve Allen, expressing its disapproval over Allen's participation in a campaign to halt nuclear testing and to outlaw capital punishment.

1961 When ABC attempts to telecast a particularly violent episode in its *Bus Stop* series, both sponsors withdraw from the show, and 25 affiliates refuse to air the program. Newton N. Minow, on becoming chairman of the FCC, condemns television programming as a "vast wasteland."

In his speech, Mr. Minow tells his audience, "You will see a procession of game shows, violence, audience-participation shows, formula comedies about totally unbelievable families, blood and thunder, mayhem, violence, sadism, murder, western badmen, western goodmen, private eyes, gangsters, more violence, and cartoons. And, endlessly, commercials—many screaming, cajoling, and offending."

1962 The first transatlantic satellite transmission is made using AT&T's Telstar satellite. *The Defenders* features an episode, "The Benefactor," dealing with the issue of abortion laws in the U.S. Ten CBS affiliates refuse to carry the program, but CBS executives hail the program as "another step in TV's march toward maturity." Senator Thomas J. Dodd, Democrat from Connecticut and chairman of the Senate Subcommittee on Juvenile Delinquency, proposes a study to determine the effects of television on children.

1963 The year in and out of television is marked and marred by the assassination of President John F. Kennedy in Dallas, Texas. On November 22, 1963, at 1:36 P.M. (EST) Don Gardiner interrupts a radio program on ABC to announce that shots had been fired at the presidential motorcade in Dallas, Texas. About four minutes later, Walter Cronkite on television interrupts a CBS soap opera with the report that President Kennedy had been wounded. From Friday to Monday, the television networks set aside their regular programming, taking entertainment and commercials off the air, to give extensive and exhaustive coverage to the historical events at hand. It is a low point for the country's history, but a high point for the power of television to bind together a disparate audience. On that Saturday, viewers of NBC-TV see Jack Ruby shoot Lee Harvey Oswald. The event becomes a tragic first for television history—the first live telecast of a killing. A viewing audience of over 100 million Americans watch President Kennedy's funeral procession on television. In this year major sponsors begin using black actors in commercials.

1965 By the end of the year, there are approximately 5 million color television sets in the U.S. There are about 3,000 TV sets in Vietnam and 100 sets in Senegal. The year brings the first filmed glimpses of the surface of the moon and the surface of Mars. ABC pays an estimated $32 million for a four-year pact with the NCAA (National Collegiate Athletic Association) to televise Saturday afternoon college football games.

1966 Over half of the 11 million TV sets sold this year are color; most network TV shows are broadcast in color. In March, the Gemini 8 space rocket has to make an emergency descent. NBC interrupts its regular showing of *Batman* to cover the incident and then receives a record number of complaints (3,600) from New York City viewers. CATV (Community Antenna Television), a forerunner of the cable television industry, grows to 1,700 systems, reaching 4 million subscribers. Subscribers are charged $5.00 a month. CBS schedules a showing of the Alfred Hitchcock movie *Psycho,* but then cancels it because network executives decide that the film is too violent for living room entertainment. ABC spends $5 million for the TV rights to two showings of *Cleopatra,* starring Richard Burton and Elizabeth Taylor.

ABC spends $3 million for the rights to televise the Academy Award–winning movie *Bridge on the River Kwai.* The showing earns a 38.3 Nielson rating (against tough competition from *The Ed Sullivan Show* and *Bonanza*). The success of this showing inspires the networks to spend millions and millions of dollars for TV rights to first class movies.

1967   The Public Broadcasting System (PBS) is formed. *Our World* is broadcast live from all five continents and beamed by satellite to 39 countries. The House Commerce Subcommittee rejects a FCC proposal for pay TV. In December, the U.S. Public Health Service opens inquiries into the possible effects of radiation leakage from color television sets.

1968   Mayor Richard Daly of Chicago attacks network television for having televised videotapes of Chicago police clubbing protesters and some newsmen on the floor of the Democratic Convention. A preliminary study by an FCC panel studying violence in television notes that in two instances violence was evidently staged for the camera.

1969   The FCC announces that it will ban all cigarette advertising from radio and television. CATV Systems with more than 3,500 subscribers are now required to provide "to a significant extent" original programming. According to polls conducted by the Roper and Harris polling surveys, television has become a major source of reliable news for most Americans. Americans favor television news over newspapers by 2 to 1.

1971 There are 98.6 million TV sets in use throughout the U.S. In 1970, there were 92.9 million TV sets in use. It is a huge one-year growth.

1972 According to *Broadcasting,* there are about 6,385 TV stations throughout the world and over 260 million TV sets; by the following year the Soviet Union will have 30 million sets. Because of the use of international satellite relays, President Nixon's visit to China is watched throughout the world. We are entering the age of international television, but even so, viewers in the U.S. do not get to see many foreign shows. McGraw-Hill Publishing Co. purchases the five television stations owned by Time, Inc. for $69.3 million.

1973 White House aide Bruce Herschensohn, addressing a "Support the President" rally in Albuquerque, N.M., criticizes the national media for its coverage of Watergate. "The media," he says, "should be subject to the same scrutiny as their target." The first round of live coverage of the Senate Watergate hearings (from May to August) consumes more than 319 network hours. In May, Valerine Perrine becomes the first actress to bare her nipples on network TV (PBS) as part of the Bruce Jay Friedman play *Steambath.*

1974 On July 4, television presents its first 60-second program. For the next two years, CBS airs a new *Bicentennial Minute* each evening.

1975 Networks create the "family hour" as a special early-evening period during which they will refrain from showing sex and violence. *The Godfather* is sold to Japanese television for an estimated $2.2 million for just one showing.

1976 Television goes all out to celebrate the bicentennial. There are 241 bicentennial specials broadcast throughout the year. The highlight is on July 4, when the three major networks provide all day coverage of the events, using more TV personnel and equipment than have ever been used before to cover a single event. NBC pays MGM $5 million for the right to telecast *Gone With the Wind*. Advertisers are charged $234,000 per minute. In July, the Viking I Probe lands on Mars, transmitting the first pictures from Mars to Earth. ABC, which has always been in third place among the big three (leading some critics to label it the Almost Broadcasting Co.), now rises to become number one in the ratings. ABC paid nearly $35 million for broadcast rights to the Winter and Summer Olympics. It telecasts 41 hours of the Winter Olympics to 31 million viewers. The Summer Olympics in Montreal attracts even more viewers.

1977　Former President Richard M. Nixon is interviewed by David Frost. Mr. Nixon frankly discusses the Watergate tapes and tells David Frost that "If the tapes had been destroyed, I believe it is likely I would not have had to go through the agony of resignation."

1980　More than 5 million U.S. homes have cable television. Johnny Carson keeps NBC happy by staying on as host of the *Tonight Show* for a salary of $5 to $7 million per year for three years.

1981　Cable television is in one-fourth of all homes in the U.S., and this year marks the beginning of nationwide distribution of videocassettes. By the next year, because of inroads being made by cable stations and the use of VCRs, network viewership is on the decline. The networks will have nearly one million fewer viewers than this year. In October, a federal appeals court rules that videotaping of copyrighted television programs is an infringement of copyright. A Supreme Court ruling makes it possible for television cameras to cover courtroom proceedings. The Reagan administration proposes that the fairness doctrine, which requires television stations to allow time for opposite viewpoints, be abolished.

1983 Between September and December, the Coalition for Better Television monitors 805 hours of prime-time television and reports that the word "hell" is used 888 times, whereas the name "God" is used only 423 times. Two years earlier, Proctor and Gamble, one of television's largest sponsors of shows, reacting to pressure from the Coalition for Better Television, lead by Mississippi clergyman the Reverend Donald B. Wildmon and joined by the Reverend Jerry Falwell and Phyllis Schlafly, announced it would no longer sponsor television programs containing racy subject matter.

Immediately following the final episode of *M*A*S*H*, New York City sets a record for the volume of water used in flushing toilets. Measuring the volume of toilet flushings after the end of a program has become one way of determining the popularity of television shows.

1984 General William Westmoreland names correspondent Mike Wallace and producer George Crile as principal defendants in a $210 million libel suit against CBS and *60 Minutes*. General Westmoreland charges that the 1982 report "The Uncounted Enemy: A Vietnam Deception" is libelous because the report accused the General, while he was in command of U.S. forces in Southeast Asia, of deliberately falsifying the body counts of enemy troops. The word "docudrama" is used to described dramatic reenactments of real life contemporary news stories.

1985 A study in *Variety* predicts that cable TV will increase its audience from 34 million American households (as of 1984) to nearly 48 million households by 1990. The word "infotainment" becomes associated with shows that attempt to provide information in an entertainment format, such as *Entertainment Tonight.*.

1986 According to the Television Bureau of Advertising the average American household watches television for over seven hours each day. Fox Broadcasting Company begins serious competition with CBS, NBC, and ABC. Fox presents ten hours of prime-time telecasting each week. The U.S. Senate votes to allow the C-Span channel to cover gavel-to-gavel proceedings of the Senate and the House of Representatives.

1987 A survey by UNESCO reveals that there are 185.3 million television sets in use throughout the U.S. According to the A. C. Nielsen Company, 43.2 million homes receive cable television shows. The Electronic Industries Associated reports that there are about 37.2 million VCRs in American households.

1988 Ninety-eight percent of all American households have at least one television set. In November, President Reagan vetoes a bill that would limit the amount of advertising shown during television programs. Three weeks earlier, the Senate passed a bill that would limit commercials on children's programs to no more than 10.5 minutes per hour on weekends and no more than 12 minutes per hour on weekdays.

1989 VCRs are in 62 percent of homes in the U.S. There is a revolution of viewing habits taking place. The big three networks of ABC, CBS, and NBC begin to experience the splintering of the viewing public. Time Inc. merges with Warner Communications to create the largest media and entertainment company in the world.

1990 The top five cable networks (ranked by millions of subscribers) are ESPN (50.1), Cable News Network (49.5), WTBS (48.4), USA Network (46.1), and MTV (44.7). Channel One debuts in 400 schools across the U.S. It presents news stories to be used in the classroom but provokes controversy because for each 12 minutes of newscast there are two minutes of commercials. CBS suspends Andy Rooney of *60 Minutes* for three months because Mr. Rooney allegedly made on-the-air comments considered derogatory to blacks and homosexuals. Rooney denies making the comments.

1991 Ted Turner is named "Man of the Year" by *Time* magazine. The war in the Persian Gulf is covered live by CNN. CNN reporters are among the last western reporters left in Baghdad. On July 17, ABC airs videotape of Baghdad during the U.S.-led air raids of the previous night. Fox Broadcasting approves advertising for condoms.

In 1991, Videoway in Montreal, Canada, produces a form of interactive TV that may be the wave of the future. With innovations developed from American technology the viewer can control what is on the screen, and, in effect, become the director of the show. For instance, during a football game any couch potato can use a device that looks like a VCR remote-control changer to alter the picture to a different camera angle by hooking in with the live feed, calling up either of two different cameras for an isolation shot, or switching to an instant replay. Viewers are also able to change the format of news shows or take part in game shows. In addition, there are other cable services available, such as educational programs, horoscopes, lottery results, stock quotations, and restaurant and shopping guides.

1992 The UNESCO survey reports 900 million television sets around the world, with 201 million sets in the U.S. NBC, which paid $401 million for the right to telecast the Summer Olympic games from Barcelona, lost nearly $100 million on its "triplecast coverage." Cable TV viewers were offered 12 hours of live coverage on three separate cable channels, but the cost for each of the packages was priced too high for most families. Texas billionaire Ross Perot announces his presidential candidacy on *Larry King Live*. Ted Turner starts his Cartoon Network on cable. Cable also introduces the Sci-Fi Channel. On November 17, 1992, *Dateline NBC* airs footage of a collision of a General Motors Corporation pickup truck in which the truck appeared to burst into flames upon impact. GM charges that NBC had rigged the test by placing remote-controlled toy rocket engines underneath the truck to make certain that the truck would catch fire. After GM files suit, NBC agrees to pay GM $2 million, the cost of GM's investigation, and issues a formal apology to the company on *Dateline NBC*.

1993   Major TV networks begin to rate shows for content after complaints of too much sex and violence. For the first time in television history, three movies about the same real person—Amy Fisher, the Long Island teenager who was sent to prison for shooting the wife of her alleged lover—aired within one week of each other. CBS and ABC both air their movies in the same time slot. Time-Warner, Inc., announces plans for a highly sophisticated Cable Television System that would provide hundreds of channels and a vast library of entertainment and services that subscribers could call up on demand.

1994   Cable's Court TV provides gavel-to-gavel coverage of the trial of Lorena Bobbitt, who sliced off her husband's penis, and is being tried for malicious wounding. The Food Network makes its debut with 24 hours of programming dedicated to food.

"Kids say their love of science is sparked more by the *Star Trek* TV series than by teachers smashing chemicals with mortar and pestle, a new survey shows." Dennis Kelly in *USA Today*, January 4, 1994

Some Highlights
and Low Points

Elvis Shown From the Waist Up

In the fall of 1956, Elvis Presley (a.k.a. "The King") appeared for the third time on *The Ed Sullivan Show*. It was a glorious moment for teenagers throughout the land, but Ed Sullivan (having allowed the singer to be shown in full-shots during his first two appearances), fearing that Elvis's hip shaking had been too suggestive and perhaps detrimental to the morals of the nation's youth, would allow the singer to be shown only in tight close-ups. (*TV Guide*, in fact, in its July 7 issue that year had subjected Elvis's "lascivious" posturings to a stern editorial.)

The Quiz Show Scandals

After a long period of rumors, the story of scandal in the quiz shows first broke in 1959. Although several shows were involved, it was *Twenty One* and its most popular contestant, Charles Van Doren, that collapsed the house of cards before a special subcommittee of the House of Representatives. Van Doren, an English teacher at Columbia University, confessed that he "was deeply involved in a deception." He had been coached on the answers to defeat Herbert Stempel, a contestant that the show's producers found to be a less popular champion. He had even been instructed "how to answer the questions, to pause before certain answers, to skip certain parts and return to them, to hesitate and build up suspense, and so forth." The trust of both public and the government of this medium was shaken, never to recover. After comparing it with baseball's Black Sox scandal of 1919, President Dwight D. Eisenhower went on to say, "What a terrible thing to do to the American public."

Interestingly, one contestant had not gone according to script. Even as the producers and sponsors were trying to get rid of her, Joyce Brothers continued to answer the questions correctly. It turned out she really had known about boxing.

The Kennedy–Nixon Debates

On September 26, 1960, 75 million Americans watched the first of the Kennedy-Nixon presidential debates. The alert and youthful Kennedy, competing against a lumbering and jowly (covered with 5 o'clock shadow) Nixon, was the clear winner on TV. On radio, however, polls showed that the audience rated the debate even. The next televised presidential debate did not take place until September 23, 1976, when Jimmy Carter took on the incumbent Gerald Ford. Now televised presidential debates have become a regular feature of American political life.

Boxing Disaster

On February 20, 1962, Benny "Kid" Paret was killed by blows received from Emile Griffith during a boxing match carried on ABC's *Fight of the Week*. Viewers were shown the final sequence again and again in slow motion. Though their weekly boxing matches had been a staple of television since its very beginning, they ended on September 11, 1964, as ABC's *Fight of the Week* showed its last bout.

Murder, American Style

On live television on November 24, 1963, Jack Ruby gunned down Lee Harvey Oswald in the basement of the police headquarters in Dallas, Texas. It is the only time there have been millions of eyewitnesses to a murder as it took place. Only 2 days before, Walter Cronkite broke into CBS regular programming (*As the World Turns*) to tell a shocked public, "In Dallas, Texas, three shots were fired at President Kennedy's motocade. The first reports say that the president was 'seriously wounded.' "

Millions followed the story of the president's death and funeral.

Get Rich Quick

On New Year's Day 1965, comedian Soupy Sales told children watching his show to go to their father's wallets and to remove "those little green pieces of paper with pictures of George Washington, Benjamin Franklin, Lincoln, and Jefferson on them. Send them to me." Children, not knowing that it was only a joke, sent in money. Outraged parents flooded the television station with calls and Soupy was suspended from his show for a week.

Nixon on Television, Again

On September 16, 1968, Richard Nixon displayed a "folksy" side by uttering the immortal words "Sock it to me" on *Laugh-In*. In his post-Watergate life, on May 4, 1977, Nixon appeared on TV in an interview with David Frost. To lure him out of a 3-year hiatus from the public eye, Nixon was rewarded with a king's ransom of a cool $1 million for the five 1-hour shows.

Man Walks on the Moon

At 10:56 P.M. EST on July 20, 1969, Neil Armstrong set foot on the moon. The astronaut tripped a string as he descended the ladder, starting a camera that sent a signal to the orbiting command module, and then to an antenna on earth, and then to the space center in Houston, and then to the networks, and then to the awaiting world—all in a fraction of a second. In the United States, 125 million viewers heard Armstrong say in his flat engineer's voice: "That's one small step for man, one giant leap for man-

kind." Around the world, more than 723 million people—
or 1 in 5—were tuned in to this "biggest show in history."

The Heidi Incident

On November 17, 1968, the New York Jets and the Oakland
Raiders met in Oakland for a regular season game. Playing
in Oakland, the Jets were leading the Raiders 32 to 29
with only 65 seconds remaining to play. It was close to 7
o'clock, and a made-for-television movie of the children's
classic *Heidi*, starring Jennifer Edwards, was scheduled to
be shown on NBC. Because it seemed obvious that the Jets
would win the football game, NBC executives decided to
cut away from the game (after a commercial) and start the
movie on time.

Thus many football fans watching the game at home
did not learn until later that the Raiders had staged a
marvelous comeback in the game's final minute. Raiders
quarterback Daryle Lamonica led his team to a 43 to 32
victory. Daryl Smith of the Raiders ran 43 yards for one
touchdown, and the Raiders scored again 9 seconds later
when Dick Christy of the Jets fumbled the kickoff. Preston
Ridlehuber scooped up the ball on the Jets' 2-yard line
and ran in for the score.

The next day, Julian Goodman, the program director
for NBC, issued a public apology for "a forgivable error
committed by humans who were concerned with the
children."

Today, it is network policy that whenever a football
game is televised in either team's home market, it stays on
the air until it's over.

A Very Public Wedding

On December 17, 1969, 48 million viewers tuned in to *The
Tonight Show* to witness Tiny Tim (Herbert Buckingham
Khaury) wed Miss Vicki (Victoria May Budinger) with a
backdrop of a 7-foot-high wedding cake and 10,000 tulips.
But after the ceremony Tiny Tim eschewed singing "Tiptoe

Through the Tulips" for his high falsetto rendition of "The Wedding Song for Miss Vicki" ("Oh won't you come and love me, O pretty Vicki mine/Oh won't you come and love me, and be my valentine. . . .") However, the 85% share garnered that night was not enough to save the marriage, as it ended in divorce in 1977. Perhaps he should have sung "Tiptoe Through the Tulips."

Madonna on Letterman

Madonna appeared on the David Letterman show March 31, 1994, and set a new low for late night television. She used the f-word about a dozen times and handed Letterman a used pair of her panties. As the studio audience started to boo her, Letterman, in spite of being insulted by his guest, handled her with restraint. The show, however, earned some of its highest ratings of the year.

Shows We Never Got to See

On June 8, 1971, Dick Cavett interviewed nutrionist J. I. Rodale for *The Dick Cavett Show*. Rodale, a leading authority on healthy eating and publisher of numerous books on good health, announced "I'm so healthy that I expect to live on and on." The words were no sooner out of his mouth when he dropped dead of a heart attack. The program was not telecast.

Reality Television

On November 18, 1993, Emilio Nunez was being interviewed by a television crew near his daughter's grave in Fort Lauderdale, Florida. When Nunez's former wife, Maritza, appeared at the gravesite unexpectedly, Nunez took out a handgun and shot her. In the interview, he had blamed his daughter's suicide on his ex-wife.

Because the shooting was captured on tape, the tape was shown on Telemundo, the Spanish-language network (whose crew had filmed the shooting) and then on *NBC Nightly News*. The tape provoked widespread debate about showing "real" violence on television.

Simpson's Longest Run

With helicopters buzzing overhead, a phalanx of police cars in tow, and crowds of onlookers, 95 million TV viewers watched the live coverage on June 17, 1994, of the white Bronco carrying former football star O. J. Simpson along the freeways of Los Angeles. The reports of his possible suicide after the murders of Nicole Simpson, his ex-wife, and Ronald Goldman, her friend, helped keep people glued to their sets all the way to his surrender in the driveway of his house in Brentwood. More people watched this event than watched the President's State of the Union message the previous January. Daytime television was virtually put on hold for the next few weeks as live court appearances by Simpson appeared on every network.

The Rise of the Commercial Networks

NBC (National Broadcasting Company) started out as a radio network in the 1920s. Its first TV broadcast was on October 30, 1931, on WXBS, New York. On April 30, 1939, it telecast President Roosevelt's message from the 1939 World's Fair in New York; and on January 12, 1940, NBC began a network broadcast with WRGB in Schenectady and what is WNBC-TV in New York today.

CBS was originally the United Independent Broadcasters. Arthur Judson had started this network in 1927 because he had trouble doing business with NBC. That same year Columbia Phonograph and Records became a partner. Then it was bought by Jerome Louchleim of Philadelphia, who changed the name to Columbia Broadcasting System. In 1929 William S. Paley bought controlling share in the company. In the late 1940s Paley succeeded in luring NBC's talent away and putting together a TV lineup that went from James Arness to Ed Sullivan with stops along the way of Lucille Ball, Jack Benny, and Jackie Gleason.

Did you know that ABC was once a part of NBC? Here's how it happened. NBC originally had two channels, the red and the blue. In 1943 the FCC ruled that NBC had to give up one of these. The Blue Network was purchased by Edward J. Noble, who renamed it the American Broadcasting Company.

Another one of the original networks was the DuMont Television Network. It was started in 1946 by Allen B. DuMont, an inventor and head of the DuMont Laboratories. Some of its best-known programs were *The Jackie Gleason Show,* Bishop Fulton J. Sheen's *Life Is Worth Living,* and the Army-McCarthy hearings. It served as the fourth network until its demise in 1955. Many of its stations later became part of the independent Metromedia Television

Fox Broadcasting Co. is the fourth commercial network nowadays. It is bankrolled by Rupert Murdoch who bought the Metromedia independents and 20th Century-Fox Studios. (The name comes from the movie studio.) This new network's first show was *The Joan Rivers Show* in November 1986. Since then it has moved to a full schedule and has registered hits such as *The Simpsons, Married . . . with Children,* and *Melrose Place.* In 1993 Fox outbid CBS for the exclusive telecast of all NFL games.

Famous TV Firsts

First transmission of image and voice over telephone lines: Secretary of Commerce Herbert Hoover; from Washington, D.C., to New York City; April 7, 1927.

First telecast of a theatrical production; *Susan and God*; June 1938.

First baseball game on TV: Columbia defeated Princeton, 2–1; May 17, 1939.

First major-league game on TV: Brooklyn Dodgers vs. Cincinnati Reds; August 26, 1939.

First football game on TV: Fordham University vs. Waynesburg College; September 30, 1939.

First telecast of a horse race: Derby at Epsom Derby; September 30, 1939.

First hockey game on TV: New York Rangers defeated Montreal Canadiens, 6–2; February 25, 1940.

First basketball game on TV: Pittsburgh over Fordham, 50–37; February 28, 1940.

First color transmission: New York City skyline; 1945.

First TV variety show: *Hour Glass*; 1946.

First network TV news program, and now longest-running program: *Meet the Press*; November 6, 1947.

First popular show for children: *Howdy Doody*; December 27, 1947.

First live telecast from the New York Metropolitan Opera: November 29, 1948.

First appearance of Marlon Brando on TV: *Actor's Studio*; January 9, 1949.

First live coverage of a horse race: The Preakness; May 14, 1949.

First successful TV sitcom for NBC: *The Aldrich Family*; October 2, 1949.

First Emmy Awards telecast: January 25, 1949.

First show to star an African-American woman: *Beulah*; Ethel Waters in title role as maid; October 3, 1950.

First regularly scheduled transmission of color TV: June 25, 1951.

First regularly scheduled coast-to-coast broadcast: President Truman at the Japanese peace treaty conference in San Francisco; September 4, 1951.

First sitcom filmed in front of a live audience: *I Love Lucy*; October 15, 1951.

First network coverage of an NFL championship game: December 23, 1951.

First live coverage of the Kentucky Derby: May 3, 1952.

First pregnant woman to play a pregnant woman on TV: Lucille Ball; 1952.

First coast-to-coast telecast of the Academy Award ceremonies: March 19, 1953.

First cover of *TV Guide* featured Desi Arnaz IV, new baby of Lucille Ball and Desi Arnaz, in April 1953.

First news program shown in color: *The Camel News Caravan*; 1954.

First televised presidential news conference: President Dwight D. Eisenhower; January 1955.

First coast-to-coast telecast of the Emmy Awards: March 7, 1955.

First show featuring rock 'n' roll: *Rock 'n' Roll Show*; May 4, 1957.

First TV show presented in stereo: *The George Gobel Show*; October 21, 1958. One channel was on TV; the other was broadcast over the radio.

First coverage of Summer Olympics: Rome; August 26, 1960.

First live coverage of a presidential news conference: President John F. Kennedy; January 25, 1961.

First transmission from a satellite: July 10, 1962; *Telstar*.

First African-American newscaster was Mel Goode, from United Nations for ABC; August 1962.

First Barbra Streisand TV special: *My Name Is Barbra*; April 28, 1965.

First *Peanuts* special: *A Charlie Brown Christmas*; December 9, 1965.

First African-American to star in a leading role and not be cast as a domestic helper: Diahann Carroll, who played a nurse in *Julia*; September 17, 1968.

First live transmission from space: Card reading "Keep those cards and letters coming in, folks" held up in *Apollo 7* command module; October 13, 1968.

First TV transmission from the moon: July 20, 1969.

First sitcom to be videotaped: *All in the Family*; January 12, 1971. Also, first to deal with taboo words and forbidden subjects.

First telecast of a night World Series game: October 13, 1971.

First color transmission from space: *Apollo 15*; July 26, 1971.

First TV drama about a gay character: *That Certain Summer* starring Hal Holbrook; November 1, 1972.

First dramatic performance of Katherine Hepburn on TV: *The Glass Menagerie*; December 16, 1973.

First guest host of *Saturday Night Live*: George Carlin; October 11, 1975.

First woman to coanchor a nightly national news program: Barbara Walters; *ABC Evening News* with Harry Reasoner; 1976.

When Max Robinson joins ABC's U.S. Network News in 1978, he becomes the first black anchorman for a major network.

First TV movie about incest: *Something About Amelia*; January 9, 1984.

First sitcom produced for pay cable TV: *Brothers*; July 13, 1984.

First person to host a new series posthumously: Alfred Hitchcock; *Alfred Hitchcock Presents*; September 29, 1985. Five years after his death, his old introductions were colorized and packaged with new shows.

First network dramatic series to be set inside a prison: *Mariah*; April 1, 1987.

First show with a zip code in the title: *Beverly Hills 90210*; October 4, 1990.

The Shows

TV Genres

Situation Comedies

The first sitcoms in the late 1940s and early 1950s—
*The Life of Riley, Amos 'n' Andy, The George Burns and
Gracie Allen Show*—were transplants from radio. Soon
they were to become the staple and backbone of the
TV schedule.

Whether it is an early *I Love Lucy* or the most recent
entry, the formula remains basically the same. The show
starts out with the characters in their normal situations.
Then something unusual or different happens to disturb
the equilibrium. After a series of funny moments and lines,
the show rolls to a happy conclusion.

The best shows had live audiences to supply the laughter. For instance, back in the 1950s *The Honeymooners* was
the hottest ticket in New York. *M*A*S*H* even tried a
show without any laughter. But what generally happens in
the sitcom biz is that a laugh track is added afterward.
Like lambs being led to slaughter, some people may be
pushed to laugh by hearing other titters and guffaws. For
other viewers, however, this may smack of manipulation.

Some of the most noteworthy sitcoms over the years
have been the following:

The Adventures of	*Happy Days*
Ozzie & Harriet	*The Mary Tyler Moore Show*

Father Knows Best

The Andy Griffith Show

Leave It to Beaver

The Dick Van Dyke
Show

The Beverly Hillbillies

All in the Family

Taxi

Cheers

Murphy Brown

Seinfeld

Westerns

The mighty western once ruled the TV airwaves. Beginning with *The Gene Autry Show, Hopalong Cassidy*, and *The Lone Ranger* in the late 1940s, the western achieved its apotheosis with *Gunsmoke* (1955–75). The western had several recognizable plots and a strong central character. This character stood tall in the saddle and remained there until police and detective shows took over the reins.

Other notable westerns have included:

The Life and Legend of
Wyatt Earp

Have Gun Will Travel

Wagon Train

Maverick

The Rifleman

Rawhide

Bonanza

Little House on the
Prairie

The year 1957 marked the height of new shows in this genre. Eleven out of the 20 Westerns aired for the first time that year. The next two years brought comparable numbers of new shows, but by 1960 only four out of 20 Westerns on the air were new programs.

Television Horses and Their Riders

Trigger: Roy Rogers
Champion: Gene Autry
Diablo: The Cisco Kid
Topper: Hopalong Cassidy
Silver: The Lone Ranger
Scout: Tonto
Buttercup: Annie Oakley
Buckskin: Kit Carson
Buttermilk: Dale Evans
Rex: Sergeant Preston
Rawhide: The Range Rider
Lucky: Dick West

Police Shows

Second only to sitcoms in popularity, the police show got its start in 1952 with *Gangbusters* and *Dragnet*. But it was *Dragnet* that set the stage for all police shows with its emphasis on gritty reality, telling it like it is, the "Just the facts, ma'am" style of Jack Webb's Joe Friday.

Since then shows have come and gone:

Highway Patrol	*The Streets of San Francisco*
Naked City	*Police Story*
The Untouchables	*Kojak*
The F.B.I.	*Police Woman*
Adam-12	*Baretta*
The Mod Squad	*S.W.A.T.*
Hawaii Five-O	*Starsky and Hutch*
McCloud	*Quincy*
McMillan and Wife	*Hill Street Blues*
The Rookies	*NYPD Blue*

And they still have their car chases and shoot-outs, their battles between good and evil.

Badges of Honor

The following are the badge numbers of some TV characters.

Badge Number	Character	Show
3	Napoleon Solo	The Man from U.N.C.L.E.
416	Captain Adam Greer	The Mod Squad
425	Lieutenant Columbo	Columbo
436	Dominic Delvecchio	Delvecchio
627	Kojak	Kojak
5712	Officer Jon Baker	CHiPs

Cop shows have certainly maintained their popularity through the 90s with the controversial NYPD Blue. The show won more Emmy nominations, 26, in one season than any other show. The show also broke new ground in male heartthrobs with the red-headed Detective John Kelly (David Caruso).

Yes sir ... I mean Sergeant

*T*hese sergeants served the force, either police or armed, faithfully (and sometimes comically):

Sergeant MacDonald: *Adam-12*
Sergeant Joe Friday: *Dragnet*
Sergeant Vince Carter: *Gomer Pyle, U.S.M.C.*
Sergeant Phil Esterhaus: *Hill Street Blues*
Sergeant Hans Schultz: *Hogan's Heroes*
Sergeant Joe Broadhurst: *McCloud*
Sergeant Pepper Anderson: *Police Woman*
Sergeant Ernie Bilko: *You'll Never Get Rich*

Detective Shows

Whether featuring a private investigator or a police detective, the detective show took up the slack left by the departure of the western. Carrying a heritage of Sir Arthur Conan Doyle, Raymond Chandler, and *film noir*, it gave rise in 1949 to *Martin Kane, Private Eye* and *The Plainclothesman*. Although the main character may range from the dapper Craig Stevens as Peter Gunn to the disheveled Peter Falk as Columbo, and the modus operandi from cerebral to gut instinct, the outcome of getting his or her man or woman remains the same. (Getting to that point, however, is where all the interest lies.)

Through the years some of the other notable detective shows have been the following:

Rocky King	*Cannon*
Inside Detective	*Barnaby Jones*
Mark Saber	*The Rockford Files*
77 Sunset Strip	*Charlie's Angels*
Hawaiian Eye	*Hart to Hart*

Ironside   Magnum, P.I.
Mannix   Remington Steele

TV Shamuses

Detective shows have been a popular staple of television programming. Here are some of the most well-known detectives and their actors:

Banacek	George Peppard
Boston Blackie	Kent Taylor
Amos Burke	Gene Barry
Cannon	William Conrad
Columbo	Peter Falk
Martin Kane	Lloyd Nolan
Kojak	Telly Savalas
Longstreet	James Franciscus
Mannix	Mike Connors
Mark Saber	Tom Conway

Medical Shows

The first doctor show was *Medic*, which premiered in 1954. With Richard Boone introducing each episode, *Medic* captured a realism that had seldom been seen before on TV. It wasn't until 1961 that two more "doctors" donned their white coats, Ben Casey and Dr. Kildare. Some of the other popular shows in this genre have been these:

The New Doctors

Marcus Welby, M.D.

Medical Center

Emergency

Lifeline

Trapper John, M.D.

St. Elsewhere

Is There a TV Doctor in the House?

Here are some of the stars who played television doctors, a popular occupation:

Doctor	Actor	Show
Galen Adams	Milburn Stone	*Gunsmoke*
Sam Beckett	Scott Bakula	*Quantum Leap*
Joe Bogart	Barnard Hughes	*Doc*
Adam Bricker	Bernie Koppell	*The Love Boat*
Ben Casey	Vince Edwards	*Ben Casey*
Doc Corkle	Eddie Mayehoff	*Doc Corkle*
The Doctor	Warner Anderson	*The Doctor*
Harlan Elldridge	Charles Durning	*Evening Shade*
Benjamin Elliot	James Franciscus	*Doc Elliot*
Joel Fleischman	Rob Morrow	*Northern Exposure*
Joe Gannon	Chad Everett	*Medical Center*
Jake Goodwill	George Peppard	*Doctors' Hospital*
Douglas Howser	Neil Patrick Harris	*Doogie Howser, M.D.*
Wayne Hudson	John Howard	*Dr. Hudson's Secret Journal*
Cliff Huxtable	Bill Cosby	*The Cosby Show*
John McIntyre	Pernell Roberts	*Trapper John, M.D.*
James Kildare	Richard Chamberlain	*Dr. Kildare*
Steven Kiley	James Brolin	*Marcus Welby, M.D.*
Richard Kimble	David Janssen	*The Fugitive*
Simon Locke	Sam Groom	*Dr. Simon Locke*
Quinn	Jane Seymour	*Dr. Quinn, Medicine Woman*
Charles Tyler	Hugh Franklin	*All My Children*

Doctor	Actor	Show
Dick Richard	Robert Picardo	*China Beach*
Jason Seaver	Alan Thicke	*Growing Pains*
Lilith Sternim	Bebe Neuwirth	*Cheers*
Alex Stone	Carl Betz	*The Donna Reed Show*
Mike Stratford	Matt Frewer	*Doctor, Doctor*
Konrad Stymer	Richard Boone	*Medic*
Michael Upton	Barry Evans	*Doctor in the House*
Marcus Welby	Robert Young	*Marcus Welby, M.D.*
Philip Chandler	Denzel Washington	*St. Elsewhere*
Michael Wise	Ed Nelson	*Doctors' Private Lives*

Hey, Sonny! Would You Get Me a Doctor?

The youngest TV doctor ever was 16-year-old Douglas Howser (played by Neal Patrick Harris) on *Doogie Howser, M.D.* For the record, Doogie spent only nine weeks in high school and graduated from Princeton University at the age of 10 before "slowing down." After that, it took the usual 4 years for Howser to graduate from medical school and 2 years for Doogie to be in his second year of residency.

Science Fiction and Fantasy Shows

Science fiction employs plots exhibiting not-as-yet developed technology, supernatural powers, and unearthly locations. Jumping off in 1949 with *Captain Video and His Video Rangers* and in 1950 with *Tom Corbett, Space Cadet* and *Buck Rogers*, newer shows have left their primitive roots behind and blasted off with such recent computer-enhanced programs as *Star Trek: The Next Generation* and *Star Trek: Deep Space Nine*.

Other science fiction shows over the years have been these:

Lost in Space   *Battlestar Galactia*
Star Trek   *Buck Rogers in the 25th*
Doctor Who   *Century*
Space: 1999

Fantasy shows include the following:

Superman   *The Six Million Dollar Man*
The Twilight Zone   *Wonder Woman*
The Outer Limits   *Mork & Mindy*
Dark Shadows   *Beauty and the Beast*
The Prisoner

The Junior Rocket Rangers' Oath of Allegiance

*W*hen *Captain Video and His Video Rangers* made its premiere on the DuMont Network in August 1949, the world became a better place and a bit more safe to live in. Video Rangers took this oath:

We as official Video Rangers, hereby promise to abide by the Ranger Code and to support forever the cause of Freedom, Truth, and Justice throughout the Universe.

Talk Shows

The talk show originated as an idea of a young programmer at NBC named Pat Weaver with *Broadway Open House* in 1950. The unscripted open format allowed for regulars Jerry Lester and Morey Amsterdam and guests to fill the silence with gags, doubletakes, and pratfalls, as well as talk. In 1951 *The Steve Allen Show* lifted the talk show to new heights as the talented Allen had the gift of gab. The next show to use unscripted talk was *Today* in 1952 with the affable Dave Garroway. After that it was Arlene Francis on *The Home Show* in 1954. Perhaps more than any other show on TV, the talk show is shaped by the personality of the host. As Kenneth Tyson once said about Johnny Carson, "There is no place in the other media for the gifts that distinguish him—most specifically, for the gift of reinventing himself, night after night, without rehearsal or repetition."

Here is a list of some of the talk shows over the years:

Tonight! (Steve Allen; 1954–57)

Tonight! America After Dark (1957)

The Tonight Show (Jack Paar; 1957–62)

The Tonight Show Starring Johnny Carson (1962–92)

The Mike Douglas Show (1965–81)

The Merv Griffin Show (1965–69)

Firing Line (1966–   )

The Joey Bishop Show (1967–69)

The Phil Donahue Show (1972–   )

The Dick Cavett Show (1969–72; 1975; 1986)

Late Night with David Letterman (1982–92)

The Arsenio Hall Show (1989–93)

The Tonight Show (with Jay Leno; 1992–   )

Late Show with David Letterman (1993–   )

Soap Operas

Daytime dramas received their epithet from the soap companies that often served as their sponsors. As James Thurber wrote:

> A soap opera is a kind of sandwich, whose recipe is simple enough, although it took years to compound. Between thick slices of advertising spread twelve minutes of dialogue, female suffering, in equal measure, throw in a dash of nobility, sprinkle with tears, season with organ music, cover with rich announcer sauce, and serve five times a week.

Soaps are heavy on characterization, human relationships, difficult predicaments, and in recent years contemporary social issues. The audiences are often lifelong as well. The characters grow and age and change right along with the viewers. They're like family.

The soap opera format originated on radio with such shows as *The Smith Family* in 1925, *Betty and Bob* in 1932, and *The Romance of Helen Trent* in 1933. When the new medium of television caught on in the late 1940s, DuMont Studios in New York experimented with *A Woman to Remember* in 1947, and in 1950 CBS debuted *The First Hundred Years*, which didn't survive to see its first anniversary. But the medium began to show true promise when in 1951 *Search for Tomorrow* and *Love of Life* were introduced, and the rest, as they say, is history. One of the first and most influential creators of soaps was Irna Phillips, whose *As the World Turns, Another World, Days of Our Lives*, and *The Guiding Light* are still on.

"I feel that soap opera is an American form. People sneer at it, but it has the basis for a truer, more meaningful drama. . . . I feel that in soap opera we have the roots for a native American drama."

—William Inge, playwright

Following are some of the most popular soap operas in America and their air dates.

Show	Network	Years Broadcast
All My Children	ABC	June 5, 1970–
Another World	NBC	May 4, 1964–
As the World Turns	CBS	April 2, 1956–
Dallas	CBS	April 2, 1978–
Dark Shadows	ABC	June 27, 1966–
Days of Our Lives	NBC	November 8, 1965–
The Doctors	NBC	April 1, 1963–
Dynasty	ABC	January 12, 1981–
The Edge of Night	CBS	April 2, 1956–
Falcon Crest	CBS	December 4, 1981–
*Faraway Hill**	DuMont	October 2, 1946–
General Hospital	ABC	April 1, 1963–
The Guiding Light	CBS	June 30, 1952–
Knots Landing	CBS	December 27, 1979–
Love of Life	CBS	September 24, 1951– February 1, 1980
One Life to Live	ABC	July 15, 1968–
One Man's Family†	NBC	November 4, 1949– June 1952; March 1954– April 1955
Peyton Place	ABC	September 15, 1964–
Ryan's Hope	ABC	July 7, 1975–
Search for Tomorrow	CBS	September 3, 1951–
The Secret Storm	CBS	February 1, 1954–
These Are My Children‡	NBC	January 31, 1949– March 4, 1949
The Young and the Restless	CBS	March 26, 1973–

**Faraway Hill is considered by some television historians to be the first network soap opera. It was broadcast simultaneously from New York and Washington, D.C.

†*One Man's Family*, which ran on radio from 1932 to 1959 for some 3,256 episodes, was the longest-running series in radio history.

‡*These Are My Children* was a 15-minute show, televised live from Chicago. It was the first continuing daytime drama on a major network.

Soaptoids

The Guiding Light   soap opera   (1952–)   CBS

The only show to graduate from radio (1937–52) to television.

As the World Turns   soap opera   (1956–)   CBS

The first words on this show were "Good morning" and "Good morning, dear" in an exchange between Nancy and Chris.

All My Children   soap opera   (1970–)   ABC

The title originated from "The great and the least, the weak and the strong, in joy and sorrow, in hope and fear, in tragedy and triumph, you are all my children."

The Young and the Restless   soap opera (1973–)   CBS

The signature song of this soap, "Nadia's Theme," is the most well known outside of soap fan circles, because in 1976, it was a hit record.

Capitol   soap opera   (1982–87)   CBS

This show, which pitted two powerful Washington, D.C., families—the McCandlesses and the Cleggs—against each other, took a page from *Romeo and Juliet* by having a McCandless fall in love with a Clegg.

It was not until the 1971–72 season that daytime drama got a special awards category for the Emmys, even though Emmy Awards began in 1948. By the 1990–91 season, the daytime awards show was primetime. Advertisers are starting to realize the name recognition of soap opera stars. Susan Lucci (the oft-married vixen Erica Kane on *All My Children*) can now be seen at all hours as the Ford spokesperson. That should be some consolation to the actress who holds the dubious honor of winning the most Emmy nominations, 12, without actually getting an award.

TV News

The first news show to have an anchorman was *CBS TV News* with Douglas Edwards in 1948. NBC followed soon afterward with *The Camel News Caravan* featuring John Cameron Swayze. The early shows were only 15 minutes long; the time was doubled in 1963 by CBS with Walter Cronkite, NBC with Chet Huntley and David Brinkley, and ABC with a variety of anchors.

In the beginning, the nightly news was a supplement to newspapers and news magazines. But nowadays most Americans get their daily dose of news through their televisions. "We do the public a service that they're not really equipped to do for themselves," said Brinkley, "by keeping track of what happens around the world and telling them about it at 6:30 or 11:30 or whatever."

One thing about TV news is that it usually shows the tougher side of life. The need for dramatic footage pushes programming decisions toward disasters rather than quiet, life-affirming topics.

In 1958, KTLA-TV began using a helicopter (known as a telecopter) to fly around Los Angeles on news assignments.

10 Movies Made for Television That You May (or May Not) Remember for the Reasons We Cite

1. *The Killers*—This film was directed by Don Siegel, and starred Ronald Reagan. Based loosely (very loosely) on Ernest Hemingway's classic short story, this film was originally made to be broadcast on NBC's "Project 120" series, but network executives felt that the film was too violent for home viewing. The movie, therefore, was placed in theatrical release.

2. *Once Upon a Savage Night*—This two-part film (originally titled *Nightmare in Chicago*) was directed for television by Robert Altman.

3. *The Adventures of Don Quixote*—Broadcast on CBS in 1973, this version of Cervantes's classic novel is notable because it stars Rex Harrison as Don Quixote and Frank Finley as Sancho Panza.

4. *Alice in Wonderland*—Produced by Irwin Allen for CBS in 1985, with a script by Pulitzer Prize–winning playwright Paul Zindel, this adaptation of the children's classic had one of the largest all-star casts in TV history. Included in the cast were: Beau Bridges as the Unicorn, Red Buttons as the White Rabbit, Sammy Davis Jr. as the Caterpillar, Carol Channing as the White Queen, Karl Malden as the Walrus, Merv Griffin as the Conductor, and Ringo Starr as the Mock Turtle. The production featured 19 songs written by Steve Allen, who also played the Gentleman in the Paper Suit.

5. *The Martian Chronicles*—Based upon the stories of Ray Bradbury, this film was broadcast as a six-

part miniseries on NBC in 1980. Rock Hudson played Colonel John Wiler, and the film marked the TV directorial debut of Michael Anderson, the director of *Around the World in 80 Days.*

6. *Flatbed Annie and Sweetpie*—In this 1979 movie about women truckers, Billy Carter, brother of President Jimmy Carter, made his screen debut.

7. *Johnny Belinda*—The 1948 movie with Jane Wyman and Lew Ayres has been adapted to television four times. The following actresses have played the Jane Wyman role:

Katherine Bard—1955
Julie Harris—1958
Mia Farrow—1967
Rosanna Arquette—1982

8. *Satan's School for Girls*—Produced by Aaron Spelling and Leonard Goldberg, this horror/mystery movie, with its titilating title, takes place at an exclusive girls' school. One of the supporting roles was played by an actress named Cheryl Jean Stoppelmoor. She later became known as Cheryl Ladd.

9. *Pursuit*—Starring Ben Gazzara and E. G. Marshall, this 1972 movie on ABC, directed by Michael Crichton (his first directorial effort), and based on a book called *Binary* by John Lange. John Lange, by the way, was a pseudonym used by Crichton.

10. *The Dain Curse*—Starring James Coburn as Hamilton Nash, this film for TV, based upon a Dashiell Hammet novel, received an Edgar Award from the Mystery Writers of America for being the best television program of 1978.

Game Shows

The game show has been a mainstay of daytime television since the debut of the medium. When it clicks, a game show is hard to beat as there is relatively little overhead. All it takes is a set, a host, some contestants, an audience, a few prizes, and a game to play. Once hooked by the toothsome congeniality of the host, the battling of wits with the contestants, and the opportunity of seeing "real" people on TV, some viewers will stay faithful for years.

Here is a spin of the dial for some of the winningest game shows and the year they began:

Beat the Clock (1950)
Break the Bank (1948)
College Bowl (1959)
Concentration (1958)
Family Feud (1976)
Hollywood Squares (1966)
I've Got a Secret (1952)
Jeopardy! (1964/1984)
Let's Make a Deal (1963)
Name That Tune (1953)
The Price Is Right (1953)

Remote Control (1987)
The $64,000 Question (1955)
To Tell the Truth (1956)
Truth or Consequences (1950)
What's My Line? (1950)
Wheel of Fortune (1953/1975/1983)
You Bet Your Life (1950)

TV Game Show Hosts You May Have Overlooked

Some game show hosts have approached their craft as a calling. Bill Cullen, Bob Eubanks, Wink Martindale, and Alex Trebek come to mind. Some others, however, have merely used it as a way station on the road to somewhere else.

Host	Show	Year of Premier
Jack Benny (comedian)	*The Big Surprise*	NBC, 1957
Al Capp (cartoonist)	*Yes and No*	NBC, 1950
Johnny Carson (talk show host)	*Earn Your Vacation*	CBS, 1954
Clifton Fadiman (author)	*What's in a Word*	CBS, 1959
Joe Garagiola (baseball player)	*He Said/She Said*	syndicated, 1969
Moss Hart (playwright)	*Yes and No*	NBC, 1950
Ernie Kovacs (comedian)	*Time Will Tell*	Dumont, 1954
Gypsy Rose Lee (exotic dancer) & Dr. Mason Gross (educator)	*Think Fast*	ABC, 1949
Roger Price (humorist)	*Droodles*	NBC, 1954
Vincent Price (actor)	*E.S.P.*	ABC, 1958
Basil Rathbone (actor)	*Your Lucky Clue*	CBS, 1952
Bill Stern (sportscaster)	*Are You Positive*	NBC, 1952
John Cameron Swayze (newscaster)	*Chance for Romance*	ABC, 1958
Mike (Myron) Wallace (newscaster)	*Majority Rules*	ABC, 1950

TV Guide's All-time Best TV

In April 1993, TV Guide asked its 14 million readers to vote on what they considered to be the all-time best TV shows. More than 65,000 readers filled out ballots. Here are some of the results of that poll.

Best family show: *Little House on the Prairie*

Best sitcom: *M*A*S*H*

Best drama: *Perry Mason*

Best soap opera: *All My Children*

Best prime-time soap: *Dallas*

Best western: *Bonanza*

Best cop show: *Hill Street Blues*

Best game show: *Jeopardy!*

Best kids' show: *Sesame Street*

Best cartoon series: *The Flintstones*

Best variety show: *The Carol Burnett Show*

Best dramatic actor: *James Garner*

Best dramatic actress: *Jane Seymour*

Best comic actor: *Jackie Gleason*

Best comic actress: *Lucille Ball*

The All-time Longest-running National Network Series (Prime Time)

Program	Number of Seasons	Years
Walt Disney's Wonderful World of Color	34	1954–88
60 Minutes	26	1968–
The Ed Sullivan Show	24	1948–71
Gunsmoke	20	1955–75
The Red Skelton Show	20	1951–71
Meet the Press	18	1947–65
What's My Line?	18	1950–67
I've Got a Secret	17	1952–76
Lassie	17	1954–71
The Lawrence Welk Show	17	1955–71

The Golden Age of Television

The early days of TV were known as the Golden Age of Television. It was a time of high excitement with live dramas on the air each week. As everything was new, there was an attitude that anything was possible as well as an air of heightened tension presenting drama live: Everyone on the set knew that everything had to go right the first time.

The Golden Age dawned on May 7, 1947, with *Kraft Television Theatre*'s production of *Double Door*. Over the next 11 years, Kraft presented a grand total of 650 plays. Kraft's success led to a tremendous number of other regularly scheduled dramatic shows, including the following:

Actors Studio   *Kaiser Aluminum Hour*

Alcoa Theatre   *Lux Video Theatre*

Armstrong Circle Theatre   *Matinee Theatre*

Breck Golden Showcase   *Medallion Theatre*

Camera Three	*Motorola TV Hour*
Circle Theatre	*Omnibus*
Climax	*Philco TV Playhouse*
Desilu Playhouse	*Playwrights 56*
Du Pont Show of the Month	*Producers' Showcase*
Elgin Hour	*Pulitzer Prize Playhouse*
Ford Startime	*Revlon Theatre*
Ford Theatre	*Robert Montgomery Presents*
Four Star Playhouse	*Schlitz Playhouse of Stars*
Front Row Center	*Special Tonight*
General Electric Theater	*Studio One*
Goodyear TV Playhouse	*Sunday Showcase*
Hallmark Hall of Fame	*The U.S. Steel Hour*

The Golden Age of Television helped produce an army of creative people who went on to work in the theater and movies. Drafting scripts were such writers as Robert Anderson, Paddy Chayefsky, Gore Vidal, Horton Foote, and Rod Serling. In the ranks of directors were John Frankenheimer, George Roy Hill, Sidney Lumet, and Arthur Penn. Some of the actors who got their starts in the Golden Age were John Cassavetes, Lee J. Cobb, James Dean, Julie Harris, Grace Kelly, Paul Newman, Sidney Poitier, Eva Marie Saint, George C. Scott, Kim Stanley, Rod Steiger, and Rip Torn.

The Golden Age of Television came to an end in 1957 or 1958. Why did the era of TV dramas disappear from view? Could it have been because the advertisers who sponsored many of the shows wanted their products associated with happy endings rather than the hard-hitting issues of realistic drama? It remains a mystery. We will probably know why the dinosaurs disappeared before we know about the demise of serious drama on television.

The 1940s

The Highest-rated Shows of the Decade

1949: *Texaco Star Theater* (NBC)

The Ed Sullivan Show   variety   (1948–71)   CBS

Called *The Toast of the Town* until 1955, the name change reflected the increased popularity of its host. Known for his uneasy demeanor and odd pronunciations ("a really big shew tonight"), "The Great Stone Face" was a favorite of impressionists for years (especially of Frank Gorshin who even did his impersonation on Sullivan's show). But Sullivan had a great eye for talent, whether it was dancing bears or Nureyev, a plate spinner or the Platters. Some of the big names who made their first TV appearances on his show were Jack Benny, Walt Disney, Jackie Gleason, Dean Martin and Jerry Lewis, and Dinah Shore; a few other acts, such as Topo Gigio and Señor Wences, never made it big off his show; and the performances of the Beatles and Elvis Presley are a part of American pop culture. The lasting popularity of this show was seen when it recently popped up in syndication.

CBS Evening News   news   (1948–   )   CBS

There have been three anchors since the start of this long-running news program: Douglas Edwards (1948–62), Walter Cronkite (1962–81), and Dan Rather (1981–   ). In 1993, Rather was teamed with co-anchor Connie Chung. However, it was in the time of Cronkite that this news show enjoyed its heyday. Uncle Walter, often called the most trusted man in America, led CBS to number one ranking in network news. Since his retirement, however, it has been another story. As Cronkite would intone at the end of his show: "And that's the way it is."

Howdy Doody children's (1947–60) NBC

Originally a radio show, this first breakthrough TV show for kids was telecast for an hour on December 27, 1947. One of the characters, Elmer, on the radio show *Triple B Ranch*, always greeted Bob Smith with, "Well, howdy doody." Later, on TV the freckle-faced marionette not only greeted Bob Smith the same way but also was given the name.

Howdy Doody quickly gained in appeal, and by spring the show had gone from 3 to 5 days a week. How far the show had skyrocketed in popularity was displayed when Howdy made a run for president of the United States in 1948. The rush for "Howdy Doody for President" buttons surpassed the demand for those of every other politico. In a mere 3 days, 14,000 requests had been received. And after only 6 weeks, a total of 100,000 buttons had been handed out.

Decked out in his fringed cowboy outfit, Buffalo Bob Smith sat at the piano to knock out a couple of songs before running a silent movie for the kids sitting in the "Peanut Gallery." (The toughest ticket in town was a seat on the show; it was not unheard of for requests to be mailed at birth.) Some of the other denizens of Doodyville were Phineas T. Bluster, the mayor; Dilly Dally, a silly carpenter; Flub-a-Dub, an amalgamation of eight different creatures; plus Howdy's sister, Heidi Doody, and his twin brother, Double Doody. There were also other humans lurking about: Chief Thunderthud (Bill "Cowabunga!" LeCornec), Princess Summerfall Winterspring (Judy Tyler, who was many a young boy's first heartthrob), and Clarabell the clown (Bob Keeshan).

Dressed up like a clown and silent except for his squeeze horn (like Harpo Marx), Keeshan once explained how TV watching in the early days was a group experience, more like movie going is today. "You see, in those days, anybody who had a set in his living room could expect a bunch of kids from the neighborhood to drop in each afternoon. It was the same with Milton Berle and his Tuesday night show," explained Keeshan. "Television shows were a home entertainment event." Keeshan did not remain a second banana for long; in 1955, he leapt to stardom as Captain Kangaroo.

"It's Howdy Doody Time."

Kukla, Fran & Ollie children's (1948–57; 1961–62; 1969–71) NBC, ABC, NBC, PBS

This show usually went on the air without a script. Burr Tillstrom, the puppeteer for Kukla (Russian for "toy"), a bald-headed clown of a puppet with a bulbous nose, and Oliver, a snaggle-toothed dragon with the official moniker of Oliver J. Dragon, interacted with the woman in front of the little stage, Fran Allison. And from time to time other Kuklapolitans were also brought into the act; most notably, Buelah the Witch, Cecil Bill, Colonel Crackie, Dolores Dragon, Fletcher Rabbit, and Madame Ooglepuss.

No children ever actually appeared on the popular children's show *Kukla, Fran & Ollie*.

The Lone Ranger western (1949–57) ABC

Once a year the first episode of this series was rebroadcast to explain how John Reid became the Lone Ranger. The only one of six Texas Rangers to survive an ambush, he was nursed back to health by Tonto, whom Reid had once helped. After donning a mask to hide his identity, the Lone Ranger along with Tonto went about making the West a safer place. On occasion, he returned to the silver mine he had once worked in with his brother for more silver bullets. Clayton Moore was the masked man (except for two years when he was played by John Hart); Jay Silverheels was Tonto; their horses were Silver ("Hi-yo Silver, away!") and Scout.

Meet the Press news (1947–) NBC

This show was originally developed by Martha Roundtree and Lawrence Spivak for radio, but 2 years later they put it on television. Roundtree was the first moderator; Spivak then held the job of moderator for 10 years. The format was as straightforward and simple then as it is now; however, that is the beauty of the show. Four members of the

Puppeteer Burr Tillstrom with his much-beloved Kukla and Ollie (Oliver J. Dragon). Kukla means "doll" in Russian.

press take turns posing questions to a politician or world leader. *Meet the Press* is the longest-running news program on TV.

The Perry Como Show   musical variety   (1948–63)
NBC, CBS, NBC

This barber from Canonsburg, Pennsylvania, became one of the most beloved tenors ever to sing on television. Comedians often poked fun at his relaxed manner, but no one made fun of his singing voice. Opening his show with "Dream Along with Me," Como then sang requests ("Letters, we get letters, we get stacks and stacks of letters") and ended with "You Are Never Far Away from Me." Along the way there were skits with comedians and numbers by other singers.

Texaco Star Theater   variety   (1948–56)   NBC

In 1948 Milton Berle did 39 live radio shows and 39 live TV shows. But it was *Texaco Star Theater* on television that was to make him famous. As another comedian of the day cracked, "Berle is responsible for more television sets being sold than anyone else. I sold mine, my father sold his. . . ."

Mr. Television was the first to change the habits of America. At 8 o'clock on Tuesday night, waiters stood around in restaurants wringing their hands and actors played to empty houses. It seemed that everyone was at home watching Uncle Miltie parading around in his outlandish getups, grinning his one-liners, watching him squirt seltzer, and listening to him call for "maaaaakeup!" During the night of the election returns in 1948, Berle's show was the only one not canceled for Truman and Dewey. Why, Berle might've pulled down even more votes than Howdy Doody, who also ran for president that year.

It appeared that neither Berle nor the other performers waiting to go on stage with their song and dance routines knew what was going to happen next on this weekly variety show. If it wasn't Carmen Miranda in person, it might be Uncle Miltie in drag as Miranda. Scripts were often torn as easily as the cheap sets in favor of ad-libbing. It was anything goes as long as the payoff was in more laughs.

No one knew what Ozzie did for a living in The Adventures of Ozzie & Harriet, one of television's longest-running comedies, but no one seemed to care. David, Harriet, Ricky, and the man in the hammock, Ozzie Nelson.

The 1950s

The Adventures of Ozzie & Harriet sitcom (1952–66) ABC

This show was so true to life that even the characters' real names were used: Ozzie, Harriet, David, and Ricky Nelson. Even the set was patterned after the Nelson family's real home in Hollywood. What was even more amazing was how in Ricky's case the line between reality and fiction became so blurred that his singing and guitar playing on

TV was parlayed into a big-time pop music career. Ricky's "A Teenager's Romance" sold millions of records. *Ozzie & Harriet* was frequently lambasted for being so blankety-blank clean-cut. But after all, Ozzie had earned his Eagle badge in the Boy Scouts at the age of 13, the youngest ever to attain that rank.

The Adventures of Ozzie & Harriet was on the air longer than any other sitcom.

Rickie: Is this all right?

Ozzie: What's that supposed to do?

Rickie: Mom told me to put on a tie.

Ozzie: Yeah, I know—but she told you to put on a shirt, too.

—*The Adventures of Ozzie & Harriet*

"Occasionally critics have complained that everyone on our show is a nice person. I don't quite understand this type of complaint. Most people are pretty nice. Harriet, David and Rick are nice people, so are most of our friends."
—*Ozzie Nelson*

The 1950s
The Highest-rated Shows of the Decade

1950: *Texaco Star Theater* (NBC)
1951: *Arthur Godfrey's Talent Scouts* (CBS)
1952: *I Love Lucy* (CBS)
1953: *I Love Lucy* (CBS)
1954: *I Love Lucy* (CBS)
1955: *$64,000 Question* (CBS)
1956: *I Love Lucy* (CBS)
1957: *Gunsmoke* (CBS)
1958: *Gunsmoke* (CBS)
1959: *Gunsmoke* (CBS)

Alfred Hitchcock Presents   drama   (1955–65)   CBS, NBC

This show had an opening sequence that few viewers wanted to miss. To characteristic theme music and a line drawing of his profile, Hitchcock entered to fill the silhouette and the air with his veddy British deadpan intro of the show and a dig at the sponsors ("a one-minute anesthetic," "calculated but confusing," "tedious"). The shows themselves were well-written, well-acted, well-directed "tales with a twist." In 1962, the show was expanded to *The Alfred Hitchcock Hour*. And in 1985, 5 years after his death, Hitchcock again appeared as the host. Colorizations of his old introductions and epilogues (the morals of evil-doing to qualm any nervous sponsors) were packaged with new shows for another run of *Alfred Hitchcock Presents*—a surprise twist that the director of the macabre himself might have relished.

"One of television's great contributions is that it brought murder back into the home, where it belongs."

—*Alfred Hitchcock*

American Bandstand music (1957–87) ABC

From 1957 to 1963 this show was on every day when the kids got home from school; for the final 24 years it was shown on Saturdays. With ageless Dick Clark as host, *American Bandstand* remained unblemished from its original format: a performer would lip-synch a hit, a couple of adolescents would rate a record, and the studio audience danced.

As the ratings proved, *I Love Lucy* was one of the most beloved shows of the 1950s. From the first two seasons, some classic episodes among fans include:

"The Freezer"—Lucy and Ethel lock themselves in a walk-in freezer.

"Lucy Does a TV Commerical"—Lucy pitches Vitameata-vegamin, "medicine" that's 23% alcohol.

"Job Switching"—Lucy and Ethel get jobs in a candy factory.

"Lucy is Enceinte"—Lucy announces her pregnancy (members of the clergy screened this episode before it aired).

The Phenomenal Rise of TV Guide

Who would have seen the need for a special magazine that would to cover TV programs when newspapers around the country listed them daily and Sunday newspapers had special supplements for the week's broadcasts? Well, that didn't stop Walter Annenberg from starting *TV Guide* back in 1953. Since then, this listing of TV programs in each geographical area, with features on performers and the TV industry, has grown to become a magazine with one of the largest circulations in the world. In 1974, *TV Guide* became the first periodical to sell a billion copies in a single year; in 1976, 20 million copies a week were sold. The success of *TV Guide* pushed Rupert Murdoch to shell out $3 billion in 1988 for its parent company, Triangle Publications. In 1993, the circulation figures were 14.5 million copies a week. However, with multiple readership this figures out to 40 million readers a week. Two innovations in 1994 are *TV Guide on Screen* (your own customized TV listings) and *TVGuideOnline* (a daily update of news about TV and entertainment). Desi Arnaz Jr., the son of Lucille Ball and Desi Arnaz, was on the cover of the first issue of *TV Guide* in April 1953.

Art Linkletter's House Party   variety   (1952–69)   CBS

This show had been on the radio for 8 years before it became the longest-running daytime variety show. Over the years the highlight was the interviews with children. Linkletter was out to show that "kids say the darndest things."

Amos 'n' Andy   sitcom   (1951–53)   CBS

A radio show for more than 20 years (President Coolidge was a fan), this show made the switch to TV with African-American actors replacing the blackfaced tradition of Freeman Gosden and Charles Correll who had created the characters. On the tube Alvin Childress was Amos Jones, Spencer Williams Jr. was Andy Brown, and Tim Moore was George "Kingfish" Stevens.

As leader of the Mystic Knights of the Sea Lodge, Kingfish was always trying to put one over on Andy. "Holy mackerel, Andy," he was wont to say. The series was narrated by Amos, a cabdriver who saw things in a more philosophical light.

Amos 'n' Andy left the air not because of poor ratings, but because many felt its humor was based on a stereotyped view of the African-American experience.

Bonanza   western   (1959–73)   NBC

This was a horse opera with a difference. Not only was it the first western in color, the Cartwrights also worked the Ponderosa in Nevada during the Civil War with shovels instead of shoot-'em-ups. Overseeing the clan was Ben Cartwright (Lorne Greene). The three half-brothers were Adam (Pernell Roberts), Hoss (Dan Blocker), and of course, Little Joe (Michael Landon). The Cartwrights were joined each week by a guest actor saddled with a story.

Broadway Open House   talk, variety   (1950–51)   NBC

The first late-night show and the forerunner of the *Tonight Show* was *Broadway Open House*. Comics Jerry Lester and Morey Amsterdam alternated nights and tried out most every skit they could recall from the vaudeville circuit. Fortunately, there were some permanent guests to help out—an announcer, two singers, an accordionist who looked like his name of Milton DeLugg, but most especially there was the drop-dead Dagmar. Wearing low-cut evening gowns, this blond bombshell perched on a high stool in the foreground was scripted as the mistress of malaprop. (She once said she rode to work on "an ominous bus.") However, it soon became apparent that to be a regular on a show with an open format, it was necessary to show a human side. This would be perfected later by the temperamental Jack Paar.

Captain Kangaroo children's (1955–84) CBS

Beginning his career as an NBC page, then playing the silent Clarabell on *Howdy Doody*, Bob Keeshan finally found his voice and his niche as the man wearing a jacket with large pockets—Captain Kangaroo. Also sharing the spotlight were Hugh Brannum as Mr. Green Jeans, a farmer, and Cosmo Allegretti as Dennis, a helper who was all thumbs. (However, behind the scenes Allegretti showed his dexterity by serving as the puppeteer.) During its record run of 29 years, characters came and went. The 1950s saw Tom Terrific and Mighty Manfred the Wonder Dog; the 1970s, Mr. Baxter and Debby; and the 1980s Slim Goodbody. But through it all, thick and thin, there was Captain Kangaroo.

College Bowl game (1959–70) CBS, NBC

From 1959 to 1962 Allen Ludden was the host of this show known as *The General Electric College Bowl*. Two college or university teams, with four students per side, answered toss-up questions to get to the meatier multiple-part questions. The winners won $1,500 in scholarship money and returned the following week; the losers returned to campus with $500 in scholarship money. In 1963, the name was shortened to *College Bowl*, and the host was Robert Earle. The game stayed the same.

Disneyland children's (1954–90) ABC

This show may have run through different names—*Disneyland, Walt Disney Presents, Walt Disney's Wonderful World of Color, The Wonderful World of Disney, Disney's Wonderful World, Walt Disney, The Disney Sunday Movie,* and *The Magical World of Disney*—but it had the staying power to last 34 seasons. Originally, Walt Disney agreed to go with the fledgling ABC if the network would invest in the amusement park. The deal worked out well for both parties.

In the early years the show itself was set up like a theme park. Tinkerbell would fly down and wave her magic wand to usher in Adventureland, Fantasyland, Frontierland, or Tomorrowland. Adventureland might feature a show such as "Sammy, the Way Out Seal;" Fantasyland might run *The Legend of Sleepy Hollow*; Tomorrowland, a documentary on space travel. But it was Frontierland's *Davy Crockett* that provided the first big sensation. Not only did Fess Parker become a household name, but "The Ballad of Davy Crockett" became an instant hit.

The Donna Reed Show   sitcom   (1958–66)   ABC

Donna Reed was nothing if not wholesome, and her show was too. Reed played Donna Stone, the wife of pediatrician Alex Stone (Carl Betz) and mother of two children. The most startling thing that her kids did in the pleasant town of Hillsdale was to record songs that turned into hits on the pop charts: Shelley Fabares's "Johnny Angel" and Paul Petersen's "My Dad" and "She Can't Find Her Keys." Also, in 1958 Buster Keaton graced the set with his first TV appearance.

Dragnet   crime   (1952–59; 1967–70)   NBC

Jack Webb was Sergeant Joe Friday and Ben Alexander was Officer Frank Smith—two cops just doing their jobs on the hot streets of Los Angeles. Friday kept things to the point ("Just the facts, ma'am"); gumshoe Smith was distractable. At the end of each show the audience was told: "The story you have just seen is true. The names have been changed to protect the innocent." And then a muscular arm chiseled "Mark VII" into stone. (No, it wasn't the model of a car but Webb's production company.) *Dum-de-dum-dum.*

Would it be that we could all find wives like Donna Stone, played by the wholesome Donna Reed.

Witness: Mr. Friday, if you was me, would you testify?

Friday: Can I wait a while?

Witness: What?

Friday: Before I'm you.

—*Dragnet*

The Ernie Kovacs Show comedy (1952–53; 1956) CBS, NBC

Ernie Kovacs was ahead of his time in his understanding of the medium of television. His use of sight gags, his use of props, his patching together of tape, and his nonsequiters would be found years later on *Laugh-In*. Once he had a room built at an angle so that what was odd seemed normal (the room itself) and what was normal seemed odd (people falling down and drinks spilling). He also employed a bagful of zany characters: poet Percy Dovetonsils, disc jockey Wolfgang Sauerbraten, and movie critic Auntie Gruesome. But the ongoing skit that is often recalled is the Nairobe Trio, a musical group whose drummer wound up beating the others on the head.

Father Knows Best sitcom (1954–63) CBS, NBC, ABC

Originally a radio show (1949–54), this Robert Young vehicle moved over to television with its star intact, where he played Jim Anderson, an insurance agent in the midwestern town Springfield. He and his wife, Margaret (Jane Wyatt), had kids with the nicknames Princess (Elinor Donahue), Bud (Billy Gray), and Kitten (Lauren Chapin). Young played the archetype of the reasonable man, a character not unlike Mr. Rogers in the way he would slip into a sweater ready for problem solving when he came in the door (in startling contrast to the tyrant of a 1970s cartoon

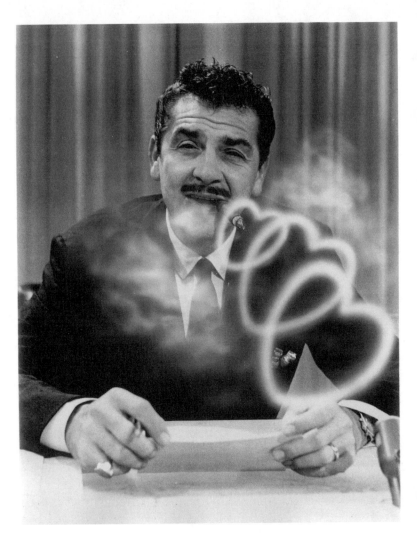

Ernie Kovaks pushed visual TV humor to the edge.

show, *Wait Till Your Father Gets Home*). Leaving the show at the peak of its popularity, Young was back on television 7 years later in another long-running blockbuster, *Marcus Welby, M.D.*

The Garry Moore Show variety (1950–51; 1958–64; 1966–67) CBS

With crew cut and bow tie, Garry Moore was a breezy relaxed host whose show served as a springboard to many

George: Gracie, how's your Uncle Harvey?
Gracie: Oh, last night he fell down the stairs with a
bottle of scotch and never spilled a drop.
George: Really?
Gracie: Yeah, he kept his mouth closed.
　　　—from The George Burns and Gracie Allen Show

up-and-coming comedians, including Don Adams, Kaye Ballard, Carol Burnett, Wally Cox, George Gobel, and Don Knotts. Others on the show were Durward Kirby, his unflappable announcer, and Allen Funt, whose *Candid Camera* was a regular feature until it became a show of its own.

The George Burns and Gracie Allen Show sitcom (1950–58) CBS

These two performers had legs (especially Burns, who has a booking planned for his 100th birthday in 1996). Beginning as vaudevillians in the 1920s, the pair moved on to radio in the 1930s and 1940s and then switched to TV in the 1950s. Although their show may have had a rigid format, there was plenty of room to maneuver for humor. Starting off with his patented cigar-in-hand monologue, Burns then introduced the latest corner Allen had painted herself into. As the episode unfolded, Burns turned to speak directly to the audience—a technique developed by William Shakespeare and used recently by Garry Shandling. The show closed with Allen becoming more and more tongue-tied until her patient husband would coax her to "say good night, Gracie."

Gunsmoke western (1955–75) CBS

Leading the stampede of adult westerns was this show that outlasted all the others. Set in 1873 in Dodge City, Kansas, it featured the 6-foot-7 James Arness as Matt Dillon. Dillon, a character modeled on John Wayne, who had been offered the role first, was very human. Unlike the earlier TV cowboys, Dillon even lost to the quick-drawing skills of the gunfighter he faced during the opening credits. However, true to character, the first gunslinger missed; Dillon didn't. James Arness stood tall for 635 episodes. The show didn't miss with the other long-term characters either. There was Milburn Stone as crusty Doc Adams and Amanda Blake as Miss Kitty Russell, the proprietor of the Longbranch Saloon. One who didn't stay the duration of the show was Dennis Weaver as Chester Goode, Dillon's deputy. Chester limped off the show after "only" 9 years.

This cast of Gunsmoke included (top to bottom) a young Burt Reynolds, Ken Curtis, Milburn Stone, Amanda Blake, and James Arness as Marshal Matt Dillon.

He was replaced by Ken Curtis as Festus Haggen, Dillon's hillbilly deputy. From 1962 to 1965 Burt Reynolds played Quint Asper, the town's halfbreed blacksmith.

The Hallmark Hall of Fame drama (1952–) NBC, CBS, PBS, ABC

Until 1955, this was a weekly show. And during the first decade there were many Shakespearean productions star-

For years, the opening segment of *Gunsmoke* featured a shoot-out on Main Street in Dodge City. After the assassinations of Martin Luther King Jr. and John F. Kennedy in the 1960s, the opening was changed to show Marshal Matt Dillon riding on the range.

ring Maurice Evans: *Hamlet, Macbeth, The Taming of the Shrew, Twelfth Night,* and *The Tempest.* It was noted at the time how more people saw Maurice Evans play the Dane in this Hallmark Hall of Fame production than had seen *Hamlet* during all the previous productions throughout all the previous centuries. Also, through the years there have been productions of *Victoria Regina, All Quiet on the Western Front, Ah! Wilderness, Lisa Bright and Dark, The Secret Garden, Stones for Ibarra, My Name is Bill W.,* and *Sarah Plain and Tall.* The Hallmark Hall of Fame continues to this day with productions debuting in peak card-buying seasons.

Have Gun Will Travel   western   (1957–63)   CBS

Richard Boone played Paladin, an unusual character for a western. Paladin (the white knight in the game of chess) was literate and cultured, a graduate of West Point. Each show began with a message that had reached him at the Hotel Carlton in San Francisco. (His calling card advertised "Have Gun Will Travel. Wire Paladin, San Francisco.") Wearing all black, Paladin would then carry out most any assignment his client had in mind. Boone played against type. Although his black pants, black shirt, and black hat were associated with evil, he most definitely was fighting for justice. Paladin was even known to turn against his clients if he found out they were corrupt.

The Honeymooners   sitcom   (1955–56; 1971)   CBS

The Honeymooners started out as a sketch on Jackie Gleason's *Calvacade of Stars* (1950–52); later it was a mainstay on *The Jackie Gleason Show* (1952–70). In *The Honeymooners* skit Ralph Kramden (Jackie Gleason), who drove a bus along Fifth Avenue for the Gotham Bus Company,

Jackie Gleason, The Great One—"Away we go!"

and Ed Norton (Art Carney), who toiled below the streets as a sewer worker for the New York City Department of Water Works, were upstairs-downstairs neighbors. (The address of 328 Chauncey Street in the Bensonhurst section of Brooklyn was Gleason's address as a kid.) Their wives, Alice Kramden (Audrey Meadows) and Trixie Norton (Joyce Randolph), worked at home. The set was the Kramden apartment.

Ralph: That's "Swanee River"?

M.C.: Yes. Now who wrote it? [*Ralph is speechless.*] Your time is almost up. Make a stab at it. Take a guess!

Ralph: Homma . . . homina . . . Ed Norton?

M.C.: Oh, I'm terribly sorry, Mr. Kramden, the right answer is Stephen Foster. But at least you have the satisfaction of knowing you have been a good contestant and a good sport. Good-by, Mr. Kramden.

—*The Honeymooners*

Originally, the scriptwriters wanted to call the show *The Beast* (an idea vetoed by Gleason). Many of the titles of their scripts were memorable ("TV or Not TV," "Dial J for Janitor," "Opportunity Knocks But"), and the writers used certain expressions for repeating elements on the show: macaroni (Ralph's blank stare), beached whale (Ralph's fainting), Kissville (the end of the show when Ralph usually exclaims to his wife, Alice, "Baby, you're the greatest!"). Kramden also had pet phrases. For example, when he became mad at Alice, he would often say, "One of these days, Alice, one of these days . . . Pow! Right in the kisser!" And for how far he was going to send her with one of his punches, he would utter, "To the moon, Alice."

Although *The Honeymooners* has been on the air regularly since 1956, there were only 39 shows in the original series. However, in 1985 Gleason released *Honeymooner* episodes that had originally been on *The Jackie Gleason Show* from 1952 through 1957. These have since been restructured into 68 thirty-minute shows. So, now there are a total of 107 episodes for fans to enjoy.

Ralph: I promise you this, Norton. I'm gonna learn. I'm gonna learn from here on in how to swallow my pride.

Ed: That ought not to be too hard. You've learned how to swallow everything else.

—*The Honeymooners*

The Huntley-Brinkley Report   news   (1956–70)   NBC

This news program was top-rated for most of its 14 years on the air. New York–based Huntley was solid and factual; Washington-based Brinkley was more temperamental and emotional. But the chemistry between these two veteran newsmen catapaulted them into the first news superstars. As a matter of fact, just make that superstars, period. A survey at the time revealed that there were more Americans who recognized Chet Huntley and David Brinkley than recognized the Beatles.

"Good night, David."
"Good night, Chet."

I Love Lucy   sitcom   (1951–57)   CBS

This show grew out of the late 1940s radio program *My Favorite Husband*, starring Lucille Ball. When CBS wanted

Lucille Ball up to her usual antics, together with William Frawley as Fred Mertz and Desi Arnaz as Ricky Ricardo.

something similar for TV, Ball complied with two stipulations: her real husband would play her spouse (not Richard Denning as in the radio show) and it would be produced by their own company, Desilu, on the West Coast.

Lucy: Gee, I'm gonna have to go on a diet. You know I could hardly get into my dress this morning?

Ethel: Hey, Lucy, wait a minute. You don't suppose . . . ?

Lucy: I don't suppose what?

Ethel: You don't suppose you're gonna have a baby?

Lucy: Oh, of course not. [*Long pause.*] A baby?!

Ethel: Yeah, baby. That's the word my grandmother made up for tiny little people.

—*I Love Lucy*

Lucille Ball starred as Lucy Ricardo, Desi Arnaz as Ricky Ricardo, her real-life bandleader husband. Their best friends and next-door neighbors in their Manhattan apartment on East 68th Street were Vivian Vance and William Frawley as Ethel and Fred Mertz.

Lucy became a show of firsts. It was the first TV series to be filmed before a live audience, the first to use three cameras, the first series produced by an independent company, and the first to be filmed on the West Coast. Another first was that it had the first birth incorporated into a TV plot. (Even pregnancy was a forbidden subject in those days.) More people tuned in to watch that show than viewed the presidential inauguration of Dwight D. Eisenhower the following day.

Ball went on to star in the subsequent shows: *The Lucille Ball–Desi Arnaz Show* (1957–60), *The Lucy Show* (1962–68), *Here's Lucy* (1968–74), and *Life with Lucy* (1986).

I Love Lucy and *The Andy Griffith Show* both went off the air when they were number one in the ratings.

Jack Benny rehearses with Groucho Marx on The Jack Benny Show.

The Jack Benny Show variety (1950–65) CBS, NBC

This show was a successful transplant from a radio program with the same premise, which Benny (birth name was Benjamin Kubelsky) had put together for his variety show. But Benny's shtick worked even better on TV—he was known as a comedian who did not say "funny *things* but one who said things *funny*." For instance, he was always maintaining that he was only 39, and there was his stinginess, as evidenced by his hanging onto the old 1928 Maxwell roadster. He was also known for the way he played the violin, which would make chimpanzees shudder and move away; the way he placed his hand on his cheek and said "Well . . ."; and other patented expressions such as "Wait a minute!" and "Now cut that out!" Two of the long-time regulars on his show were Eddie Anderson, who played his valet, Rochester, and Don Wilson, who was his announcer and friend. On *The Jack Benny Show*, as with the recent *It's Gary Shandling's Show*, there often seemed to be a fine line between television and real life.

Jack Benny: What's your name?

Mel Blanc: [in a "Mexican" voice] Sy.

Benny: Sy?

Blanc: Si.

Benny: And your sister?

Blanc: Sue.

Benny: What does she do?

Blanc: Sew.

Benny: Sew?

Blanc: Si.

—*The Jack Benny Show*

Lassie children's (1954–71) CBS

This series was spawned by *Lassie Come Home*, Eric Knight's best-selling 1940 novel. Over the 17 years that *Lassie* ran, six male collies trained and owned by Rudd Weatherwax played the part. For the first 10 years Lassie

A Show by Any Other Name

Creating the correct name for a television show is not as simple as it looks. Some of our favorite shows started life with a different name. Here is a list of the original titles selected for some well-known shows.

Today: The Rise and Shine Review

The Brady Bunch: The Brady Brood

Leave It to Beaver: Wally and the Beaver

Peter Gunn: Gunn for Hire

McHale's Navy: McHale's Men

What's My Line?: Occupation Unknown

It Takes a Thief: Once a Crook

Monty Python's Flying Circus: Gwen Dibley's Flying Circus

The Flintstones: The Flagstones

Toast of the Town: You're the Top

The Partridge Family: Family Business

Charlie's Angels: The Alley Cats

The Six Million Dollar Man: Cyborg

Dynasty: Oil

All in the Family: Those Were the Days

lived on a farm with a small boy in Calverton, and for the next 4 years she lived with a forest ranger; finally Lassie was on her own. She (he) even met up with a male collie and had puppies. Of the many two-footed members of the cast over the years, two stand out: Jon Provost as Timmy and June Lockhart as Ruth Martin.

Leave It to Beaver sitcom (1957–63) CBS, ABC

Jerry Mathers played the all-time younger brother, Theodore Cleaver, nicknamed the Beaver. He lived in Mayfield with his parents, Ward (Hugh Beaumont), an accountant, and June (Barbara Billingsley), a housewife, and his older brother, Wally. Only 7 when the series began (his brother was 12), the Beaver wrestled with problems that would be welcomed by any parent faced with today's headlines. *Leave It to Beaver* is one of those shows (like *Star Trek*) that became even more popular after it went into syndication.

Make Room for Daddy sitcom (1953–57) ABC

Danny Thomas played Danny Williams, a character who was as close to reality as the first name. Danny was a nightclub entertainer who juggled his career with being a father. When the real Danny came off the road, his real kids would holler, "Make room for Daddy!" Thus the birth of the show.

The TV kids were Rusty Hamer as Rusty and Sherry Jackson as Terry. His first wife on the show, Margaret, was Jean Hagen; his second wife, Kathy, was Marjorie Lord. (Her "daughter" by an earlier marriage was Angela Cartwright as Linda.) The birdlike Hans Conreid was Uncle Tonoose; Bill Dana was Jose Jimenez, the elevator man. When the show moved to CBS in 1957, the name was changed to *The Danny Thomas Show*. It continued until 1964.

Danny: Let's play horsey.

Terry: Okay, Daddy. Here's two dollars—put it on Count Flash in the seventh.

—*Make Room for Daddy*

Danny Thomas, star of Make Room for Daddy.

The Many Loves of Dobie Gillis sitcom (1959–63) CBS

Based on a popular book by Max Shulman, this series professed to show what it was like to be an aging adolescent of that time. Dobie Gillis (Dwayne Hickman) was the son of a grocer who was struggling with the old question of what life is all about. Frequently he could be seen underneath the statue of *The Thinker* in the local park trying to figure it all out. One thing he did aspire to was life in the fast lane. If only he had enough money he felt he would be able to win the status, the fancy cars, and the beautiful women that naturally followed. His best friend, Maynard G. Krebs (played by Bob Denver) was a sweat-shirted beatnik who exerted even less effort than Dobie. Even when Gillis and Krebs graduated from high school, tried a stint in the army, and enrolled in a local junior college, their lives remained basically the same. Tuesday Weld and Warren Beatty, two actors who went on to bigger and better things, got their starts on this show.

Dobie: Write 'Dear Alumni.'

Maynard: How do you spell it?

Dobie: A-L-U-M-N-I—

Maynard: No . . . ! 'Dear.'

Dobie: I'll write it.

—*Dobie Gillis*

Maverick western (1957–62) ABC

James Garner was Bret Maverick, a card shark who would just as soon walk away from a fight. He also had an eye for the ladies and a sense of humor. This ability to poke fun at himself and others was what made this show stand tall. For instance, one episode called "Gunshy" was a take-off on *Gunsmoke*. Another spoofed *Bonanza*. Joe Wheelwright (as played by Jim Backus), the patriarch of Subrosa Ranch, was doing his darndest to find mates for his three lamebrain sons: Moose, Henry, and Small Paul.

The Mickey Mouse Club children's (1955–59) ABC

Produced by—who else?—Walt Disney, there were more than 40 children who wore mouse ears and their names on their shirts to perform as Mouseketeers over the 4-year run of this show. (Can anyone remember another name besides Annette, who grew up to be the Annette Funicello of the "beach blanket" movies?) Each day of the week, Monday through Friday, had its own feature: "Fun with Music Day," "Guest Star Day," "Anything Can Happen Day," "Circus Day," and "Talent Roundup Day." And, of course, the show's theme song was the classic "M-I-C . . . K-E-Y . . . M-O-U-S-E."

The Millionaire drama (1955–60) CBS

Each week John Beresford Tipton would dispatch his secretary, Michael Anthony (Marvin Miller), from his Silverstone estate to deliver a check for $1 million to some unsuspecting person. The only requirement was that the exact amount of the check and the donor not be divulged. The point of the show was to see how receiving a million tax-free dollars would affect someone's life. For some characters the money was a blessing; for others it was a curse. "What would *you* do if you had a million dollars?"

Our Miss Brooks sitcom (1952–56) CBS

Eve Arden was Connie Brooks, an English teacher at Madison High School. She was loved by some—especially one student, Walter Denton (Richard Crenna)—and disliked by others—most particularly the principal, Osgood P. Conklin (Gale Gordon). Miss Brooks had her preferences, too: Philip Boynton (Robert Rockwell), the biology teacher. In an attempt to pump life into the series, Miss Brooks found a new job at Mrs. Nestor's Private Elementary School, but the show's popularity shrunk along with the size of her new students.

Miss Brooks: Anything special you want for dinner?

Mr. Boynton: I'm not fussy. I'll love whatever you put on my plate. I'll be there at seven.

Miss Brooks: Fine—I'll be on your plate.

—*Our Miss Brooks*

Perry Mason   drama   (1957–66)   CBS

Erle Stanley Gardner, a lawyer turned writer, created the Perry Mason character first for his novels, then for a radio show that ran from 1943 to 1955. Next, it was TV for the defense attorney, who, played by Raymond Burr, lost only 1 case out of a total of 271 to the prosecuting attorney Hamilton Burger (William Talman). Mason would usually win the courtroom case by a withering cross-examination that would cause the guilty party to break down and confess. To help the viewers understand how the defense attorney had figured out what had happened, Mason would explain it all at the end of the show to his private investigator Paul Drake (William Hopper) and to his secretary Della Street (Barbara Hale). *Perry Mason* defined the public's perception of lawyers until *L.A. Law* went to court in the 1980s. The show's popularity continues in reruns, and in a series of made-for-TV films.

Peter Gunn   detective drama   (1958–61)   NBC, ABC

Craig Stevens was such a smooth, suave operator as Peter Gunn, and handsome too, that some barbershops of that time advertised a Craig Stevens cut. In addition to Stevens, there was the lovely Lola Albright who played his girl-friend, Edie Hart, the featured singer down at Mother's, a jazz place that provided the hangout for the actors and the action. Lieutenant Jacoby (Herschel Bernardi) could also be found there and at crucial moments to help Gunn. But it was Henry Mancini's music that was such an instrumental part of the show and that lingers in the memory like the final chord of a vibraphone. Mancini's cool jazz was released as two enormously popular albums: *The Music from Peter Gunn* and *More Music from Peter Gunn*.

The Phil Silvers Show sitcom (1955–59) CBS

Phil Silvers was Master Sergeant Ernie Bilko from the motor pool at Fort Baxter, Kansas. Bilko's routine was to try to bilk his unwitting underlings, especially Private Duane Doberman (Maurice Gosfield), and his superiors, most notably Colonel John Hall (Paul Ford). His get rich schemes gave the first episode its title "You'll Never Get Rich," which became a permanent subtitle to the program a few weeks later. In syndication, the title was changed once again to *Sergeant Bilko*. A major movie of this TV show has been announced—with Steve Martin to star. Another one of Bilko's schemes?

Sergeant Bilko of *The Phil Silvers Show (You'll Never Get Rich)* was given his name because of its association with the word *bilk* and in honor of Steve Bilko, a minor league player who once hit 61 home runs. Phil Silvers was a great baseball fan, and in fact, New York Yankees stars Yogi Berra, Whitey Ford, and Gil McDougald all made their TV debuts on his show.

Playhouse 90 drama (1956–60) CBS

These 90-minute plays, presented live before an audience, represented the apex of the Golden Age of Television. (However, by 1958 videotape was already starting to be used.) Some of the more memorable presentations were

Private One: Bilko'll get his.

Private Two: Oh, he's already got his and he's got yours too.

—*The Phil Silvers Show*

Rod Serling's *Requiem for a Heavyweight* (starring Jack Palance as a washed-up fighter), William Gibson's *The Miracle Worker* (Patty McCormack and Teresa Wright), Joseph Conrad's *Heart of Darkness* (Oscar Homolka and Eartha Kitt), and Ernest Hemingway's *For Whom the Bell Tolls* (Jason Robards Jr. and Maria Schell). Over the years it won 11 Emmys—for best actor, actress, teleplay, show, series, and program achievement.

The Red Skelton Show comedy variety (1951–71) NBC, CBS, NBC

After a 10-year stint on radio, this red-headed son of a circus clown made a smooth transition to a 20-year career on TV. (David Rose and His Orchestra were with him the whole time.) After his opening monologue and appearances by his guests, Skelton got down to the heart of the show: his line-up of characters. Some of his best were Sheriff Deadeye, Freddie the Freeloader, Clem Kadiddlehopper, Willie Lump-Lump (a drunk), Cauliflower McPugg (a boxer), and The Mean Widdle Kid.

Rocky and His Friends cartoon (1959–61) ABC

Rocky, a squirrel, and Bullwinkle, a moose, fought an unending battle with Cold War–era villains Mr. Big and his assistants Boris Badenov and Natasha. In addition to these adventures, there were also the regular features of *Fractured Fairy Tales* and *Bullwinkle's Corner*. This series turned out to be so big that it was transmogrified into *The Bullwin-kle Show*, a series that ran from 1961 to 1973.

The Roy Rogers Show   western   (1951–57)   NBC

Roy's real name may have been Leonard Slye and his hometown Cincinnati, but after moving to California and becoming a member of the Sons of the Pioneers, he was destined to become "King of the Cowboys." Astride his horse, Trigger, Roy made the Double R Bar Ranch run as smoothly as his shaven face. Oh, he received help from his wife, Dale Evans, "Queen of the West," on her horse, Buttermilk, from their German shepherd, Bullet, and from their ranch hand, Pat Brady, in his jeep, Nellybelle. "Happy trails to you . . ."

Sea Hunt   adventure   (1957–61)   syndicated

Lloyd Bridges was ex-navy frogman Mike Nelson who went into business for himself as an underwater investigator. Whether he was working for the government or an insurance company, whether he was looking for a downed plane or an escaped criminal, Bridges stayed under water as long as it took. And with the expertise of underwater photographer Lamar Boren that was usually more than half of each 30-minute show.

Search for Tomorrow   soap opera   (1951–86)   CBS, NBC

Starting out as a mere 15-minute show, this was the first of many TV soap operas. (They are called "soap" operas because they were once primarily sponsored by soap companies.) Characteristically, these shows drag on because they are usually shown during the workday. It's important that you can miss part of them, or even whole shows, and still know what's going on.

   Although soaps may not always seem realistic, they do deal with current problems. In fact, they can even serve as a barometer for society's attitudes toward issues such as extramarital affairs, single parenthood, spouse beating, etc. In addition, soap families are sometimes more permanent than real families. Certain characters are on a show for decades and age just as real people do. Along with the feeling of "at least there's someone whose life is more messed up than mine," this helps account for audience loyalty.

See It Now documentary (1952–55) CBS

Television's *See It Now* grew out of radio's *Hear It Now*. One of the striking similarities of both shows was in the writing. "Writing for television is not unlike writing for radio," wrote host Edward R. Murrow and producer Fred Friendly. "It must be the language of speech, lean copy, sparing of adjectives, letting the pictures and the action and the indigenous sound create the mood, and then maybe a few words—the fewer the better." Murrow ended *See It Now*, as well as the later *Person to Person*, with his signature sign-off that still echoes today: "Good night, and good luck."

77 Sunset Strip detective drama (1958–64) ABC

The name of this show and its finger-snapping hit song came from the address of the detective agency headed by Stu Bailey (Efrem Zimbalist Jr.), a smooth-talking Ivy League Ph.D., and his partner, Jeff Spencer (Roger Smith). Next door at Dino's was car-parking attendant Gerald Lloyd Kookson III better known as Kookie (Ed Byrnes), who eventually outshadowed everyone else. Kookie caught on with the younger generation in the same way that Fonzie (Henry Winkler) did in the 1970s. It was not only Kookie's long-haired good looks ("Kookie, Kookie, Lend Me Your Comb," a song featuring Byrnes and Connie Stevens became a hit) but also his language—"Kookie-isms" such as "the ginchiest" (the greatest), "piling up the Z's" (sleeping), and "a dark seven" (a bad week). Realizing his importance to the show, Byrnes walked out in 1960 and was hired back the next year as a partner in the detective agency. The success of *77 Sunset Strip* gave rise to other action adventure series, including *Hawaiian Eye* and *Surfside Six*.

The $64,000 Question game (1955–58) CBS

The parent of this show was radio's *The $64 Question*.

Can You Answer the Very First $64,000 Question?

*T*he very first $64,000 question to be asked on television was this: "Describe the menu served at Buckingham Palace on March 21, 1939, when King George VI and Queen Elizabeth entertained the president of France and his wife."

> *Answer:*
> *Château d'yquem*
> *Maltaise sauce*
> *Filet de truite saumonée*
> *Madeira Sercial*
> *Consommé quenelle*

However, on TV the stakes were raised a thousandfold. With Hal March as host, contestants started off with a question worth only $64, and from then on the worth of each answer doubled. When the $8,000 level was reached, the contestant went into the isolation booth. This was where the show captured its audience: with anxiety-producing music playing in the background, the viewers sweated it out along with the contestant.

Some of the contestants who won the top prize were 11-year-old Robert Strom whose category was science, a shoemaker from the Bronx named Gino Prato whose field was opera, and Joyce Brothers (who had not yet received her Ph.D.) who answered questions about boxing. Why did she pick boxing? She felt it was an area that did not have an overwhelming number of records and statistics, so it could be mastered with relative ease. Also, she was nobody's Palooka.

Superman action (1952–57) syndicated

Superman had a long history before the TV show. Born as

Superman (George Reeves) defends the honor of Lois Lane (Phyllis Coates).

a comic book, it also had a life in the funny papers and then a radio show (with Bud Collyer as Superman). On television George Reeves was mild-mannered Clark Kent, the reporter at *The Daily Planet* who stepped into a phone booth to change into his Superman persona. His love interest was, of course, another reporter at the paper, Lois Lane (Phyllis Coates for the first year, Noel Neill afterward). His only other weakness was kryptonite, a mineral from his native planet of Krypton. Otherwise, his superpowers were employed to solve the crimes of Metropolis. The low-tech special effects may be comical these days (jumping onto mattresses and wires for the flying scenes), but there was something so magical about these characters that they returned in *Lois and Clark* during the 1993 TV season.

This Is Your Life testimonial (1952–61) NBC

Ralph Edwards moved this radio show to TV where it was even more successful as people—sometimes celebrities, sometimes common folk—were surprised (usually) by his

"This is your life." As Edwards clutched the book of his guest's life, some of the highlights were recounted with periodic visits from people from the past. One of the most talked-about shows was when Lillian Roth, a recovering alcoholic, was honored.

Today   news   (1952–   )   CBS

Today, hosted by Dave Garroway, went on the air at 7 A.M. on January 14, 1952. (Because every show has always been at least 2 hours, *Today* has been on the air more hours than any other program.) Pat Weaver put a Polonius-like spin to his words when he outlined the show's philosophy: "What the people should know today, which is what happened yesterday as reported today plus what is actually happening now and is going to happen momentarily." One of the initial problems with the show was the time slot. Previously, television had been considered to be like sex and booze—you shouldn't touch it till after sundown.

Typical of the show's early live interviews was this exchange (reported in full):

INTERVIEWER: "How's the navy going these days, Admiral?"
FECHTELER : "Guess it's all right. It was there last night all right, when I left it."
INTERVIEWER: "Thank you very much, sir. Ladies and gentlemen, you have just heard from Admiral William Fechteler, chief of naval operations down here at the Pentagon in Washington. And now we return you to Dave Garroway in New York."

The show had survived numerous controversial changes in hosts and an onslaught of imitators to remain the top-rated morning show.

The Tonight Show   talk, variety   (1954–   )   NBC

Steve Allen was the original host of *Tonight*, spinning off from announcer Gene Rayburn and conductor Skitch Henderson with his unique brand of humor. Allen's musical talents and his quick wit attracted a loyal following. His gift of gab was in evidence as he wandered about in the audience or did "man on the street" interviews, not to

Crowds stood outside the window at Rockefeller Center to greet Dave Garroway, the original host of Today. In 1994, NBC revived the idea of having a live audience standing outside the window at Rockefeller Center.

Hosts of *Today*

Dave Garroway	January 1952–July 1961
John Chancellor	September 1961–October 1962
Hugh Downs	October 1962–October 1971
Frank McGee	October 1971–April 1974
Jim Hartz (Barbara Walters, cohost 1974–1976)	April 1974–June 1976
Tom Brokaw (Jane Pauley, cohost 1976–1992)	August 1976–December 1981
Bryant Gumbell (Chris Wallace, cohost 1982; Deborah Norville, cohost 1992; Katie Couric, cohost 1992–)	January 1982–

mention when he talked the U.S. Marines into landing on Miami Beach. When Allen cut back to 3 days a week, Ernie Kovacs was on for the other 2 days. And when Allen left in 1957, the show became *Tonight! America After Dark* with Jack Lescoulie. Patterned after the *Today* show, it lasted only 6 months.

The next full-time host was so successful that the show was renamed *The Jack Paar Tonight Show*. Emotional and unpredictable, Paar's forte was interviewing. With Hugh Downs as his announcer and Jose Melis as his bandleader,

Paar surrounded himself with people who liked to talk. One of the most notable was Alexander King who was a hilariously spellbinding raconteur. One memorable evening in 1960, Paar walked off the set when NBC censors objected to a joke he had told. The censors were shocked by the term *water closet*. Paar left for good in 1962 and was replaced by Johnny Carson.

The Tonight Show Starring Johnny Carson was on the air for just shy of 30 years. Introduced with a long "Heeere's Johnny" by sidekick Ed McMahon, Carson delivered his opening monolog, and then visited with people in the news or showbiz or off-beat personalities. Sometimes there were skits that fell flat, but that was the whole point. The show was comforting because you could count on what to expect. In one of the most closely watched transitions in television history, in 1992 Johnny was replaced by Jay Leno.

Twilight Zone   science fiction   (1959–64)   CBS

Three-time Emmy Award–winner Rod Serling was the host and chief writer of this series. (Of the 151 shows, Serling penned 89.) *Twilight Zone* is a show that, like *The Honeymooners* and *Star Trek*, has gained momentum through the years. Many fans watch their favorites over and over, episodes such as "The Dummy" (Cliff Robertson), "The Hitchhiker" (Inger Stevens), "Nightmare at 20,000 Feet" (William Shatner), "Nothing in the Dark" (Robert Redford), "People Are Alike All Over" (Roddy McDowall), and "Time Enough to Last" (Burgess Meredith). The stories, more often than not, have ironic twists. For instance, in "Time Enough to Last," Meredith was a bank teller who wished he had time enough to read. One day he went into the bank's vault with a book, and when he came back out the world had been laid to waste by a nuclear blast. He now certainly had the time, but unfortunately, he stepped on his reading glasses. The viewers of *Twilight Zone* relish the "fifth dimension, beyond that which is known to man."

The Untouchables   crime   (1959–63)   ABC

This show had its basis in fact. A Chicago newspaper had

Rod Serling himself hosted <u>Twilight Zone</u>, but the first choice had been Orson Welles.

labeled Elliot Ness and his group of fellow U.S. Treasury agents, who had captured Al Capone, "The Untouchables." The facts, however, ended there. This was nothing unusual, except that with narration by Walter Winchell the show purported to be other than what it was. Among the thugs that Ness (played by Robert Stack) and his gang reined in were Buggs Moran (Lloyd Nolan), Legenza (William Bendix), Mad Dog Coll (Clu Gulager), and Nate Selko (Peter Falk). The audience was not tuning in for historical accuracy but rather for its first real dose of violence on TV.

Groucho: Tell me. I understand that men of the cloth are not of great means. How can you afford a vacation here on the West Coast?

Clergyman: Well, Groucho, I just had a windfall.

Groucho: Oh? Have you tried Alka-Seltzer?

—*You Bet Your Life*

You Bet Your Life game (1950–61) NBC

Groucho Marx ran with this show for 3 years on radio before it was transplanted to television. With his bow tie, mustache, cigar, and his deadpan gaze, Groucho worked well in the visual medium. The show was actually rather simplistic: Two contestants were given money that they could increase if they answered questions correctly (they lost money if they were wrong). There was also a wild card thrown in, a mangy duck that would flop down from the ceiling for an added $100 if they said the secret word. But all of this was just an excuse for Groucho to dispense his wit. He would interview the contestants and usually show them to be anything but masters of their fate. As George Fenneman, the announcer, said in introducing the host: "the one, the only—Groucho Marx."

Your Show of Shows   comedy variety   (1950–54)   NBC

Growing out of the 1949 *Admiral Broadway of Revue*, Sid Caesar and Imogene Coca starred in this weekly 90-minute live show that was the heart of the Golden Age of Television. It grew into an ensemble with the comedic talents of Carl Reiner and Howard Morris and the writing talents of Woody Allen, Mel Brooks, Larry Gelbart, and Neil Simon. Some of Caesar's memorable characters were Progress Hornsby, a jazz musician; Professor Sigmund von Fraidy Katz, a scholar; Giuseppe Marinara, a filmmaker; and Somerset Winterset, a writer. Together Coca and Caesar were the unideal couple, the Hicklenloopers, and did takeoffs on movies, such as "From Here to Obscurity." (Who can forget the two tussling about on stage getting drenched with buckets of water?)

Wagon Train   western   (1957–65)   NBC, ABC

Ward Bond, who had starred as Major Seth Adams in the movie *The Wagonmaster*, recreated the role 7 years later for this TV show. He helped pioneers make the trek from St. Joseph, Missouri, to the West until his death in 1960. The new wagon master, Chris Hale, was played by John McIntire. The focus of each show was determined by the week's guest.

What's My Line?   quiz, panel   (1950–67)   CBS

The granddaddy of all panel shows (a genre that includes *I've Got a Secret*, *To Tell the Truth*, and *Masquerade Party*) was *What's My Line?*—a show that stayed on the air for more than 25 years. The idea behind this Mark Goodson––Bill Todman show was simple. A panel of celebrity "experts" would guess the occupation of a guest by asking questions, to which the guest would answer yes or no.

What's My Line? was originally meant to be a serious, straightforward show. ("Will you sign in please," instructed the solemn-faced John Daly, the host.) However, during auditions the comedic possibilities immediately became apparent. That's why one of the most memorable panels consisted of the sensible Dorothy Killgallen, the witty Arlene

Some People Who Appeared on What's My Line? as Either Contestants, Panelists, or Mystery Guests

Edward Albee: playwright
Edward Villella: ballet dancer
Norman Rockwell: painter
Beverly Sills: opera singer
Marcel Marceau: mime
Jesse Owens: track athlete
Lillian Gish: movie actress
Satchel Paige: baseball player
Agnes DeMille: choreographer
Frank Zappa: rock musician

Francis, the punning Bennett Cerf, plus the droll Steve Allen, a guest panelist for a year and a half. (Allen's enduring question "Is it bigger than a breadbox?" originated during this time.)

What's My Line? ran longer than any other prime-time panel show. It was on CBS from 1950 to 1967.

Early Television Bloopers

In the formative years of television broadcasting, when shows were telecast live, there were, as you might well imagine, numerous errors, gaffes, bloopers, mistakes, and general all-round mayhem that sometimes got transmitted to the screen. (*TV Guide*, in fact, offered free tickets to TV shows to viewers who spotted mistakes.) Among the bloopers that occurred during some of the shows of the early 1950s were these.

In one show, Ellery Queen thought there was a gas leak, so what did he do? He looked for the gas leak with his cigarette lighter. Dumb detective or what?

Lloyd Nolan was being held at gunpoint by a man in a chauffeur's uniform. Suddenly, the actor swung at the chauffeur with his right hand, and knocked the man to the ground. "You were always a sucker for a left hook," Nolan snarled.

On *One's Man Family*, Claudia was supposed to look at her wristwatch to see what time it was. "7:10," she announced. Unfortunately, she wasn't wearing a watch.

On *Studio One*'s production of *Mutiny on the Nicolette*, the captain of the ship used a road map to navigate with.

On *Theater of Music Classics*, Bob Bryer played a record to advertise a phonograph. After he removed the record from the machine, the music continued to play.

The early television series *Mama (I Remember Mama)* was broadcast on CBS from 1949 to 1956. The series concerned a Norwegian family living in San Francisco at the turn of the century. The show was sponsored by Maxwell House, and episodes during the first 3 years showed Mama opening a can of Maxwell House coffee. Unfortunately, at the time the stories were taking place, vacuum-packed cans were not yet being used.

On *Playhouse of the Stars*, Charleton Heston was shown typing away on a battered typewriter. The television camera angle, however, made it clear that there was no ribbon in the typewriter.

On *Your Hit Parade*, a man and a woman were shown riding a Ferris wheel. The man is seen tossing an ice-cream cone away. According to the script, the ice-cream cone was to hit another man in the eye, but the camera was quicker than the actor, because audiences at home were treated to the sight of the actor taking an ice cream cone and sticking it into his eye.

In 1954, a man by the name of George Poper appeared on the television show *Strike It Rich*. For his hard-luck story, he won all of $65, but when a kinescope of the show was telecast in Austin, Texas, Poper was quickly recognized by law enforcement officers. Poper had been a fugitive from an indictment of embezzlement; he was promptly arrested.

The Highest-rated Shows of the Decade

1960: *Gunsmoke* (CBS)

1961: *Wagon Train* (NBC)

1962: *The Beverly Hillbillies* (CBS)

1963: *The Beverly Hillbillies* (CBS)

1964: *Bonanza* (NBC)

1965: *Bonanza* (NBC)

1966: *Bonanza* (NBC)

1967: *The Andy Griffith Show* (CBS)

1968: *Rowan and Martin's Laugh-In* (NBC)

1969: *Rowan and Martin's Laugh-In* (NBC)

The 1960s

The Addams Family   sitcom   (1964–66)   ABC

This unlikely sitcom, inspired by Charles Addams's cartoons in *The New Yorker*, has become a cult classic. With a castle full of offbeat characters—Morticia (Carolyn Jones), Gomez (John Astin), Uncle Fester (Jackie Coogan; had he really once been the fresh-faced kid in Charlie Chaplin's *The Kid?*), Lurch (Ted "You rang?" Cassidy, who also played Thing, the hand), Grandmama (Blossom Rock), and children Pugsley (Ken Weatherwax) and Wednesday (Lisa Loring)—this nuclear family (meaning it could blow up at any time) turned normal sensibilities upside down. As Morticia once cooed to Gomez as she batted her eyes: "I've been yours since that first day you carved your initials in my leg." Its popularity was translated to the big screen in the features *The Addams Family* (1992) and *Addams Family Values* (1993).

Cosmetic Saleslady: Say, maybe you could help me make a sale. . . . What kind of powder does your mommy use?

Wednesday: Baking powder.

Cosmetic Saleslady: I mean on her face.

Wednesday: Baking powder.

—*The Addams Family*

The Andy Griffith Show   sitcom   (1960–68)   CBS

This rural sitcom featured the warm humanitarianism of Griffith's Andy Taylor, "the sheriff without a gun." As Taylor described Mayberry, North Carolina, it was "just a little town. We hang around, get up in the morning and go to work and come home. For entertainment, we have television and movies, and we take rides in the car out of town on Sundays." Andy's son, Opie (Ron Howard), and Aunt Bee (Frances Bavier) completed the family circle. In contrast, Andy's deputy was Barney Fife (Don Knotts), who tried to do everything according to the regulations. Gomer Pyle (Jim Nabors) pumped gas until he went off to his own show, *Gomer Pyle, U.S.M.C.*; Don Knotts went on to *The Don Knotts Show*.

No Longer the First on Your Block

In 1968 Americans began buying more color televisions than black-and-white sets. That year 5.8 million color sets were sold versus 5.5 million black-and-white sets.

The Avengers spy drama (1966–69) ABC

This stylish sleuth show was born during the James Bond era and tried to outdo Bond at his own game. It featured Jonathan Steed as the debonair Patrick Macnee, a British secret agent decked out in three-piece suit and bowler. His first female partner was Honor Blackman, who played Pussy Galore in *Goldfinger*, and his last was Linda Thorson. But it was the leather-jumpsuited and booted Diana Rigg, an actress capable of casting off sparks of intelligence with a mere glance, who defined the role of Mrs. Emma Peel. In their 51 episodes together Macnee and Peel outdid the villains of the world without once losing their humor or misplacing their sense of propriety.

Batman adventure (1966–68) ABC

This 1939 comic book character came to life on the TV screen as high camp. Batman (Adam West) had both his parents killed by thugs, so he was obsessed with stopping criminals. The Caped Crusader was assisted by Robin (Burt Ward), the Boy Wonder. The Dynamic Duo responded to calls from the police commissioner on the batphone or by batsignal to track down their many archenemies: the Black Widow (Tallulah Bankhead), Catwoman (Julie Newmar, Lee Meriwether, Eartha Kitt), Chandel (Liberace), Egghead (Vincent Price), the Joker (Cesar Romero), King Tut (Victor Buono), Lola Lasagne (Ethel Merman), Louie the Lilac (Milton Berle), Lucky Pierre (Pierre Salinger), Mr. Freeze (George Sanders, Otto Preminger, Eli Wallach), the Penguin (Burgess Meredith), or the Riddler (Frank Gorshen). The first year this high camp production was shown on two separate nights each week and was so popular that both shows were ranked in the top 10—yet it was off the air only 2 years later!

Ben Casey medical drama (1961–66) ABC

Vince Edwards played the title role of the dashing brain surgeon at County General Hospital. (You knew the show was dealing with serious issues when the voice after the opening credits intoned: "Man, woman, birth, death, infinity. . . .") Although Dr. Casey seemed to know practically everything there was to know in the field of medicine, he still needed an occasional pep talk from Dr. David Zorba, played by savvy Sam Jaffe, the chief surgeon who served as Casey's conscience.

The Beverly Hillbillies sitcom (1962–71) CBS

The storyline of this sitcom was rather simple. After oil was discovered on Jed Clampett's (Buddy Ebson) Appalachian spread, the patriarch moved his clan to Beverly Hills. The cast included Granny (whose given name was Daisy Moses), his mother-in-law (Irene Ryan), his daughter Elly May (Donna Douglas), and his nephew, Jethro Bodine (Max Baer Jr., the prize fighter's son). The clash of cultures was made especially apparent in the Clampetts' dealings with their banker and his secretary, the stiff Miss (Jane) Hathaway (Nancy Kulp). The unsophisticated humor made this the number-one show during its first 2 years. However, by the end of its run city slickers had stopped watching the show and it was viewed primarily by people in the sticks, by other—er—hillbillies.

Bewitched sitcom (1964–72) ABC

Samantha Stevens (Elizabeth Montgomery) was not a typical housebound housewife. Because she was also a witch, all she had to do was wiggle her nose and her every wish would come true. Samantha was married to an earthbound husband who worked for an ad agency, Darrin Stephens (Dick York, Dick Sargent), a match that her mother, Endora (Agnes Moorehead)—also a witch—could never quite fathom. (Nominated for five Oscars and six Emmys, Moorehead could never quite win either.) The couple eventually had a daughter, Tabitha, played by twins Erin and Diane Murphy.

The Brady Bunch sitcom (1969–74) ABC

This sitcom about Mike and Carol Brady (Robert Reed and Florence Henderson) with three sons and three daughters from previous marriages set the standard for what a "typical" American family was like. With Ann B. Davis as Alice, their housekeeper-referee, the trivial concerns of the Bradys were enough to make any viewer feel like a stranger in a strange land. The bunch included Greg (Barry Williams), Marcia (Maureen McCormick), Peter (Christopher Knight), Jan (Eve Plumb), Bobby (Michael Lookinland), and Cindy (Susan Olsen).

Candid Camera comedy (1960–67) CBS

The genesis for this show began during World War II when Allen Funt was sitting around the barracks one day and began recording the candid comments of GIs. After the war, Funt got his *Candid Microphone* on radio, and later the idea was turned into *Candid Camera* on TV. Funt (along with his main co-host, Durwood Kirby) seemed to take genuine delight setting up traps for unsuspecting people who would then be "caught in the act of being themselves." Then it was "Smile, you're on *Candid Camera*."

The Carol Burnett Show comedy variety (1967–79) CBS

One of the secrets of the longevity of this show was Carol

BARRY WILLIAMS

Barry Williams penned _Growing Up Brady_ about his years as a teen dream Greg Brady on _The Brady Bunch._

herself. From her opening sequence of fielding questions from the audience to her farewell ear tug, it was Burnett who held it all together. A comedian who can sing, dance, act, mimic, mime, and exude a feeling of genuine warmth,

Burnett was joined by a company of regulars—Harvey Korman, Lyle Wagonner, Tim Conway, and Vicki Lawrence—for such ongoing skits as "Ed and Eunice" (marital unbliss), "Mr. Tudball and Mrs. Wiggins" (problems at the office), and "As the Stomach Turns" (a satire of soaps). There were also musical numbers by guests as well as by Burnett. After Harvey Korman left in 1977, the ratings began to slip and, two years later, the show was off the air. *The Carol Burnett Show* was revived for a short run in 1991, but the audience was no longer there.

Dark Shadows Gothic soap opera (1966–71) ABC

This first occult soap opera starred Jonathan Frid as Barnabas Collins, a 200-year-old vampire who resided in an old mansion, Collinwood, in Collinsport, Maine. Other regulars on the show were a werewolf (Quentin Collins), a witch (Angelique), a monster (Jeb Hawkes), and a warlock (Nicholas Blair). There was also a Dr. Julia Hoffman (Grayson Hall) who tried to cure Barnabas of his penchant for sinking his fangs into unsuspecting necks. ("Do you mind if I invite myself in for a drink?") As many of the characters had previous and unusually long lives, there were many extended historical flashbacks. *Dark Shadows* was afterschool camp (90% of the audience was teenagers) that became a long-standing cult favorite.

The Defenders legal drama (1961–65) CBS

Growing out of a 1957 *Studio One* production starring Ralph Bellamy and William Shatner, this weekly dramatic series featured E. G. Marshall and Robert Reed, as the father-son lawyer team of Preston & Preston. Kenneth, the son, had recently graduated from law school, and he had much to learn from his father, Lawrence, not only about the intricacies of law but about life. The script did not shy away from controversial issues, treating such topics as abortion, illegal immigration, and mercy killing. (Sounds like today's newspaper.) Marshall won 2 Emmys; the show, 11.

The Dick Van Dyke Show sitcom (1961–66) CBS

Conceived by Carl Reiner, this sitcom featured Dick Van Dyke as Rob Petrie, the head writer for *The Alan Brady Show*, and Mary Tyler Moore as his wife, Laura. The Petries were a couple never seen on sitcoms before: a man and wife who were intellectual equals. The show was also noteworthy for seeing Rob Petrie at his job writing for a comedy TV show. He didn't just walk out of the house in the morning and return at night. Also prominent in the cast were Morey Amsterdam and Rose Marie as comedy writers Buddy Sorrell and Sally Rogers, Richard Deacon as producer Mel Cooley (the butt of many jokes), Carl Reiner as star Alan Brady, and Jerry Paris as Jerry Helper, the Petries' next-door neighbor in New Rochelle.

Dr. Kildare medical drama (1961–66) NBC

This TV show had a long genesis. It began as a series of short stories by Frederick Shiller Faust in the 1930s, followed by movies, and then a radio show. But the biggest splash of all was created by Richard Chamberlain as Dr. James Kildare. (He was a far cry from Vince Edwards on *Ben Casey*, the other medic on the air.) Whenever the idealistic Kildare needed advice, there was the sagacious Raymond Massey as Dr. Leonard Gillespie at Blair General Hospital. In the beginning, Kildare was an intern trying to win the approval of the older doctors. When Kildare became a doctor, the focus switched to his patients and their lives. By the end of the series the episodes continued over several shows, more in the style of a soap opera.

The F.B.I. police drama (1965–74) ABC

J. Edgar Hoover gave his imprimatur to this show starring Efrem Zimbalist Jr. as Inspector Lewis Erskine, William Reynolds as Agent Tom Colby, and Philip Abbott as Agent Arthur Ward. Hoover liked the show so much, how the smooth, buttoned-down Zimbalist always got his man, that he opened up F.B.I. headquarters in Washington, D.C., for the filming of background scenes.

The Flintstones animated sitcom (1960–66) ABC

Animated by Hanna-Barbera, *The Flintstones* can be viewed as a Stone Age takeoff on *The Honeymooners*. Fred Flintstone would return home after a hard day at the rock quarry to his wife, Wilma, who looked after their daughter, Pebbles, their split-level cave, and Dino, their pet dinosaur. (Wilma enjoyed playing her Stoneway piano; Fred his "rock" music.) Their best friends were the Rubbles: Barney (Mel Blanc supplied this voice); Betty; and their adopted son, Bamm Bamm. One of the first color cartoons on TV, *The Flintstones* was geared for adults as much as children. Not only was it shown during prime time but it also included characters from pop culture (Lollobrickida, Perry Masonry, and TV host Ed Sullystone). A popular show in reruns, *The Flintstones* made it to the big screen in 1994.

The Fugitive drama (1963–67) ABC

David Janssen was Dr. Richard Kimble, the fugitive. Sentenced to die for the murder of his own wife, Kimble maintained that a one-armed man had actually done the killing. A train wreck on the way to his execution allowed Kimble to escape, only to be doggedly pursued for four years by Lt. Philip Gerard (Barry Morse). Each episode showed Kimble in one odd job after another as he used his time on the lam in an attempt to track down the real killer, Fred Johnson, played by Bill Raisch, as well as stay out of the clutches of the law. At the conclusion of the series, Kimble was cornered by the one-armed killer atop a water tower. Gerard was able to hear the killer's confession before the lieutenant shot him to save Kimble's life. It was such a compelling show, as if Albert Camus were let loose in the ABC studios, that it was resurrected in 1993 as a major motion picture starring Harrison Ford.

Get Smart sitcom (1965–70) NBC

Developed by Mel Brooks and Buck Henry, this spy spoof featured Don Adams in the leading role as Maxwell Smart, who was anything but. Agent 86 (bartender's lingo for cutting off a drinker) was joined by Barbara Feldon as

Agent 99 in an attempt to keep the evil forces of K.A.O.S. at bay. Fortunately for the good guys (Smart's shoe telephone always seemed to be ringing at the wrong time), Agent 86 always seemed to land on both feet. As he would often say when trying to convince someone of his plans, "Would you believe . . . ?" This stock phrase became part of the jargon of the 1960s. The show began with one of the best opening sequences created for television as Smart passed through a series of slamming doors before disappearing into a phone booth.

Sanchez: [*putting Max before an angry firing squad*] Would you like a blindfold? A last cigarette?

Max: No. I'm trying to break the habit.

—*Get Smart*

Gilligan's Island   sitcom   (1964–67)   CBS

Nobody expected a show about the shipwreck of the *Minnow* (with its two crew members and five passengers) on an uncharted island in the South Pacific to be the whale of a hit it was. Some may not have expected it to last much longer than the 3 hours of the *Minnow*'s original cruise; however, it kept the cast busy for the next 3 years: Bob Denver as the hapless Gilligan, Alan Hale Jr. as the obtuse Skipper Jonas Grumby, Tina Louise as the sexy movie star Ginger Grant, Dawn Wells as the girl next door Mary Anne Summers, Russell Johnson as high-school science teacher Professor Roy Hinkley, Jim Backus as the snobbish millionaire Thurston Howell III, and Natalie Schaefer as his blustery wife, Lovey. This show has sometimes been pointed to as exhibit number one that TV really is "a vast wasteland." At other times, it has been held up as evidence that TV gives the customers what they want.

In any case, the shenanigans of Gilligan proved extremely popular.

Hawaii Five-O police drama (1968–80) CBS

Jack Lord as Steve McGarrett, the head of the crime unit, and James MacArthur as Dano Williams, his assistant, tracked one criminal after another among the palm trees. At the end of this longest-running crime show ever, the diabolical Wo Fat (Khigh Dhiegh) is captured. The title refers to Hawaii's status as the 50th state.

Hogan's Heroes sitcom (1965–71) CBS

On the low end of the scale of funny ideas for sitcoms would probably be life in a German POW camp. But that was the situation of *Hogan's Heroes* as Colonel Robert Hogan (Bob Crane) and the other "prisoners" of Stalag 13 had the run of the camp and practically lived in luxury while their captors, the buffonish Sergeant Hans Schultz (John Banner) and the crotchety Colonel Wilhelm Klink (Werner Klemperer) unwittingly watched. Attempts at escape formed a frequent plot line.

The Hollywood Squares game (1966–80) NBC

Celebrities, particularly Cliff Arquette and Wally Cox, sitting in a three-level tic-tac-toe set would be asked questions by host Peter Marshall. The contestant (of the two playing) who had picked the celebrity would listen to the answer (the more ridiculous the better) and agree or disagree. Sitting at the center square was the outrageous Paul Lynde. A show for the dentist's chair.

I Dream of Jeannie sitcom (1965–70) NBC

When astronaut Captain Tony Nelson (Larry Hagman) discovered an ornate bottle when forced down on a desert island, inside was a 2,000-year-old genie (Barbara Eden), who promptly proclaimed him "master" for setting her free. Returning home to Cocoa Beach, Jeannie complicated Nelson's life. Whenever someone approached, she would disappear, so that the NASA psychiatrist, Dr. Alfred Bellows (Hayden Rorke), overhearing Hagman, thought he was suffering from exposure. The only other person who ever saw Jeannie was Nelson's best friend, Captain Roger Healey (Bill Daily). And what Jeannie didn't see were the strange customs of 20th-century American culture.

I Spy   spy drama   (1965–68)   NBC

In a gadget-free secret agent series, Robert Culp played Kelly Robinson, a top-ranked tennis player, who traveled around the world for tournaments and espionage with his trainer, Bill Cosby as Alexander Scott. No rubdown artist with linament, Scott was a Temple University graduate fluent in languages and a Rhodes scholar to boot. Indeed, Cosby was the first African-American to star regularly in a dramatic series, and he was the winner of three consecutive Emmy Awards.

Ironside   police drama   (1967–75)   NBC

After *Perry Mason* ground to a halt, Raymond Burr found another star vehicle as Robert Ironside, the one-time chief of detectives of the San Francisco Police Department who had been paralyzed by a bullet to his spine. Confined to a wheelchair, Ironside proved that his mind still worked even if his legs didn't. Transported to the scene of the crime in a souped-up police van, Ironside was ably helped out by Sergeant Ed Brown (Don Galloway), Mark Sanger (Don Mitchell), Policewoman Eve Whitfield (Barbara Anderson), and later Policewoman Fran Belding (Elizabeth Bauer).

Jeopardy!   game   (1964–75;   1978–79;   1984–   )   NBC, syndicated

In *Jeopardy!* Merv Griffin developed a game show that stood the genre on its head: instead of giving answers, contestants come up with the questions for the answers provided. One of the draws of this show is that the average viewer at home is able to participate (more than in conventional quiz shows) in trying to outdo the contestants. The host from 1964 to 1979 was Art Fleming; since 1984 it has been Alex Trebek.

The Jetsons animated sitcom (1962–83) ABC

The Jetsons was *The Flintstones* rocketed into the Space Age. (It was also made by the same folks at Hanna-Barbera.) After a day at Spacely Space Sprockets, George journeyed home in his atomic bubble to the Skypad Apartments, where he was met by Jane, his wife; Judy and Elroy, their children; and Astro, their dog. Although only 24 episodes had been released, *The Jetsons* was shown from 1963 to 1983. In 1985, 41 new shows were added, enough to blast off this syndicated series into the 21st century.

Julia sitcom (1968–71) NBC

In the first starring role for an African-American woman since *Beulah* (Ethel Waters, 1950–52; Louise Beavers, 1952–53), Diahann Carroll portrayed a nurse (Beulah had been a maid). In addition to being a professional, Julia Baker was a single mother raising a 6-year-old (Marc Copage). (Julia's pilot husband had been killed in combat in Vietnam.)

Lost in Space science fiction (1965–68) CBS

The space family Robinson blasted off on a 5-year mission to explore Alpha Centauri. However, on board was enemy agent Dr. Zachery Smith (Jonathan Harris) who sabotaged the steering mechanism so that they were all lost in space. The Robinson family—Dr. John Robinson (Guy Williams); his wife, Maureen (June Lockart); Judy (Marta Kristen); Will (Billy Mumy); and Penny (Angela Cartwright)—went planet hopping in hopes of finding some friendlies to help them return home. Also, trying to help out was the Robot ("It does not compute") played by Bob May.

McHale's Navy sitcom (1962–66) ABC

This was the navy version of *The Phil Silvers Show*. Instead of Fort Baxter, Kansas, the setting was the south seas; yet, the tension with those in command was the same. Lieutenant Commander Quinton McHale (Ernest Borgnine) led his outrageous PT crew against the straight-laced Captain Wallace B. Binghamton (Joe Flynn), who had also assigned Ensign

Charles Parker (Tim Conway) to this hopeless cause. After 130 episodes McHale was still holding all the aces.

The Man from U.N.C.L.E. spy drama (1964–68) NBC

This show, spawned by Ian Fleming's novel *Goldfinger*, featured Napoleon Solo (Robert Vaughn) and Ilya Kuryakin (David McCallum) as agents from U.N.C.L.E. (United Network Command for Law and Enforcement), dispatched by their boss, Alexander Waverly (Leo G. Carroll), to do battle around the world. Solo, an American, and Kuryakin, a Russian, were fighting something bigger than democracy versus communism. They were up against the evil empire of T.H.R.U.S.H.

Mannix crime (1967–75) CBS

Mannix was one of the first shows to prove that violence is a ratings winner. Detective Joe Mannix (Mike Connors) had a penchant for settling things using nothing fancier than his fists. By show's end, bodies were sometimes stacked like so much cord wood, giving rise to a Bob and Ray parody titled *Blimmix*.

Marcus Welby, M.D. medical drama (1969–76) ABC

Robert Young played the ultimate family doctor, more concerned with the well-being of his patients than with anything else (except perhaps the Nielsen ratings). James Brolin played his younger, brasher associate, Steven Kiley.

Mission: Impossible drama (1966–73) CBS

At the opening of each episode, the leader of the Missions Impossible Force would play a tape: "Your mission, should you decide to accept it, is. . . . This tape will self-destruct in five seconds." Then James Phelps (Peter Graves) would select his people, Cinnamon Carter (Barbara Bain), Rollin Hand (Martin Landau), and others to carry out an intricate plan against some small Communist country or big organized crime outfit. (When the show was revived for the 1988 season, a laser disc was used instead of an audiotape; however, by 1990, the show itself had self-destructed.)

Mr. Novak drama (1963–65) NBC

John Novak (James Franciscus), an idealistic English teacher at Jefferson High School, found himself up against either students who didn't want to learn or a system that disliked innovation. His principal was Albert Vane (Dean Jagger), who later became the superintendent of schools and was replaced by Martin Woodridge (Burgess Meredith). Though few would have thought a show about a high school teacher would make for sexy viewing, *Mr. Novak*'s popularity paved the way for other shows about teachers.

Mister Ed sitcom (1961–65) CBS

Wilbur Post (played by Alan Young) was an architect fed up with the city. When he purchased a home and barn in the country for himself and his wife, Carol (Connie Hines), he wound up with more than he bargained for. In the barn was a palomino who went by the moniker of Mister Ed who could—you guessed it—talk. Why had he never talked before then? Well, Mister Ed had simply never run into anyone worth talking to, of course. Post's life was further complicated by the fact that Mister Ed (his voice was provided by Allan "Rocky" Lane, a former actor in westerns) refused to talk to anyone but him.

Mister Ed registered two firsts: It was the first noncartoon TV show out of the gate to feature a talking animal, and it was the first TV show to graduate from syndication to prime time.

Wilbur: How does hay taste to a horse?

Ed: Tastes terrible.

Wilbur: It does? Why are you eating it?

Ed: I don't see you offering me pizza.

—*Mister Ed*

Here are some guest stars who appeared as themselves on Mister Ed

Leo Durocher: baseball coach

Clint Eastwood: actor

Zsa Zsa Gabor: actress

Sandy Koufax: baseball Hall-of-Famer

George Burns: entertainer

John Roseboro: baseball player

Sharon Tate: actress

Mae West: actress

Moose Skowron: baseball player

Mister Rogers' Neighborhood children's (1967–75; 1979–) PBS

Fred Rogers began as a Presbyterian minister from Pittsburgh who used stories, songs, and puppets to get through to kids. From there he went to NBC's *The Children's Corner* and *MisteRogers' Neighborhood* on Canadian TV, and finally to the show as it is known today. Children respond to this kindly man who speaks gently and slips into a sweater and slippers on the homey set. They are also comfortable with such regulars as Mr. McFeely, "the Speedy Delivery Man," and even learn things when they travel by toy trolley to visit everything from apiaries to zoos. *Mr. Rogers' Neighborhood* is now the longest-running children's show on TV.

The Mod Squad crime (1968–73) ABC

In the days following the Chicago riots at the Democratic convention, it was easy (if you were under 30) not to trust anyone over 30. Into this mood slipped *The Mod Squad*, three hippies who had been in minor scrapes with the law (Peggy Lipton as Julie Barnes, Clarence Williams III as Linc Hayes, and Michael Cole as Pete Cochrane) and had been recruited to be cops to infiltrate the counterculture and bust criminals over 30.

The Monkees sitcom (1966–68) NBC

Sired by the Beatles' *A Hard Day's Night* (1964) and *Help!* (1965), this sitcom used many of the same techniques from those film classics: clips from other films, distorted focus, fast and slow motion, and non sequiturs. But the real breakthrough of the series was in the commercial exploitation of the youth market. Of the four selected for the series, Davy Jones, Mickey Dolenz, Peter Tork, and Michael Nesmith, the first two were actors and the second two had been folk singers. Professional musicians dubbed their playing, and the singing and sound was so manufactured in the studio that their later live concerts left audiences confused and disappointed. During the run of the show, however, the Monkees churned out one hit single ("I'm a Believer," "Last Train to Clarksville," and "Words") and album after another, outselling even the Beatles.

Monty Python's Flying Circus comedy (1969–74) BBC

"And now for something completely different." This show, veddy British and in the tradition of *The Goon Show, Beyond the Fringe*, and *That Was the Week That Was* was first seen in the United States after its British run ended in 1974. It featured Graham Chapman, John Cleese (his father had changed their surname from Cheese), Eric Idle, Terry Jones, and Michael Palin. (Terry Gilliam, an American, designed the surreal animation.) *Monty Python* poked fun at talk show hosts, documentaries, professionals, religion, the military—everyone and everything else. There was a Minister of Silly Walks, a Society for Putting Things on Top of Things, a Twit of the Year, and a Summarize Proust contest. As Cleese once remarked, "The nicest thing anyone ever said about [the show] is that they couldn't watch the news after seeing it."

The Munsters   sitcom   (1964–66)   CBS

Fred Gwynne was Herman Munster, a seven-foot Franken-
stein monster look-alike, Yvonne DeCarlo was Lily, his
vampire wife, and Al Lewis was Grandpa, an aging Count
Dracula type, in this far cry from the iconoclastic *Addams
Family*. The addresses present a clue as to the differences
between these two shows: the Munsters' 1313 Mockingbird Lane versus the Addams's 000 Cemetery Lane. The
Munsters were attempting the impossible task of fitting in
as a regular family in the neighborhood, whereas the Ad-
damses relished their oddball eccentricity.

My Three Sons   sitcom   (1960–65; 1965–72)   ABC, CBS

Second to *The Adventures of Ozzie & Harriet* as the longest-
running sitcom, *My Three Sons* starred Fred MacMurray as
Steve Douglas, an aeronautical engineer and the widowed
father of three boys, Mike (Tim Considine), Robbie (Don
Grady), and Chip (Stanley Livingston). Helping out at 837
Mill Street was William Frawley as "Bub" O'Casey, Steve's
father-in-law. When Frawley died in 1965 (he went to
Ireland in the script), he was replaced by William Demar-
est as Uncle Charley. (The other changes and replacements
in the cast, as with many American families, approached
critical mass.) In 1967, the family moved to North Hollywood; the next year, Robbie married and had triplets, and
the story possibilities became as variable as a soap opera.
As Marvin Kitman once observed on *The Marvin Kitman
TV Show:* "The Douglas family—and their neighbors the
Nelsons (Ozzie and Harriet), the Andersons ("Father
Knows Best") and the Donna Reed family—was the place
where a viewer could escape from the reality of his own
house. On that Great Block in the Sky, fathers never yelled
at their kids, mothers never threw dishes or uttered pro-
fanities, nobody ever hit his children unreasonably or worried about making a living."

Peyton Place   drama   (1964–69)   ABC

Based loosely on Grace Metalious's book of the same name,
this show explored the sordid affairs and skeletons in clos-

ets in this small New England town. Constance MacKenzie (Dorothy Malone) was the bookstore owner whose daughter, Allison, had been sired by a man who had been sent away to prison. Allison (Mia Farrow) fell in love with wealthy Rodney Harrington (Ryan O'Neal) who was later brought up on a murder charge. (Farrow and O'Neal both got their start in this series.) And so on through a hundred characters breezed this first soap opera to be shown at night.

The Prisoner mystery (1968–69) CBS

The actor Patrick McGoohan (who was also the creator, producer, writer, and director of this series) was being held prisoner. However, Number 6, as he was called, didn't know why, or even who his captors were. All he knew for sure was that he and others (all of them were apparently former spys who knew too much) were in a beautiful and mysterious village patrolled by Rover (actually meteorological balloons). Number 6 did not want to lose his individuality and didn't crack when Number 2 attempted to have him brainwashed. His only ally was the silent Butler, played by Angelo Muscat. At the end of this Kafkaesque series of only 17 shows, McGoohan escapes. The message? We are all prisoners.

Route 66 drama (1960–64) CBS

Tod Stiles (Martin Milner) was a young man from money and Yale and Buzz Murdock (George Maharis) was a graduate of the school of hard knocks, but they shared in common a 1960 Corvette as they roamed the highways of the U.S.A. in search of adventure and meaning. Accompanied by Nelson Riddle's jazzy theme and in 1963 by the replacement of Maharis by a disenchanted Vietnam vet named Linc Case (Glenn Corbett), there was still tight writing and acting, a Corvette, and the Kerouacian call of the open road.

Rowan and Martin's Laugh-In comedy (1968–73) NBC

In addition to Dan Rowan and Dick Martin, some of the

prominent regulars on this running gag of a show were Ruth Buzzi, Judy Carne, Henry Gibson, Goldie Hawn, Arte Johnson, Flip Wilson, Lily Tomlin, and JoAnne Worley. Rated as the number-one show for its first two seasons, *Laugh-In* even affected the language of the times: "Beautiful downtown Burbank," "Here comes de judge," "Look that up in your Funk and Wagnalls," "The devil made me do it," "Verrrry interesting," "Sock it to me," and "You bet your sweet bippy."

Sesame Street   children's   (1969–   )   PBS

Produced by the Children's Television Workshop, this show established new ways to teach children about numbers, letters, grammar, and life. (When Will Lee who played Mr. Hooper died, the show dealt with the issue of death and dying.) One of the show's methods is to use the quick-cut techniques of advertising to stimulate and keep interest (the show is also "sponsored" by a particular letter or number). The show was home to the Muppets, created by Jim Henson (Bert and Ernie, the Cookie Monster, Grover, Kermit the Frog, Miss Piggy, and Oscar the Grouch), who went on to enormous celebrity in their own right in books, film, TV specials, and their own *The Muppet Show*.

60 Minutes   news magazine   (1968–   )   CBS

The first and still most successful of the magazine shows, *60 Minutes* begins with the sound and sight of a ticking stopwatch followed by previews of each of the three or more segments of investigative reporting. Later, after each segment has been shown—whether it be a profile of a leading personality or an exposé of corrupt politics—the ticking stopwatch shows how much time remains. Except for Mike Wallace who has been a correspondent since the beginning, there have been personnel changes over the years. The most recent crew features Ed Bradley, Steve Kroft, Morley Safer, Leslie Stahl, Andy Rooney, and of course, Wallace. (Its alums include Diane Sawyer, Harry Reasoner, and Dan Rather.) Don Hewitt, the creator of the show, has been the executive producer ever since its origin.

Desiree Casado plays Gaby on <u>Sesame Street.</u> Photo ©
James J. Kriegsman Jr.

The Smothers Brothers Comedy Hour   comedy
(1967–69)   CBS

Guitar-playing Tom played dumb, bass-playing Dick appeared bright, and the two often talked over youthful competition ("Mom always liked you best"). But as time went by they began to throw out a brand of humor and satire that made TV execs nervous and censors itchy. Even Pat Paulson's "If nominated I will not run, and if elected I will not serve" was a problem because CBS worried that it would bring on a claim for equal time by the less comedic presidential candidates. Equally troublesome to the execs ("The network is for what they are doing; it simply becomes a matter of degree") was an appearance by Pete Seeger singing a Vietnam protest song, "Waist Deep in the Big Muddy" and a message about Mother's Day that ended with "Please talk peace." After one too many last straws the series was replaced by the ho-hum *Hee Haw*. Perhaps the media isn't all that liberal after all.

Star Trek   science fantasy   (1966–69)   NBC

Because of the celestial regard many have today for Gene Roddenberry's creation, it is often overlooked that this show ranked no higher than fifty-second during its initial run. But the U.S.S. *Enterprise* always had a bigger goal: "to seek out new life and new civilizations." Beginning in Stardate 1312.4, the five-year mission of the starship as envoy of The United Federation of Planets, the governing body over the majority of known planets, led the crew to the far reaches of the universe. With William Shatner as Captain James T. Kirk, Leonard Nimoy as Mr. Spock, DeForrest Kelley as Dr. Leonard "Bones" McCoy, James Doohan as Lt. Commander Montgomery "Scotty" Scott, Walter Koenig as Ensign Pavel Chekov, George Takei as Lt. Hikaru Sulu, and Michelle Nichols as Lieutenant Uhura, the crew sailed on to cult status and no fewer than six feature films. The dashing Captain always got the female, whether or not she was human—humanoid was usually close enough—and seemed to be constantly getting the bad news that "He's dead, Jim." Spock's logical Vulcan mind struggled with his human side (his mother was human), which broke through in such episodes as "This Side of Paradise." Bones found teasing Spock irresistible, and Nurse Chapel found him irresistible—period. The chief engineer was never asked to "Beam me up, Scotty." Uhura and Kirk indulged in TV's first interracial kiss, and Uhura kept her cool as a high-ranking officer despite the skin-tight micro-mini dress with thigh-high boots that was female crewmembers' standard uniform. The crew took on not only Klingons and Romulans with the *Enterprise*'s phasers and photon torpedoes, but also battled Greek gods in "Who Mourns for Adonis?," their barbarian counterparts from an alternate universe in "Mirror, Mirror," and a most unusual witch and warlock in "Cat's Paw." Kirk, Spock, and McCoy time traveled in "City on the Edge of Forever," and who could forget our fine, furry friends of "The Trouble with Tribbles."

That Was the Week that Was   satire   (1964–65)   NBC

Known as "TW3," this British import was a show of political satire that took no prisoners, whether it was Washington or the Vatican. Its barbs against Barry Goldwater, however, may have led to the show's early demise, for TW3 was frequently preempted by Republican speeches. By election time, viewers had learned to turn to the competition on the other two channels. TW3 can be viewed as a forerunner to *Saturday Night Live* and *SCTV Comedy Network*.

The Virginian   western   (1962–71)   NBC

Based on the Owen Wister western novel, this was the first of the 90-minute dramas. It starred James Drury as the Virginian, a ranch hand with no other name, who stood witness to the approach of the civilization that would eventually wipe out the cowboy's way of life. Other regulars were Doug McClure as a cowpoke named Tampas and Lee J. Cobb as Judge Henry Garth, the first owner of Shiloh Ranch.

The Wild, Wild West   western   (1965–70)   CBS

This show, James Bond in chaps, featured Robert Conrad

as James T. West, a special agent for President Ulysses S. Grant during the 1870s, and his sidekick, Ross Martin as Artemus Gordon, an expert in disguises and dialects. Traveling about in a specially appointed railroad car, West and Gordon extricated themselves from one sticky situation after another in carrying out their assignments. Their most difficult adversary, their version of Sherlock Holmes's Professor Moriarty, was a dwarf named Dr. Miguelito Loveless, played by Michael Dunn.

The 1970s

Monday Night Football sports (1970–) ABC

Even people who do not ordinarily watch football tune in to football on Monday nights. It probably has to do with the fatigue factor after a day of work as well as the sportscasters. In the early years it was Frank Gifford doing the play-by-play and Howard Cosell and Don Meredith doing the color commentary. Nowadays it is still Frank Gifford joined by Al Michaels and Dan Dierdorf.

All in the Family sitcom (1971–83) CBS

This sitcom ran almost as long as *The Adventures of Ozzie & Harriet*, but the two shows were polar opposites. *All in the Family* created a revolution in television. No one had ever seen anything before like producer Norman Lear's blue-collar family that freely spoke their minds. *Any* controversial subject could find its way into the script: abortion, homosexuality, quotas. The language regularly included offensive racial epithets. (This certainly was light-years away from *The Moon Is Blue* days when the mere mention of the word *virgin* created shock waves in the entertainment industry.)

Archie Bunker (Caroll O'Connor) was a blue-collar worker who remained in blissful ignorance of his prejudices. (Although O'Connor seemed born to play this role, Mickey Rooney had originally turned it down.) "Look, Archie Bunker ain't no bigot," O'Connor would intone. "I'm

Awards for the Decade (1960–1970) from Time Magazine's "TV Most" Awards

Starting in 1970 (for the year 1969), *Time* magazine started its own awards for television. Some of these awards took note of television's low moments as well as its highs, and a few of the awards were humorous or outrageous in nature. In its first year of the awards, *Time* cited the "Top of the Decade" (1960–1969).

First Kennedy-Nixon debate (1960)

FCC Chairman Newton Minow's "Vast wasteland" speech (1961)

Lee Harvey Oswald murdered by Jack Ruby on camera (1963)

First instant replay adds new dimension to sports coverage (1963)

Vietnam War becomes the first in history to be brought directly into the living room (1964)

A black, Bill Cosby, costars in NBC series, *I Spy* (1965)

All network shows are now broadcast in color (1967)

Peter Goldmark of CBS Labs announces invention of Electronic Video Recording (EVR) (1968)

Television shows men on the Moon (1969)

Vice President Spiro Agnew attacks the networks (1969)

the first to say—it ain't your fault you're colored!" Also living under Archie's roof in Queens, New York, with Archie's baby "goil" Gloria (Sally Struthers) was his son-in-law, Mike Stivic (Rob Reiner). Stivic was studying sociology at a nearby college and bringing home no bacon. ("I tell ya, Gloria married the laziest white man I ever seen.") To Archie, Mike was simply "Meathead." Indeed, Mike's liberal leanings were often as unexamined as Archie's reactionary views. Gloria often defended her husband against Archie's salvos, but it was Edith Bunker (Jean Stapleton) who held the family together. "Dingbat," as Archie often referred to his wife, had an unqualified love that conquered all.

As in real life, the show changed with the years. Bea Arthur, who played Edith's cousin Maude Findlay, moved on to *Maude* (1972–78); Sherman Helmsley opened up his dry-cleaning establishment on his own show, *The Jeffersons* (1975–85); Mike and Gloria moved away (seen in *Gloria* (1982–83); and Archie realized his dream of his own bar on *Archie Bunker's Place* (1979–83).

No Strings

The theme song of *All in the Family* was "Those Were the Days" (also the name of the pilot). Written by Lee Adams and Charles Strouse, it was recorded for a song by Carroll O'Connor and Jean Stapleton—only $800—because that was all there was left in Norman Lear's budget.

Barney Miller sitcom (1975–82) ABC

Once called "the Keystone Cops under the ethnic quota system," Barney Miller (Hal Linden) sent his motley crew out from their 12th Precinct in Greenwich Village to cover the local capers. The cast included Phil Fish (Abe Vigoda), Nick Yemana (Jack Soo), Stanley "Wojo" Wojohowicz (Max Gail), Ron Harris (Ron Glass), Arthur Dietrich (Steve Landesberg), Carl Levitt (Ron Carey), Inspector Luger (James Gregory), and Chano Amengule (Gregoy Sierra). There were no high-speed car chases in this low-tech show: it was all gabbing and jabbing around the station house. The dialogue showed these men in blue had feet very much made of clay.

The Highest-rated Shows of the Decade

1970: *Marcus Welby, M.D.* (ABC)
1971: *All in the Family* (CBS)
1972: *All in the Family* (CBS)
1973: *All in the Family* (CBS)
1974: *All in the Family* (CBS)
1975: *All in the Family* (CBS)
1976: *Happy Days* (ABC)
1977: *Laverne & Shirley* (ABC)
1978: *Three's Company* (ABC)
1979: *60 Minutes* (CBS)

Columbo   police drama   (1971–90)   NBC

Peter Falk proved the old cliché that you can't judge a book by its cover. Shabby and unshaven and wearing a rumpled raincoat that looked like he had slept in it, Falk appeared to be an unlikely candidate to solve any crime whatsoever. As it turns out, however, Lieutenant Columbo is not only up to the task, but he is one of the cagiest members of the L.A.P.D. Although he appears to be oblivious to the facts of the case, he finally skewers his culprit with an unassuming question beginning "Just one more thing. . . ." The show survives in reruns and several prime-time movies.

Dallas   drama   (1978–91)   CBS

Chockablock with colorful characters and knee-deep in convoluted plots, *Dallas* remained a popular show for over a decade. Leading the way were Larry Hagman who played a snake-skinned J. R. and Patrick Duffy as his brother

Bobby who possessed every good trait that J. R. lacked. Some other prominent members of the cast were Barbara Bel Geddes (1978–84, 1985–90) and Donna Reed (1984–85) as Eleanor (Miss Ellie) Southworth Ewing, Victoria Principal (1978–87) as Pamela Barnes Ewing, Linda Gray (1978–89) as Sue Ellen Ewing, Jim Davis (1978–81) as John Ross (Jock) Ewing, Steve Kanaly (1978–88) as Ray Krebbs, Charlene Tilton (1978–85, 1988–90) as Lucy Ewing, Priscilla Presley (1983–88) as Jenna Wade, and Ken Kercheval as Cliff Barnes. The plots revolved around the family down home at the Southfork ranch: the Ewings feuding with the Barneses (Bobby had married a Barnes to complicate things); the Ewings fighting other families; the Ewings scrapping with each other; and J. R. versus everybody.

On November 21, 1980, *Dallas* ran the show that answered the question, "Who Shot J. R.?" About 80% of the TV viewers that night were watching, millions of dollars had been bet. The answer: Kristin Shepard, J. R.'s sister-in-law, a discarded mistress pregnant with J. R.'s child.

Bobby Ewing: Fight? Sue Ellen doesn't fight. She takes it all inside. That's why she's the one who always gets hurt."

—*Dallas*

Happy Days sitcom (1974–84) ABC

This show grew out of Ron Howard's character in an appearance on *Love, American Style* and in the movie *American Graffitti*. If it had stopped with the Cunningham family, Dad Howard (Tom Bosley), Mom (Marion Ross), and sister Joanie (Erin Moran), it would have been Ozzie and Harriet all over again, but Henry Winkler as the Fonz

(Arthur Fonzarelli) pushed it to the edge. The goodness of Richie Cunningham (Howard) was balanced by the wild unpredictable nature of the Fonz. Winkler even made leather jackets fashionable.

The success of *Happy Days* led to three spinoffs: *Laverne & Shirley* (1976–83), *Mork & Mindy* (1978–82), and *Joanie Loves Chachi* (1982–83).

The Jeffersons sitcom (1975–85) CBS

This was a spinoff from *All in the Family* in more ways than one. George Jefferson (Sherman Hemsley) was the African-American equivalent of Archie Bunker. When Jefferson's dry-cleaning business became successful, George quickly moved his wife, Louise (Isabel Sanford), and their son, Lionel (played by either Damon Evans or Mike Evans), out of Archie's neighborhood in Queens to Manhattan's Upper East Side. But like Oedipus, he ran smack into his problems instead of away from them. George's prejudices were severely tested when Lionel fell in love with Jenny (Berlinda Tolbert), the daughter of a mixed marriage (Helen Willis played by Roxie Roker and Tom Willis played by Franklin Cover). Eventually, Lionel and Jenny married, had a child, and before the show had run its course were divorced. By the end George had found a sanctuary in Charlie's Place, a bar that he bought with— who else?—Tom Willis.

Florence: [wearing a bright red dress] Do you think this color suits me?

George: Sure—it's loud, isn't it?

—*The Jeffersons*

Kojak police drama (1973–78) CBS

Telly Savalas was Lieutenant Theo Kojak in a role so identified with the actor that one might expect him always to
be sucking on a lollipop and exclaiming, "Who loves ya,
baby." Kojak was assigned to Manhattan South, a tough
beat in New York City, and working for his one-time partner, Captain Frank McNeil (Dan Frazer). The main reason
that Kojak has never been promoted is that he does not
play the game. He is the archtype of the outsider: a person
who is within the system but maintains his own integrity,
his own sense of who he is. Along with the realistic portrayal of what police work is like, this perspective helps
to account for the worldwide popularity that this show
enjoyed.

The Mary Tyler Moore Show sitcom (1970–77) CBS

The comedic events of this show swirled around Mary
Richards (Mary Tyler Moore), an associate producer at
Channel 12 in Minneapolis who came to represent the new
woman of the 1970s–independent and in the workplace.
(During one show Mary's mother reminded her husband,
"Don't forget to take your pill"; Mary replied, "I won't."
When Lou Grant, played by bearish Ed Asner, asked
Mary's religion during her job interview, she informed him
that the question was illegal. Then he asked if she were
married. "Presbyterian," chirped Mary.) The supporting
cast included the obtuse anchorman Ted Baxter (Ted
Knight), the schmoozing news writer Murray Slaughter
(Gavin MacLeod), the on-the-make "Happy Homemaker"
Sue Ann Nivens (Betty White), the looking-for-love neigh-
bor Rhoda Morgenstern (Valerie Harper), and the snoopish
Phyllis Lindstrom (Cloris Leachman). The supporting cast
was so accomplished that they went off to shows of their
own: *Lou Grant, The Love Boat, The Betty White Show,
Rhoda, Phyllis.*

M*A*S*H sitcom (1972–83) CBS

This 1970 Robert Altman film was transformed into one
of the most successful sitcoms ever, an unlikely fortune

for a show that demonstrated the futility of war during the Vietnam War era. *M*A*S*H* (the acronym stands for mobile army surgical hospital) also had the good fortune of being shown on Saturday night between *All in the Family* and *The Mary Tyler Moore Show*. Set during the Korean War, the show featured Alan Alda (who won Emmys for acting, directing, and writing) as Captain Benjamin Franklin Pierce, a surgeon better known as "Hawkeye"; Wayne Rogers as "Trapper," Captain John McIntyre; Loretta Swit as Major Margaret Houlihan, at one time known as "Hot Lips"; Larry Linville as Major Frank Burns; Harry Morgan as Colonel Sherman T. Potter; Jamie Farr as the cross-dressing Corporal Maxwell Klinger; Gary Burghoff as Corporal Walter O'Reilly, "Radar"; and William Christopher as Father Francis Mulcahy.

Some of the episodes were even experimental, using a documentary style, a first-person narrative, and real-time (the time elapsed during the show's 30 minutes). The final episode, a 2.5-hour special, was a landmark in Americana. "Goodbye, Farewell, Amen" was watched by 125 million viewers.

You're in Good Company, Sir

The penchant of Corporal Maxwell Klinger (played by Jamie Farr) for peignoirs, gowns, and boas on *M*A*S*H* was based on comedian Lenny Bruce's similar strategy to get discharged from the U.S. Navy.

Radar: [interrupting conversation between Hot Lips and Colonel Potter] Excuse me . . .

Hot Lips: Will you butt out!!! This is man talk!!!

Radar: I'm sorry, sir.

—*M*A*S*H*

G.I.: I hear you guys are terrific doctors, but you don't go by the book.

B. J.: Sure we do.

Hawkeye: But our book has pictures of naked people playing volleyball.

—*M*A*S*H*

Masterpiece Theatre drama (1971–) PBS

Introduced for years by the erudite British-turned-American host Alistair Cooke, *Masterpiece Theatre* has become so much an institution it almost parodies itself. (The mantle has recently been passed on to *New York Times* columnist Russell Baker.) Sitting in an elegant if obviously prefabricated parlor, the host's insightful commentary actually adds something to understanding the production. And what productions they have been over the past two decades. Some of the top-notch offerings have included: *The First Churchills* with Susan Hampshire; *Elizabeth R* with Glenda Jackson; *Upstairs, Downstairs* with Jean Marsh; *I, Claudius* with Derek Jocobi; *Silas Marner* with Ben Kingsley; *Therese Raquin* with Kate Nelligan; *The Jewel in the Crown* with Peggy Ashcroft; and *Middlemarch*.

The Muppet Show variety (1976–81) syndicated

Jim Henson's Muppets have always appealed to adults—

their debut was on *The Tonight Show* in 1957—and this show proved it. Each week Kermit the Frog tried to pull together the variety show of muppets (the word is a combination of marionette and puppet) to go along with the featured guest (for example, Rudolph Nureyev dancing with Miss Piggy to "Swine Lake"). However, it was the Muppets themselves who have appealed to 235 million people in more than 100 countries—an audience far less critical than Statler and Hilton, the two old codgers who always had a box seat in the *The Muppet Show* theater. The Muppets also make regular appearances on *Sesame Street*.

The Odd Couple   sitcom   (1970–75)   ABC

Based on Neil Simon's play, this half-hour sitcom threw two divorced childhood chums together to share an apartment—the fastidious photographer Felix Unger (Tony Randall) and the messy sportswriter Oscar Madison (Jack Klugman). Although the pair seemed well mismatched, Art Carney and Martin Balsam had been the first choices for the series. Much of the humor centered on domestic discord and barbs at ex-wives Gloria Unger (Janis Hansen) and Blanche Madison (played by Klugman's wife, Brett Somers).

The Paper Chase   drama   (1978–1979; 1983–1986)   CBS, PBS, Showtime

This series originally featured first-year law students struggling to get through the class on contracts taught by Professor Charles W. Kingsfield Jr. John Houseman played Kingsfield in such an imperious manner that it is not only the young man from Iowa, James T. Hart (played by James Stephens), who withers under his questioning—viewers occasionally feel nervous that he might call on them! The first year of law school was covered in *The Paper Chase*, the year-long series that was first shown on CBS and later aired on PBS. The second year of the show and law school as well as *The Paper Chase: The Third Year* appeared years later on Showtime. At long last Hart finally graduated and upgraded his employer from a pizza parlor to a law firm.

Police Story police drama (1973–77) NBC

This series was noteworthy for its realistic portrayal of police work and its guest stars that included Tony Lo Bianco, Don Meredith, Lloyd Bridges, and David Cassidy. This was due to Joseph Wambaugh, the creator, former police officer, and author of such classic books as *The Onion Field* and *The Choir Boys*. It also gave rise to the spin-off program of *Police Woman* with Angie Dickinson as Sergeant Pepper Anderson.

Rhoda sitcom (1974–78) CBS

Valerie Harper had played Rhoda Morgenstern on *The Mary Tyler Moore Show*. However, when she returned home to New York City from Minneapolis, Rhoda (and the writers) decided she should stay. Rhoda fell in love with Joe Gerard (David Groh), a rocky romance that led to marriage. (Upon seeing Rhoda in her wedding dress, a blasé neighbor asked, "What's new?") The focus of the show then switched to the angst of her sister, Brenda (Julie Kavner). Rhoda's marriage ultimately crashed on the rocks to emphasize the humor of being single in the big city.

Roots dramatic special (1977) ABC

Based on the book by Alex Haley and shown on eight consecutive nights, this 12-hour ABC special followed the story of Kunta Kinte in West Africa in the 1750s through his enslavement and arrival in America. The special went on to cover the plight of his family to the freeing of his great-grandson after the Civil War. LeVar Burton was featured as the young Kunta Kinte and James Amos portrayed the adult Kinte known as Toby. The large cast included Louis Gossett Jr., Leslie Uggams, Ben Vereen, Cicily Tyson, and Edward Asner. This series had the highest Nielsen rating of any miniseries; the final installment was seen by more than 100 million people in the United States.

Saturday Night Live comedy variety (1975–) NBC

Developed by Dick Ebersol and produced by Lorne Michaels, the cast roster of *SNL* reads like a hall of fame of young comics:

Dan Aykroyd	Garrett Morris
Jim Belushi	Bill Murray
John Belushi	Eddie Murphy
Dana Carvey	Mike Myers
Chevy Chase	Don Novello
Billy Crystal	Joe Piscopo
Jane Curtin	Randy Quaid
Julia Louis-Dreyfus	Gilda Radner
Jon Lovitz	Martin Short
Dennis Miller	

Over the years some of the famous skits have included Chase ("Good evening, I'm Chevy Chase and you're not") and Miller in "Weekend Update"; Radner as Ba Ba Wawa, Emily Litella, and Rosanne Rosanna-Dana; John Belushi as the Samurai warrior; Belushi and Aykroyd as the Blues Brothers; Novello as Father Guido Sarducci; Crystal as Fernando ("You look mah-velous!"); Steve Martin and Aykroyd as "two wild and crazy guys"; Curtin and Aykroyd as The Coneheads; Carvey as the Church Lady ("Isn't that special"); Lovitz's lying Tommy Flanagan ("That's the ticket!"); and Myers and Carvey as Wayne and Garth. In addition to the cast and the fine writing, the spoofs of commercials, and the short films (Mr. Bill was a crowd pleaser), part of the excitement has been that *Saturday Night Live* is just that—live—a throwback to *Your Show of Shows* during the Golden Age of Television. The show also features a celebrity guest host and a popular musical group. Some of the memorable guest hosts have been Candice Bergen, George Carlin, Buck Henry, Ed Koch (former mayor of New York), Steve Martin, Ron Nessen (presidential press secretary), Paul Simon, and Lily Tomlin. Musical groups have ranged from little-known bands to front runners such as Blondie, Kate Bush, Tracy Chapman, Devo, Living Color, Roy Orbison, and the Rolling Stones. An appearance on *SNL* is usually worth an increase of 250,000 album sales.

SCTV Comedy Network   sitcom   (1977–80; 1981–83)
syndication

A Canadian show in the tradition of *Saturday Night Live*, the initials stand for Second City TV and the show is a satire of the medium. One of the memorable skits was the "Great White North," featuring two hunters sitting around watching the tube, guzzling beer, and saying little about nothing. The genesis of the skit was that every show produced in Canada had to include some Canadian-oriented content. Cast members included John Candy, Joe Flaherty, Eugene Levy, Andrea Martin, Rick Moranis, Catherine O'Hara, and Martin Short.

Taxi   sitcom   (1978–83)   ABC, NBC

This "men's" comedy was set in a taxi garage ruled by the dispatcher, Louie DePalma (Danny DeVito), a tyrant who instructed his drivers not to pick up the handicapped because you could pick up four "normal" fares in the same period of time. The only taxi driver who actually considered himself to be a cabbie, Alex Reiger (Judd Hirsch), was a person unmarked by career drive ("My shorts have more ambition that I do"). He listened to the others who were only "temporarily" hacking until they got their big breaks. There was Tony Banta (Tony Danza), a boxer; Bobby Wheeler (Jeff Conaway), an actor; and Elaine Nardo (Marilu Henner), an art dealer. Also in the cast were Latka Gravis (Andy Kaufman), Simka Gravis (Carol Kane), the "Reverend" Jim Ignatowski (Christopher Lloyd), whose brain waves had been burnt by too much acid, and John Burns (Randall Carver).

Bobby: Have you ever experienced loss of consciousness, hallucination, dizzy spells, convulsive disorders, fainting, or periods of loss of memory?

Jim: Hasn't everyone?

Bobby: Mental illness or narcotic addiction?

Jim: That's a tough choice.

—*Taxi*

The 1980s

ABC News Nightline news (1980–) ABC

This show was started in 1980 as a nightly vigil in response to the Iranian hostage crisis with Frank Reynolds as host. One night Ted Koppel filled in for Reynolds, and like Lou Gehrig substituting for Wally Pip, Koppel has been the host ever since. The format of *Nightline* is to treat one topic of the day in depth, with an introductory feature and interviewees representing different sides of an issue. Koppel occasionally takes a break, and Chris Wallace or Cokie Roberts often fills in.

Brideshead Revisited drama (1982) PBS

Produced by Granada Television and written by John Mortimer, this elaborate production took America by storm when its 11 episodes were first shown. The acting, costumes, scenery, music, and haunting voice-over are spellbinding; the Evelyn Waugh story, riveting. The audience is drawn in by the lavishness of Brideshead Castle (Castle

The Highest-rated Shows of the Decade

1980: *Dallas* (CBS)
1981: *Dallas* (CBS)
1982: *60 Minutes* (CBS)
1983: *Dallas* (CBS)
1984: *60 Minutes* (CBS)
1985: *Dallas* (CBS)
1986: *Dallas* (CBS)
1987: *The Cosby Show* (NBC)
1988: *The Cosby Show* (NBC)
1989: *The Cosby Show* (NBC)

Howard in Yorkshire) and the opulence of the Marchmain family just as Charles Ryder (Jeremy Irons) is when he first visits the family's son and his Oxford classmate Sebastian Flyte (Anthony Andrews). The rest of the cast features Claire Bloom, John Gielgud, Simon Jones, Phoebe Nichols, Laurence Olivier, and Diana Quick.

Cagney & Lacey   police drama   (1982–88)   CBS

This was not just another detective show—the two leads were women. Detective Mary Beth Lacey (Tyne Daly) was married and a mother; detective Chris Cagney (Sharon Gless) was single. These two became fast friends and so popular with the public that when the show was canceled, a write-in campaign brought them back.

Cheers   sitcom   (1982–93)   NBC

This Boston bar "where everybody knows your name" is what everyone always wanted in a local pub. The owner and bartender, Sam Malone (Ted Danson), is an ex-ballplayer for the Red Sox and a Hall of Fame ladies' man. He mainly hankers after Diane Chambers (Shelley Long), a prudish intellectual. Their relationship catapults star-crossed lovers into a new art form. ("Last night I was up until two in the morning finishing Kierkegaard," says Diane. "I hope he thanked you," replies Sam.) Other people dispensing drinks and advice were Ernie "Coach" Pantusso (Nicholas Colasanto), who died during the 1985 season and was replaced by the impossibly thick Woody Boyd (Woody Harrelson); Carla Tortelli (Rhea Perlman), a single mother of a large brood; and manager Rebecca Howe (Kirstie Alley), who later became Sam's love interest when Diane left the show to write her novel. The regulars on the other side of the bar were accountant and sometime house painter/decorator, Norm Peterson (George Wendt), who is greeted each day with a shout of "Norm!" as he settles onto his customary stool. The proud wearer of the postal uniform and mamma's boy Cliff Clavin (John Ratzenberger) in one episode gets to test his inexhaustible supply of trivia on *Jeopardy* in categories like "Stamps of the World" and "Celibacy." And Diane's first jilted finance (before Sam), psychiatrist Frasier Crane (Kelsey Grammar) finally finds a mate in Dr. Lillith Sternim (Bebe Neuwirth) when she mesmerizes him by letting loose her tight bun. Frasier went on to star in his own show.

TV Guide Picks the 10 Top Television Personalities of the 1980s

1. Bill Cosby
2. Larry Hagman
3. Oprah Winfrey
4. Ronald Reagan
5. Joan Collins

6. Ted Koppel
7. Vana White
8. David Letterman
9. Michael J. Fox
10. Tom Selleck

Cheers Facts:

At 26 Emmys, *Cheers* ties for second place with *Hill Street Blues* for the highest number of Emmys won. However, at 109 nominations, *Cheers* beat out *M*A*S*H* for the most. *Cheers* has had its share of famous guest stars. Going beyond the usual entertainment personalities, the show has featured the Chairman of the Joint Chiefs of Staff, Admiral William Crowe, Senator Gary Hart, former Speaker of the House Tip O'Neil, and baseball player Wade Boggs.

China Beach   war drama   (1988–91)   ABC

This tightly written show spun around nurse Colleen McMurphy (Dana Delany) as she tried to hold the body and soul of herself and others together at the evacuation center near Da Nang on the South China Sea. *China Beach* tried to do with the Vietnam War what *M*A*S*H* had done with the Korean War: show the stupidity of war and still be entertaining. Though a critical favorite, *China Beach* struggled for an audience.

Coach   sitcom   (1989–   )   ABC

Craig T. Nelson is Hayden Fox, the football coach at Minnesota State University. Between the Screaming Eagles and the women in his life, he has his hands full. Also on hand are Jerry Van Dyke as Assistant Coach Luther Van Dam and Shelley Fabares as Christine Armstrong.

The Cosby Show   sitcom   (1984–93)   NBC

This show was a far cry from the original portrayal of the African-American family on television. Wearing his fabulous sweaters and his rubbery face, Bill Cosby combined his deadpan humor and sensitivity (along with some of his ideas about how to raise kids) into the character of

Heathcliff (Cliff) Huxtable, a well-to-do obstetrician and father of a large upscale family. Also in the cast were his wife, Claire Huxtable (Phylicia Rashad), and children, Sondra (Sabrina Le Beauf), Denise (Lisa Bonet), Theo (Malcolm-Jamal Warner), Vanessa (Tempestt Bledsoe), and Rudy (Keshia Knight Pulliam). The show achieved phenomenal popularity among viewers across the demographic spectrum and was the most highly rated television program for four years before it went off the air in 1993.

According to *Forbes* magazine, the highest-paid male entertainer on TV for the 1988–89 season was Bill Cosby with $95 million. The highest-paid female entertainer during that year was Oprah Winfrey who pulled down $55 million.

Dynasty drama (1981–89) ABC

What *Dynasty* lacked in characterization and story, it made up for in lavish sets and costumes. The basic plot turned on Blake Carrington's (John Forsythe) two wives: his present wife, Krystle (Linda Evans), who was always in competition with his first wife and mother of their three children, Alexis Colby (Joan Collins). Krystle was blond goodness; Alexis was dark evil.

Family Ties sitcom (1982–89) NBC

Two graduates of the 1960s, Elyse Keaton (Meredith Baxter Birney) and Steven Keaton (Michael Gross) are parents to a new generation of yuppy-minded kids: Alex (Michael J. Fox), Mallory (Justin Bateman), Jennifer (Tina Yothers), and Andrew (Brian Bonsall). After the laughter from the clash between generations began to die down, the show shifted gears to highlight the kids as they grew up. It especially focused on Michael J. Fox, who had become a star after Spielberg's *Back to the Future* movie. (The fan magazines had a field day when Fox and his first girlfriend on the show, Tracy Pollan, were married.)

The Golden Girls sitcom (1985–) NBC

Created to reflect the aging of the population in the United States, this series of four women over 50, who live together, shows that aging is a natural process. The cast includes Dorothy Zbornak (Bea Arthur), a teacher; Rose Nylund (Betty White), a counselor; Blanche Devereaux (Rue McLanahan), an art gallery employee; and Sophia Petrillo (Estelle Getty), Dorothy's 80-year-old mother. The humor sometimes revolves around Maalox and hot flashes, but at bottom it demonstrates that older people are people, too. Just older.

Hill Street Blues police drama (1981–87) NBC

Produced by the award-winning team of Michael Kozoll and Steven Bochco, *Hill Street Blues* was a critic's darling but took several seasons to establish its audience, even facing cancellation before achieving its ultimate popularity. In charge of the Hill Street Station in an unnamed American city was Captain Frank Furillo (Daniel J. Travanti); however, he was less in charge of his personal life with ex-wife Fay Furillo (Barbara Bosson) and lover Joyce Davenport (Veronica Hamel). This show had the courage to realize that it isn't always the good guys who win. As Sergeant Phil Esterhaus (Michael Conrad) said at the end of each roll call, "And, hey—let's be careful out there." The show was famous for its ensemble acting, carrying plot lines from one episode to the next, and its familiar theme song. It eventually won 26 Emmys.

The Jewel in the Crown drama (1984) PBS

This Granada production converts Paul Scott's *Raj Quartet* into one of the best literary adaptations ever. The struggle between England and India is played out in a love triangle between British police superintendent Ronald Merrick (Tim Pigott-Smith) and Hari Kumar (Art Malik), an English school–educated Indian, competing for the affections of Daphne Manners (Susan Wooldridge), a young woman visiting from England. Just as the larger themes shed light on the plight of these individuals, the personal story played out against the backdrop of the struggle between England and India illuminates the larger saga. When presented on public television it achieved the kind of cult status that viewers would drop all their plans to be home to watch.

Kate & Allie   sitcom   (1984–89)   CBS

Kate & Allie is a female version of *The Odd Couple* with *The Brady Bunch* thrown in for good measure. Kate McArdle (Susan Saint James) and Allie Lowell (Jane Curtin) are divorcées who decide to share an apartment in Greenwich Village with their three children. Kate is the flashy one who works; Allie is the down-to-earth one who stays home. The built-in complications are dating, working, and raising children.

L.A. Law   legal drama   (1986–94)   NBC

Created by Steven Bochco and Terry Louise Fischer, *L.A. Law* seemed to do for lawyers what Bochco's *Hill Street Blues* did for police officers. "It is a much easier show to make than *Hill Street* . . .," said Bochco. "Also, it's primarily an internal show. We're not going to be fighting in the streets. . . ." *L.A. Law* also differed dramatically with earlier shows about lawyers such as *Perry Mason* and *Owen Marshall*. "Those shows compressed the process to such an enormous degree," observed Bochco, "they lost the reality of the system and how it works. The decision we've made is to not condescend to the material or to the audience." Some of the cases involved such topical issues as adultery, AIDS, computer hacking, divorce settlements, dating services, and endorsements. By mixing the personal and professional lives of a large ensemble cast with overlapping plot lines, the audience found themselves caught up in the story and came away with what amounted to an empathy for these privileged and driven professionals.

The ensemble cast included:

Arnie Becker: Corbin Bernsen
Douglas Brackman Jr.: Alan Rachins
Ann Kelsey: Jill Eikenberry

Michael Kuzak: Harry Hamlin

Stuart Markowitz: Michael Tucker

Leland McKenzie: Richard Dysart

Roxanne Melman: Susan Ruttan

Tommy Mullaney: John Spencer

Jonathan Rollins: Blair Underwood

Victor Sifuentes: Jimmy Smits

Benny Stulwicz: Larry Drake

Grace Van Owen: Susan Dey

Late Night with David Letterman talk, variety (1982–) NBC, CBS

There were a lot of viewers between the ages of 18 and 34 who stayed up until 1:30 A.M. to watch the iconoclastic Letterman. He used television in a way that Ernie Kovacs would've appreciated: the "Top Ten" lists on wacky subjects, the show that revolved 360 degrees during the hour, "Stupid Pet Tricks," the use of the "Thrill Cam." There were also guests to interview, Calvert DeForest as the ridiculously boring Larry "Bud" Melman, and a spotlight on Paul Shaffer and the World's Most Dangerous Band. In 1993 Letterman moved to CBS when NBC went with Jay Leno to replace Johnny Carson on *The Tonight Show*. The show was renamed *Late Show with David Letterman* and is the front runner in the late-night talk show wars.

David Letterman's salary for the 1993–94 season was $14 million, or $57,142.86 per hour.

Lonesome Dove miniseries (1989) CBS

This Peabody Award–winning miniseries transfers Larry McMurtry's novel into an eight-hour saga of a cattle drive from Lonesome Dove, Texas, to Montana. In addition to the scenery of Big Sky country are the wonderful performances of Robert Duvall as the philosphical Gus McCrae,

Rick Schroeder (left) reprises his role as Newt Dobbs, and Jon Voight stars as Captain Woodrow Call, in A Return to Lonesome Dove. Barbara Hershey stars as Clara Allen and William Petersen is former Texas Ranger Gideon Walker.

Tommy Lee Jones as the tight-lipped Woodrow F. Call, and Anjelica Huston as Clara Allen. A second miniseries, *A Return to Lonesome Dove* continuing the saga, aired in 1993, starring Barbara Hershey and William Peterson.

Long Ago and Far Away children's (1989–) PBS

Hosted by the mellifluous-voiced James Earl Jones, this series is an easy show for parents to sit down and watch with their children. The stories, whether adaptations of classics or originals, and films, whether animated, Claymation, puppets, or live action are so entertaining and well done (mostly by overseas production companies) that one is reminded of the wonderful possibilities of television.

The MacNeil-Lehrer Newshour   news   (1983–   )   PBS

Together, Robert MacNeil, based in New York, and Jim Lehrer, based in Washington, have presented an hour of news analysis each weekday evening that has consistently outshone the dramatic irrelevance of many news programs. The program begins with a look at the day's headlines and moves to in-depth interviews, profiles, and "essays." *MacNeil-Lehrer* goes in for the talking heads instead of dramatic news footage, but oh, what talking heads they are—heads of state, wheeler dealers in Congress, people in the know. The prototype of this show was *The MacNeil-Lehrer Report*, a half-hour show that was on PBS from 1976 to 1983.

Miami Vice   police drama   (1984–89)   NBC

Detectives Sonny Crockett (Don Johnson) and Ricardo Tubbs (Philip Michael Thomas) decked out in pastel sport jackets and t-shirts rock around Miami in fast sports cars chasing drug dealers and an occasional skirt. From time to time Crockett and Tubbs reported in to their unimpressed superior, Lieutenant Martin Castillo (Edward James Olmos). The show was high on production values and low on script, but its fast-paced MTV style and music by Jan Hammer appealed to the same type audience that had been blissed out in front of *Starsky and Hutch* in the 1970s. The show set a certain visual standard in both television and fashion and launched Don Johnson to superstardom.

Moonlighting   comedy drama   (1985–89)   ABC

Cybill Shepherd is Maddie Hayes, an ex-model who once advertised Blue Moon shampoo; Bruce Willis is David Addison, an investigator for her Blue Moon Detective Agency. When she is rooked out of her money by her manager, Maddie discovers that one of her few assets is this detective agency. Before she can sell it, Addison convinces her to become his partner. Although Hayes is sophisticated and Addison is streetwise, eventually they fall in love, prolonging the romantic tension as long as possible. But what raises everything to another level is the witty dialogue, the shows within shows (takeoffs on *The Taming of the Shrew* and *It's a Wonderful Life*), and the in-jokes about production delays and the feuding between the two stars. The show revived Shepherd's career and made Willis a prime-time heartthrob.

Murder, She Wrote drama (1984–) CBS

Angela Lansbury plays Jessica Fletcher, a widow living in Cabot Cove, Maine, who turned to mystery writing during her later years. In addition to traveling, one of her passions is solving the crimes that take place around her. The show is tightly written so it is necessary for the audience to pay strict attention if they want to solve the mystery along with Fletcher. Although she is a four-time Tony winner (*Mame, Dear World, Gypsy*, and *Sweeney Todd*) and *Murder, She Wrote* was in the top ten for the first five years of its run, Angela Lansbury has been nominated eleven times but has not won an Emmy for her portrayal of Jessica Fletcher.

Murphy Brown sitcom (1988–) CBS

Candice Bergen stars as the Betty Ford Clinic alumna who is still a driven personality and veteran reporter for *F.Y.I.*, a weekly TV news-magazine show set in Washington. When Murphy Brown decided to have a child out of wedlock in the fall of 1991, the show became a bellwether campaign issue in the 1992 presidential race when Vice President Dan Quayle claimed it was typical of the wrong-headed, anti-family liberal thinking of his opponents. The show incorporated Quayle's real-life response into the plot line and needless to say had great fun at his expense. Other cast members include Murphy's young producer Miles Silverberg (Grant Shaud), reporter and ex-beauty queen Corky Sherwood (Faith Ford), reporter Frank Fontana (Joe Regalbuto), anchor Jim Dial (Charles Kimbrough), and the Phil of Phil's Place (Pat Corley). *Murphy Brown* has pulled down two Emmys as the outstanding comedy, while Bergen has raked in three as the outstanding comedy actress.

Mystery! mystery (1980–) PBS

Some of the sterling shows on this series have been John

Mortimer's *Rumpole of the Bailey* with Leo Kern as the crusty Horace Rumpole, *The Adventures of Sherlock Holmes* with a quirky and brilliant Jeremy Brett as Holmes and a bemused David Burke as Watson, *Inspector Morse* with John Thaw as the Mozart-loving inspector, and *Prime Suspect* with Helen Mirren as Detective Jane Tennison.

With imaginative opening credits by Edward Gorey and hosted by Vincent Price and then Diana Rigg, *Mystery!* has become a much-beloved staple of public television.

Newhart   sitcom   (1982–90)   CBS

Following on the heels of *The Bob Newhart Show*, this sitcom finds Newhart as Dick Loudon, a one-time ad executive and more recently a writer of do-it-yourself books, who has "retired" to Vermont to become the owner of the Stratford Inn. (The inn shown is actually the Waybury Inn near Middlebury.) Dick and his wife, Joanna (Mary Frann), are joined by maid Stephanie Vanderkellen (Julia Duffy), who can't seem to get anything right, George Utley (Tom Poston), an eccentric handyman, and three even odder businessmen brothers, Larry (William Sanderson), Darryl (Tony Papenfuss), and the "other brother" Darryl (John Volstad). As if that isn't enough, Dick later hosts a local talk show produced by Michael Harris (Peter Scolari), and the characters on the *Vermont Today* show bring out the best of blank stares and double-takes from Bob Newhart. "I've been doing the same thing for 25 years," ponders the bemused Newhart, "and I'm still getting away with it."

Newhart also had two shows in the 1960s and 1970s called *The Bob Newhart Show*. One was a comedy-variety show—Newhart opened with a monologue on a telephone that ended with "Same to you, fella"—that ran from 1961 to 1962; the other was a sitcom with Newhart as a Chicago psychologist that ran from 1972 to 1978. For the 1990s, the show was simply called *Bob*, where this time the main character was a cartoonist.

Roseanne   sitcom   (1988–)   ABC

In this wildly successful series, Roseanne (Roseanne Barr Arnold) and Dan Conner (John Goodman) are a wisecracking blue-collar couple with three difficult kids. The Conners are everything less than perfect, representing a more realistic display of family foibles than earlier too-good-to-be true predecessors such as the Huxtables on *The Cosby Show.* The roots of the humor for the blue-collar Conners reach back to *The Honeymooners* and *All in the Family. Roseanne* is consistently a top-rated show and has received numerous Emmys.

The most expensive sitcom for the 1993–94 season was *Roseanne* at a hefty $900,000 per episode.

The Simpsons cartoon (1989–) Fox

Starting out as a segment on *The Tracey Ullman Show*, this portrait of a family of misfits quickly grew into the most popular animated show since *The Flintstones*, appealing to adults and kids alike. The counterculture Simpsons are about as far removed from the Huxtable clan on *The Cosby Show* as possible. Homer, the father, is an inspector at the nearby nuclear plant, who spends his time as unconstructively as possible, preferably drinking or bowling. At home the family consists of blue-haired Marge, tiny tot Maggie, sister Lisa, and spike-haired Bart. Bart's name is a respelling of Brat, and that's exactly what he is. Like his father, he does as little as possible ("Underachiever, and proud of it, man!"). Whether he's scraping by in fourth grade or tooling around town on his skateboard, Bart is every parent's quintessential nightmare. But hey, "don't have a cow, man!"

Star Trek: The Next Generation science fantasy (1987–94) syndicated

When Gene Roddenberry revived this show 18 years after the end of the original *Star Trek*, he decided to cast it 78 years later in the 24th century. After all, who could ever replace William Shatner as Captain Kirk and Leonard

Phrases Written by Bart Simpson on His School Chalkboard

I will not aim at the head.

My name is not Dr. Death.

I will not defame New Orleans.

Organ transplants are best left to professionals.

I will not yell "She's dead!" during roll call.

I saw nothing unusual in the teacher's lounge.

My homework was not stolen by a one-armed man.

I will not xerox my butt.

I will not do that thing with my tongue.

I will not belch the national anthem.

I will not fake rabies.

I did not see Elvis.

Nimoy as Mr. Spock? Now no one will be able to replace the Shakespearean actor Patrick Stewart as Captain Picard. In the new series, the USS *Enterprise* is grander, the special effects are state of the art, the shows are more diverse, and the crew is larger and more nonhuman. The cast includes Jonathan Frakes as Commander William Riker, LeVar Burton as Lieutenant Geordi La Forge, Michael Dorn as Lieutenant Worf, Gates McFadden as Dr. Beverly Crusher, Marina Sirtis as Counselor Deanna Troi, Brent Spiner as Lieutenant Commander Data, Colm Meaney as Transporter Chief Miles O'Brien, and Whoopi Goldberg as Guinan.

St. Elsewhere   medical drama   (1982–88)   NBC

St. Eligius is a big hospital in Boston that takes on all the problems that other hospitals choose to ignore. Except for

The New York Times reported on July 24, 1994, that "Like a character in one of its science-fiction plots, *Star Trek: The Next Generation* knew from the day it was born the approximate day it would die." To maximize profits on the lucrative Star Trek franchise, Paramount planned on producing only seven seasons of *Next Generation*. The *Times* television critic noted that "Because of the economics of the television business, the end of the seventh season appeared to be the show's moment of maximum profitability." By ending new production at 182 episodes, Paramount could charge the most per episode for reruns (stations must buy rerun rights to all episodes in one package deal), avoid costly contract renegotiations for stars, and begin filming *Next Generation* movies. Fans need not fear that their TV dose is at an end. To supplement the third Star Trek series *Deep Space Nine*, already on the air, a new Star Trek, *Voyager*, is scheduled to begin January 1995. Paramount will no doubt push the ongoing mission to where no profits have gone before.

the white coats, this show bears little similarity to *Dr. Kildare* and *Ben Casey*. The doctors have shortcomings and their patients do not always pull through, any more than they do in real life. Produced by the *Hill Street Blues* company, *St. Elsewhere* won Emmys but never broke into the top ten in the ratings. Still there was a loyal audience out there to tune in to the weekly trials of Ed Flanders as chief of staff Dr. Donald Westphall, William Daniels as the brilliant Dr. Mark Craig, Bonnie Bartlett as Mrs. Craig, Norman Lloyd as crusty Dr. Daniel Auschlander, David Birney as heartthrob Dr. Ben Samuels, Howie Mandel as Dr. Wayne Fiscus, Barbara Whinnery as Dr. Cathy Martin, David Morse as Dr. Jack Morrison, Cynthia Sikes as Dr. Annie Cavanero, Stephen Furst as Dr. Elliot Axelrod, and Denzel Washington as Dr. Philip Chandler.

Shogun miniseries (1980) NBC

This 12-hour miniseries based on James Clavell's historical novel featured Richard Chamberlain as English navigator John Blackthorne, who becomes assimilated after being shipwrecked off the coast. Several of the plots have to do with feuding warlords, the encroachment of the West, a love affair between Blackthorne and a married woman of the aristocracy, and Blackthorne's attempt to become the first Westerner to achieve the status of a Shogun. Toshiro Mifune starred as the warlord Toranaga and Yoko Shimada as the beautiful Lady Mariko. When *Shogun* was rebroadcast in 1983, narration by Orson Welles was added.

thirtysomething comedy drama (1987–91) ABC

Written by Ed Zwick and Marshall Herskovitz, this show was aimed squarely at baby boomers. There were seven main characters—two couples and three singles. The ensemble cast included ad exec Michael Steadman (Ken Olin) and his wife, Hope (Mel Harris), Elliot Weston (Timothy Busfield) and his wife, Nancy (Patricia Wettig), city administrator Ellyn Warren (Polly Draper), photographer Melissa Steadman (Melanie Mayron), and teacher Gary Shepherd (Peter Horton). The couples sometimes wanted to be single; the singles sometimes wanted to be part of a couple; and all of them talked a lot. (In real life actors Patricia Wettig and Ken Olin were married.) If you could relate to the self-analysis of these characters, *thirtysomething* was a show that spoke to you. Otherwise, it might have seemed much ado about nothing.

The Thorn Birds miniseries (1983) ABC

This 10-hour miniseries was second only to *Roots* in total number of viewers. Starring in Colleen McCullough's best-selling novel set in sprawling Australia was Richard Chamberlain as Ralph de Bricassart, a priest trying to choose between his love for God and Maggie Carson, a beautiful woman played by Rachel Ward. Other stars in the cast were Barbara Stanwyck as Mary Carson, Jean Simmons as

Fee Cleary, Richard Kiley as Paddy Cleary, and Christopher Plummer as Archbishop Contini-Verchese.

The Tracey Ullman Show comedy variety (1987–90) Fox

In this one-woman vehicle, this British comedian amply demonstrated her ability to be funny, to sing, to dance, and to act. In her ongoing skits as a bored secretary, a teenager being raised by two gay men, a worker down at the post office, and others, Ullman revealed an uncanny ability to capture the accents and mannerisms of her characters. Another staple of the show as an odd family called the Simpsons that served as a segue between skits and later claimed their own show.

War and Remembrance miniseries (1988; 1989) ABC

This miniseries based on Herman Wouk's novel was even more extravagant than the earlier miniseries based on Wouk's *The Winds of War*. *War and Remembrance* lasted 30 hours, was shown in November (depicting years 1941 to 1943) and May (1943 to 1945), and cost $110 million. This time Robert Mitchum as Victor "Pug" Henry and Polly Bergen, his wife, were joined by a cast that included Sir John Gielgud, Peter Graves, Jane Seymour, and Michael Woods. Poor ratings tolled a deathknell for the extravagant miniseries.

The Winds of War miniseries (1983) ABC

This 18-hour miniseries was just as ambitious as Herman Wouk's lengthy novel about the events from the 1939 Nazi invasion of Poland to the bombing of Pearl Harbor in 1941. It took 14 months to film the 1,785 scenes in 267 locations in six different countries at a cost of $40 million. Robert Mitchum was Victor "Pug" Henry; Polly Bergen played his wife.

The Highest-rated Shows of the Decade

1990: *Cheers* (CBS)
1991: *Cheers* (CBS)
1992: *Roseanne* (ABC)
1993: *Home Improvement* (ABC)
1994: *Home Improvement* (ABC)

The 1990s

Beverly Hills 90210 sitcom (1990–) Fox

The jumping off point for this popular show was the Walsh family's move from Minneapolis to Beverly Hills. The first order of business for the Walsh twins, Brenda (Shannon Doherty) and Brandon (Jason Priestly), was to fit in at West Beverly Hills High School. Since then, the Walshes and their new friends have had their shot at many of the social issues that confront teenagers today: alcohol abuse, date rape, drugs, safe sex, and suicide. Of course, there are still some of those other problems that were dealt with by a quieter and gentler society (*Leave It to Beaver* days perhaps): getting along with others, being popular, pulling down good grades, etc. The show's popularity was aided by its attractive cast, which also includes heartthrob Luke Perry as Dylan Baker. Fox followed up this series with the even hotter *Melrose Place*.

Dave's World sitcom (1993–) CBS

Harry Anderson plays Dave Barry, the syndicated columnist whose observations of daily life are a staple to millions of newspaper readers. On the first show, Anderson said to his TV son Tommy (Zane Carney): "Sometimes you've got to do things you don't want to do if you want to make a difference." "But I don't want to make a difference," replied Tommy. "I want to be like you."

Evening Shade sitcom (1990–) CBS

Burt Reynolds plays Wood Newton, the coach of the losing high school football team in Evening Shade, Arkansas. Newton and his wife, Ava (Marilu Henner), the prosecuting attorney, have four children, and her father, Evan Evans (Hal Holbrook), is the publisher of the newspaper. Others in the superb cast are Elizabeth Ashley as Ava's Aunt Frieda Evans, Charles Durning as Dr. Harlan Elldridge, Michael Jeter as a math teacher, and Ossie Davis as Ponder Blue, owner of Ponder Blue's Barbecue Villa, where most of the denizens of Evening Shade hang out. "They say there's not much to see in a small town," drawls Ponder Blue, "but what you hear makes up for it." The series is produced by President and Hilary Clinton's longtime Arkansas pals Harry and Linda Bloodworth-Thomason.

Gabriel's Fire drama (1990–92) ABC

James Earl Jones is Gabriel Bird, a one-time cop in Chicago who had been forced to shoot his white partner to prevent him from shooting a mother and her child. Bird was sent to prison for life for his partner's death, but his case was taken up by Victoria Heller (Laila Robins), who was able to get him released after 20 years. Bird worked for Heller that year as a private investigator; however, his anger was smoldering too close to the surface. So, the following year the show was changed to *Pros and Cons* and a Bird who looked on the positive side of life.

Home Improvement sitcom (1991–) ABC

In this popular offering, Tim Taylor (Tim Allen) has a home improvement show on a local TV station where he dispenses his customary advice of "more power." Visual aids and sex appeal are provided by Heidi (Debbi Dunning), the Tool Time Girl. However, when "The Tool Man" comes home, he is all thumbs. Patricia Richardson plays wife Jill Taylor; their three children are Zachery Ty Bryan as Brad, Jonathan Taylor Thomas as Randy, and Taran Smith as Mark.

I'll Fly Away legal drama (1991–93) NBC, PBS

In this distinguished series created by the same team who produced *Northern Exposure*, Forrest Bedford (Sam Waterston) is the district attorney in the small southern town of Bryland with three children to raise on his own after his wife is hospitalized. Into his life arrives the quietly determined Lilly Harper (Regina Taylor), through whose eyes we view the African-American experience in the South in the early Civil Rights era. Though the show received uniformly glowing reviews from critics, it was dropped by NBC in 1993, but is being shown in reruns on public television.

In Living Color comedy variety (1990–) Fox

This satirical show, the brainchild of Keenan Ivory Wayans, is something like *SCTV*, poking fun at perceptions of blacks in the media and popular culture with a largely African-American cast. In addition to frequent jibes at Arsenio Hall and Oprah Winfrey, there are skits about gay film critics ("Men on Film"), hard-working West Indians, scam artists, and winos. The cast includes several members of the Wayans family, and every show is punctuated with rapid-fire dance numbers by the "fly-girls."

Lois & Clark: The New Adventures of Superman
adventure (1993–) ABC

Good enough to have once been on the Buffalo Bills roster, Dean Cain brings a rugged athleticism and a sense of joy rather than melancholy to the part of the man from Krypton. But this new man with the *S* on his chest is still hanging out in the *Daily Planet* newsroom trying to catch the eye of reporter Lois Lane (Teri Hatcher), who still doesn't recognize that Clark is Superman minus the cape.

Just as good is the cast swirling around them: Lane Smith as Perry White, Michael Landes as Jimmy Olson, and John Shea as Lex Luthor.

Northern Exposure   comedy drama   (1990–   )   CBS

Rob Morrow is Joel Fleischman, a young doctor who is paying back the state of Alaska for funding his medical education by setting up his practice in the backwoods town of Cicely. When not dreaming of returning to his native New York City, Fleischman is trying to fit in with local lights such as vivacious bush pilot Maggie O'Connell (Janine Turner), New Age deejay Chris Stevens (John Corbett), chamber of commerce president Maurice Minnifield (Barry Corbin), bar owner and mayor (in that order) Holling Vincoeur (John Cullum), and Holling's wife, Shelly Tambo Vincoeur (Cynthia Geary), who is 40 years his younger. The popular show succeeds on the basis of its offbeat topics and ensemble cast and has earned numerous Emmy Awards.

NYPD Blue   police drama   (1993–   )   ABC

Steven Bochco and David Milch have a *Hill Street Blues* for New York City in the 1990s. The writing is taut with a few salty words thrown in along with a glimpse of the gluteus maximus. The star hands down is David Caruso as red-headed Detective John Kelly. Part of the reason for his charisma may seem unusual for a cop show: Kelly's a good listener. Other prominent members of the cast include his partner, Detective Andy Sipowicz (Dennis Franz), who is lifting himself out of alcoholic despair, and Detective Janice Licalsi (Amy Brenneman), who found herself forced to commit two murders. In 1994, *NYPD Blue* received 26 Emmy nominations—a record for any nominated show.

Picket Fences   drama   (1991–   )   CBS

This is a show with a heart, a show that deals with tough issues, a show with something to say ("We're not here on this earth long, people; we have to learn to love better").

The setting is Rome, Wisconsin (pop. 30,000). It's a nice picket-fence kind of place to live for Sheriff Jimmy Brock (Tom Skerritt) and his physician wife, Jill (Kathy Baker), and their three children: Zack (Adam Wylie), Kimberly (Holly Marie Combs), and Matthew (Justin Shenkarow). But even so life keeps everyone hopping because there seems to be as much incest, murder, pornography, and general mayhem as you would find in any large city. In 1993 *Picket Fences* corralled Emmy Awards for best drama, best actor (Tom Skerritt), and best actress (Kathy Baker). *Picket Fences* may be to the 1990s what *Hill Street Blues* was to the 1980s, *All in the Family* was to the 1970s, *The Dick Van Dyke Show* was to the 1960s, and *I Love Lucy* was to the 1950s.

Seinfeld sitcom (1990–) NBC

Jerry Seinfeld plays himself in this Emmy Award–winning show about the life of a stand-up comic in New York City. What happens in "real" life between Seinfeld and his ex-girlfriend, Elaine (Julia Louis-Dreyfus), his best friend, George (Jason Alexander), and his next-door neighbor Kramer (Michael Richards) becomes material for his comedy act on stage. Seinfeld, of course, owes a debt to Garry Shandling. On the *It's Garry Shandling's Show*, Shandling was a stand-up comic who lived at home. (The set was his home in Sherman Oaks in a blurring of the line between fiction and reality.) And Shandling, in turn, is indebted to George Burns. On the old *Burns and Allen Show*, George would turn away from the action, cigar in hand, to talk directly to the audience in a technique known as "breaking the fourth wall."

Star Trek—Deep Space Nine science fiction (1992–)

"Gene [Roddenbury] used to say, somewhat in kidding," remembers executive producer Michael Piller, "to communicate what he wanted to do with *Star Trek*, that space was like the old west, and that *Star Trek* was like *Wagon Train*."

Deep Space Nine features characters developed in *Star Trek: The Next Generation* and is a working out of the many conflicts that exist between warring cultures of the Cardassians, Klingons, and Romulans.

Some TV Lists

TV Shows and Their Spin-offs

Original Series	Spin-off Show
Dallas	Knots Landing
Happy Days	Laverne & Shirley
	Mork & Mindy
	Joanie Loves Chachi
All in the Family	Maude
	The Jeffersons
	Gloria
Petticoat Junction	Green Acres
The Tracey Ullman Show	The Simpsons
Booker	21 Jump Street
Maude	Good Times
Who's the Boss?	Living Dolls
Hill Street Blues	Beverly Hills Buntz
The Cosby Show	A Different World
The Mary Tyler Moore Show	Rhoda
	Phyllis
	Lou Grant
The Andy Griffith Show	Gomer Pyle, U.S.M.C.
	Mayberry, R.F.D.
M*A*S*H	Trapper John, M.D.

Professions of Characters in Television Shows

Jim Anderson (*Father Knows Best*): insurance salesman

Tony Banta (*Taxi*): taxi driver and boxer

Ted Baxter (*The Mary Tyler Moore Show*): TV news anchor

Sister Bertulle (*The Flying Nun*): nun

Blanche (*Golden Girls*): art gallery assistant

Murphy Brown (*Murphy Brown*): TV news magazine anchor

Al Bundy (*Married . . . with Children*): shoe salesman

Archie Bunker (*All in the Family*): dock foreman for the Pendergast Tool and Die Co.

Joe Calucci (*Calucci's Department*): supervisor for the New York state unemployment office

Cliff Clavin (*Cheers*): letter carrier

Bob Collins (*The Bob Cummings Show*): fashion photographer

Dave Crabtree (*My Mother, the Car*): lawyer

Phil Fish (*Barney Miller*): detective

Dr. Fraser Crane (*Cheers*): psychiatrist

Louie De Palma (*Taxi*): taxi dispatcher

Florence (*The Jeffersons*): maid

Florida (*Maude*): housekeeper

Ginger Grant (*Gilligan's Island*): actress

Robert Harley (*The Bob Newhart Show*): psychologist

Hazel (*Hazel*): maid

Heathcliff "Cliff" Huxtable (*The Cosby Show*): obstetrician

George Jefferson (*The Jeffersons*): owner of a dry-cleaning establishment

Clark Kent (*The Adventures of Superman*): newspaper reporter

Gabe Kotter (*Welcome Back, Kotter*): high school teacher

Ralph Kramden (*The Honeymooners*): bus driver

Lois Lane (*Superman*): newspaper reporter

Sam Malone (*Cheers*): bartender

Rhoda Morgenstern (*The Mary Tyler Moore Show*): window dresser at Hempel's department store

Herman Munster (*The Munsters*): funeral director

Tony Nelson (*I Dream of Jeannie*): astronaut

Ed Norton (*The Honeymooners*): sewer worker

Robinson J. Peepers (*Mr. Peepers*): junior high school biology teacher

Norm Peterson (*Cheers*): accountant

Major Benjamin Franklin "Hawkeye" Pierce (*M*A*S*H*): army surgeon

Wilbur Post (*Mister Ed*): architect

Ricky Ricardo (*I Love Lucy*): band leader and singer

Mary Richards (*The Mary Tyler Moore Show*): associate producer of television news for station WJM-TV

Fred Sanford (*Sanford and Son*): junk dealer

Homer Simpson (*The Simpsons*): worker at nuclear power plant

Cosmo Topper (*Topper*): vice president of the National Security Bank

---

According to the U.S. Bureau of Labor Statistics in 1992, the most common occupation in the U.S. is salesperson, but on prime time television the number-one occupation is police officer, followed by doctor and lawyer.

Abbreviations in the Titles of TV Shows

Here's what the abbreviations mean in the titles of some shows.

C.P.O Sharkey (1976–78). Don Rickles starred as Chief Petty Officer Sharkey.

B.A.D. C.A.T.S (1980). The show's title stands for burglary auto detail, commercial auto thefts. This show, starring Asher Brauner as Officer Nick Donovan and Michelle Pfeiffer as Officer Samantha Jensen, lasted for only five episodes.

M*A*S*H (1972–83). The show centered around a mobile army surgical hospital. One of the all-time great situation comedies, it starred Alan Alda, Wayne Rogers, and Loretta Swit.

S.W.A.T. (1975–76). This police drama, about a special weapons and tactics team, featured Steve Forrest as Lieutenant Dan ("Hondo") Harrelson.

T.H.E. CAT (1966–67): Robert Loggia played Thomas Hewitt Edward Cat in this adventure series.

THE MAN FROM U.N.C.L.E. (1964–68). This adventure series starred Robert Vaughn as Napoleon Solo, who worked for the United Network Command for Law and Enforcement.

Phone Numbers of Some Television Characters

Phone numbers of television characters start with 555, because that is the prefix set aside by telephone companies for such use. If you dial these numbers, you will reach directory assistance.

The Harts of *Hart to Hart*: 555–1271

Mary Richards of *The Mary Tyler Moore Show*: 555–2321

Tony Baretta of *Baretta*: 555–2368

Captain B. J. Hunnicut of *M*A*S*H*: 555–2657

Stevens family of *Bewitched*: 555–6161

Ted Baxter of *The Mary Tyler Moore Show*: 555–8737

Brady family of *The Brady Bunch*: 555–6161

Kate Columbo of *Mrs. Columbo*: 555–9861

Jim Rockford of the *Rockford Files*: 555–2368

Fred Sanford of *Sanford and Son*: 555–1079

Lew Archer of *Archer*: 555–4141

Janie Sommers of *The Bionic Woman*: 555–2368

Theme Songs of Noted Television Shows

"Love in Bloom," by Leo Robin and Ralph Rainger: *The Jack Benny Show*

"Plink, Plank, Plunk," by Leroy Anderson: *I've Got a Secret*

"The Ballad of Paladin": *Have Gun Will Travel*

"Flight of the Bumble Bee," performed by Al Hurt: *The Green Hornet*

"Gentle on My Mind," by John Hartford: *The Glen Campbell Goodtime Hour*

"Gobelues": *The George Gobel Show*

"Melancholy Serenade," by Jackie Gleason:
   The Jackie Gleason Show
"The Beat Goes On" *The Sonny and Cher Comedy Hour*
"Back in the Saddle Again," by Ray Whitley and Gene
   Autry: *The Gene Autry Show*

Billboard Magazine's Top TV Theme Songs

Ranking	Song	Composer	Show	Year
#1	"Miami Vice"	Jan Hammer	*Miami Vice*	1985
#1	"Welcome Back"	John Sebastian	*Welcome Back, Kotter*	1976
#1	"S.W.A.T."	Rhythm Section	*S.W.A.T.*	1975
#2	"Believe It or Not"	Joey Scarbury	*The Greatest American Hero*	1981
#3	"Dragnet"	Ray Anthony Orchestra	*Dragnet*	1953
#3	"Secret Agent Man"	Johnny Rivers	*Secret Agent*	1966
#4	"Hawaii Five-0"	The Ventures	*Hawaii Five-0*	1969
#5	"Happy Days"	Pratt and McClain	*Happy Days*	1976
#5	"Makin' It"	David Naughton	*Makin' It*	1979
#8	"Peter Gunn"	Ray Anthony Orchestra	*Peter Gunn*	1959
#10	"Hill Street Blues"	Mike Post	*Hill Street Blues*	1985
#10	"The Rockford Files"	Mike Post	*The Rockford Files*	1975
#10	"Three Stars Will Shine Tonight"	Richard Chamberlain	*Dr. Kildare*	1962

Hollywood and Television

Television and movies don't quite go together like a horse and carriage, but numerous films have dealt with television in its myriad forms. One of the earliest sound movies to show television in action is the 1933 comedy *International House* with W. C. Fields, George Burns, Gracie Allen, and Bela Lugosi. In the movie, Rudy Vallee and Cab Calloway are shown on a television screen.

Here are some other movies television fans might consider.

Murder by Television (1935)

The Glass Web (1953)

A Face in the Crowd (1957)

The Groove Tube (1974)

The Front (1976)

Network (1976)

My Favorite Year (1982)

The King of Comedy (1983)

Ginger and Fred (1985)

Terrorvision (1986)

Broadcast News (1987)

Switching Channels (1988)

Some successful television programs have spawned movie versions. Here are some popular shows that have led to big-screen features.*

Dragnet (1954/1987)

Gunn (based on *Peter Gunn*) (1967)

Superman (1978)

The Untouchables (1987)

Star Trek: The Motion Picture (1979)

Batman (1989)

---

* Of course, there were films of *Batman* and *Superman* in the 1940s.

The Addams Family (1991)

Wayne's World (1992)

Dennis the Menace (1993)

The Coneheads (1993)

The Beverly Hillbillies (1993)

The Fugitive (1993)

The Flintstones (1994)

Maverick (1994)

TV Animals

Bullet: Roy Rogers's dog.

Cleo: Jackie Cooper's upstaging basset hound on *The People's Choice*.

The Critters: Elly May's menagerie on *The Beverly Hillbillies*. There was a bloodhound (Duke), a cat (Rusty), another dog (Skippy), a pigeon (Homer), a skunk (Smelly), a rooster (Earl), and a hippopotamus.

Lassie: collie star of her own show. (Actually, Lassie was played by a series of male dogs.)

Mister Ed: the talking horse on the show of the same name. "Time and Ed wait for no man," this horse once philosophized.

Rex: Sergeant Preston's horse on *Sergeant Preston of the Yukon*.

Rin Tin Tin: German shepherd who starred in his own show.

Yukon King: Sergeant Preston's dog on *Sergeant Preston of the Yukon*.

Arnold Ziffel: the pig on *Green Acres*. Eddie Albert once complained that he was that "fellow on television with that pig."

Grin and Bear It

On February 10, 1979, a comedy adventure series—*B. J. and the Bear*—about a young trucker named B. J. (Billie Joe) McCay, made its premiere on NBC.

So here's the question with the obvious answer: What kind of animal was "the Bear" in the series? "The Bear" was a chimpanzee. (Don't ask us. We don't make these things up.) Actually, the chimp was named Bear in honor of Billie Joe McCay's favorite football coach, Paul "the Bear" Bryant.

Read All About It

Here's a list of newspapers that were read by characters on TV shows.

Los Angeles Daily Blade: Dear Phoebe
The Morning Express: Crime Photographer
The Daily Planet: The Adventures of Superman
Los Angeles Sun: The Debbie Reynolds Show
Center City Examiner: The Front Page
The Evening Shade Argus: Evening Shade
Today's World (a magazine): *The Doris Day Show*
The Daily Bugle: The Amazing Spider-Man
The Los Angeles Tribune: Lou Grant

What a Difference a Roman Numeral Makes

Most readers of American literature know who Edgar Allan Poe is, but who in television was Edgar Allan Poe IV?

Edgar Allan Poe IV was Lex Luthor's father in *The Adventures of Superman* (1988–92).

Famous Wheels

Cars, spaceships, and other vehicles have come to assume characters of their own in many shows. The following are some of the more well-known examples.

Maxwell: *The Jack Benny Show*

Corvette: *Route 66*

Thunderbird: *77 Sunset Strip*

Porter: *My Mother the Car*

U.S.S. *Enterprise: Star Trek*

Batmobile: *Batman*

Jupiter II: Lost in Space

Searcher: Buck Rogers in the 25th Century

Viper: *Viper*

Kit: *Knight Rider*

I Don't Usually Talk to Strangers

As in real life, TV characters meet and mingle at the local watering hole. Here are some local favorites and who hangs out there.

Archie Bunker's Place: Edith Bunker and Murray Klein

Cheers: Sam Malone and Diane Chambers

Copra Club: Danny Williams and Uncle Tonoose

Grant's Tomb: Fred Costello and Phil Bracken

Mother's: Peter Gunn and Lieutenant Jacoby

Moe's: Homer Simpson

Tropicana: Desi and Lucy

Addresses of TV Characters

Morticia and Gomez Addams (*The Addams Family*): 000 Cemetery Lane, Cemetery Ridge

Anderson Family (*Father Knows Best*): 607 Maple Street, Springfield

Stuart Bailey and Jeff Spencer (*77 Sunset Strip*): 77 Sunset Strip (office 101)

Jack Benny (*The Jack Benny Program*): 366 North Camden Drive, Beverly Hills, CA

Bundy Family (*Married . . . with Children*): 9674 Jeopardy Lane, Chicago

Archie and Edith Bunker (*All in the Family*): 704 Houser Street, Queens, New York

George Burns and Gracie Allen (*The Burns and Allen Show*): 312 Maple Drive, Beverly Hills and Suite 2216, St. Moritz Hotel, New York City

Roseanne and Dan Connor (*Roseanne*): 714 Delaware Street, Lanford, IL

Dorothy, Rose, Blanche, and Sophia (*The Golden Girls*): 6151 Richmond Street, Miami Beach

Fred and Wilma Flintstone (*The Flintstones*): 345 Stone Cave Road, Bedrock

Peter Gunn (*Peter Gunn*): 351 Ellis Park Road and Mother's, Los Angeles

Mary Hartman (*Mary Hartman, Mary Hartman*): 343 Bratner Avenue, Fernwood, OH

Hazel (*Hazel*): 123 Marshall Road (somewhere on the East Coast)

Cliff and Clair Huxtable (*The Cosby Show*): 10 Stigwood Avenue, Brooklyn, NY

Stella Johnson (*Harper Valley PTA*): 769 Oakwood, Harper Valley, OH

Gabe and Julie Kotter (*Welcome Back Kotter*): 711 East Ocean Parkway, Brooklyn, NY

Laverne and Shirley (*Laverne and Shirley*): 730 Hampton Street, Apt. A, Milwaukee

Ann Marie (*That Girl*): 344 West 78th Street, New York City

Mork and Mindy (*Mork and Mindy*): 1619 Pine Street, Boulder, CO

The Munsters (*The Munsters*): 1313 Mockingbird Lane

Nelson Family (*The Adventures of Ozzie and Harriet*): 822 Sycamore Road, Hillsdale, CA

Paladin (*Have Gun, Will Travel*): Hotel Carlton, San Francisco

Rob and Laura Petrie (*The Dick Van Dyke Show*): 148 Bonnie Meadow Road, New Rochelle, NY

Wilbur Post (*Mister Ed*): 17230 Valley Spring Lane, Los Angeles

Lucy and Rickey Ricardo (*I Love Lucy*): 623 East 68th Street, New York City

Chester A. Riley (*The Life of Riley*): 5412 Grove Street, Del Mar Vista, CA (also 1313 Blue View Terrace, Los Angeles)

Samantha and Darrin Stevens (*Bewitched*): 1164 Morning Glory Circle, Westport, CT

"Tool Time" (*Home Improvement*): P.O. Box 32732, Minneapolis, MN 48252

Cosmo Topper (*Topper*): 101 Maple Drive

Felix Unger and Oscar Madison (*The Odd Couple*): 1049 Park Avenue, Apt. 1102, New York City

Walsh Family (*Beverly Hills 90210*): 933 Hillcrest Drive, Beverly Hills

The Awards

The Emmys

On January 25, 1949, the National Academy of Television Arts and Sciences (NATAS) presented its first Emmy Award. The name *Emmy*, chosen by NATAS president Harry Lubcke, refers to the Immy, a nickname for the image orthicon tube used in TV image transmission.

Invented by physicist Vladimir Zworykin, this was a tube that allowed cameras to be used in the studio without the intense light previously required. Zworykin's invention was once dramatically demonstated in Madison Square Garden for nonbelievers. After the arena was plunged in darkness, a man on horseback lit a candle. The camera was able to transmit the picture with the illumination of that single candle.

In 1948, only six Emmy Awards were presented. Louis McManus, who designed the award—a statuette of a winged woman holding an atomic globe—was one of the recipients. Beginning in 1954, many Emmys were bestowed on technological innovations and expertise, but these have been weeded out here so that this listing of the Emmy Awards would not take over like kudzu. In addition, the actual wording of the individual categories has been eliminated. For example, the Emmy Winner for "Outstanding Program Achievement in the Field of Educational and Public Affairs Programming" in 1961–62, *David Brinkley's Journal*, has been grouped into the less precise but certainly more concise category of "Outstanding Programs." However, even with this editing, there were still

72 Emmys handed out in 1989–90 for outstanding programs, actors, supporting actors, directors, writers, and individual achievements.

It is also noteworthy that following a split between the Hollywood chapter and the national organization in 1976–77, the Emmys were divided into two categories, prime time and daytime. The prime-time awards became the bailiwick of the Academy of Television Arts and Sciences (ATAS); whereas the daytime awards fell to the National Academy of Television Arts and Sciences (NATAS).

Here is a year-by-year listing of the major awards.

The Awards

1948

Outstanding TV Personality: Shirley Dinsdale (and puppet Judy Splinters) (KTLA)
Most Popular TV Program: *Pantomime Quiz* (KTLA)
Best Film Made for TV: *The Necklace*, (*Your Show Time*) (NBC)
Special Award: Louis McManus, designer of the Emmy Award

1949

Best Live Show: *The Ed Wynn Show* (CBS)
Best Kinescope Show: *Texaco Star Theater* (NBC)
Outstanding Live Personality: Ed Wynn (CBS)
Outstanding Kinescope Personality: Milton Berle (NBC)
Best Film Made for TV: *The Life of Riley* (NBC)

1950

Best Variety Show: *The Alan Young Show* (CBS)
Best Dramatic Show: *Pulitzer Prize Playhouse* (ABC)
Best Game Show: *Truth or Consequences* (CBS)
Best Actor: Alan Young (CBS)
Best Actress: Gertrude Berg (CBS)

1951

Best Dramatic Show: *Studio One* (CBS)
Best Comedy Show: *The Red Skelton Show* (CBS)
Best Variety Show: *Your Show of Shows* (NBC)
Best Actor: Sid Caesar (NBC)
Best Actress: Imogene Coca (NBC)
Best Comedian: Red Skelton (NBC)

1952

Best Dramatic Show: *Robert Montgomery Presents* (NBC)
Best Variety Show: *Your Show of Shows* (NBC)
Best Mystery, Action, or Adventure Show: *Dragnet* (NBC)
Best Sitcom: *I Love Lucy* (CBS)
Best Actor: Thomas Mitchell
Best Actress: Helen Hayes

1953

Best Dramatic Show: *U.S. Steel Hour* (ABC)
Best Sitcom: *I Love Lucy* (CBS)
Best Variety Show: *Omnibus* (CBS)
Best Actor: Donald O'Connor, *Colgate Comedy Hour* (NBC)
Best Actress: Eve Arden, *Our Miss Brooks* (CBS)
Best Mystery, Action, or Adventure Show: *Dragnet* (NBC)

1954

Best Dramatic Show: *U.S. Steel Hour* (ABC)
Beat Sitcom: *Make Room for Daddy* (ABC)
Best Variety Show: *Disneyland* (ABC)
Best Actor: Danny Thomas, *Make Room for Daddy* (ABC)
Best Actress: Loretta Young, *The Loretta Young Show* (NBC)
Best Mystery, Action, or Adventure Show: *Dragnet* (NBC)

1955

Best Dramatic Show: *Producers' Showcase* (NBC)
Best Mystery, Action, or Adventure Show: *Disneyland* (ABC)
Best Comedy Show: *The Phil Silvers Show* (CBS)
Best Variety Show: *The Ed Sullivan Show* (CBS)

Best Actor: Phil Silvers, *The Phil Silvers Show* (CBS)
Best Actress: Lucille Ball, *I Love Lucy* (CBS)

1956

Best Single Show: *Requiem for a Heavyweight* (*Playhouse 90*) (CBS)
Best Series (½ hour): *The Phil Silvers Show* (CBS)
Best Series (1 hour): *Caesar's Hour* (NBC)
Best Actor: Robert Young, *Father Knows Best* (NBC)
Best Actress: Loretta Young, *The Loretta Young Show* (NBC)

1957

Best Single Show: *The Comedian* (*Playhouse 90*) (CBS)
Best Dramatic Show: *Gunsmoke* (CBS)
Best Comedy Show: *The Phil Silvers Show* (CBS)
Best Musical, Variety, Audience Participation, or Quiz Show: *The Dinah Shore Chevy Show* (NBC)
Best Actor: Robert Young, *Father Knows Best* (NBC)
Best Actress: Jane Wyatt, *Father Knows Best* (NBC)

1958—59

Best Single Show: *An Evening with Fred Astaire* (NBC)
Best Dramatic Show (1 hour): *Playhouse 90* (CBS)
Best Dramatic Show (1 hour): *The Alcoa Hour/Goodyear Playhouse* (NBC)
Best Comedy Show: *The Jack Benny Show* (CBS)
Best Musical or Variety Show: *The Dinah Shore Chevy Show* (NBC)
Best Western Show: *Maverick* (ABC)
Best Actor (Dramatic): Raymond Burr, *Perry Mason* (CBS)
Best Actress (Dramatic): Loretta Young, *The Loretta Young Show* (NBC)
Best Actor (Comedy): Jack Benny, *The Jack Benny Show* (CBS)
Best Actress (Comedy): Jane Wyatt, *Father Knows Best* (CBS and NBC)

1959—60

Best Comedy Show: *Art Carney Special* (NBC)
Best Dramatic Show: *Playhouse 90* (CBS)

Best Variety Show: *The Fabulous Fifties* (CBS)
Best Actor: Robert Stack, *The Untouchables* (ABC)
Best Actress: Jane Wyatt, *Father Knows Best* (CBS)
Best Performance in a Variety or Musical Show: Harry Belafonte, *Tonight with Belafonte* (*The Revlon Revue*) (CBS)

1960—61

Best Single Show: *Macbeth* (*Hallmark Hall of Fame*) (NBC)
Best Comedy Show: *The Jack Benny Show* (CBS)
Best Variety Show: *Astaire Time* (NBC)
Best Actor: Raymond Burr, *Perry Mason* (CBS)
Best Actress: Barbara Stanwyck, *The Barbara Stanwyck Show* (NBC)
Best Performance in a Variety or Musical Show: Fred Astaire, *Astaire Time* (NBC)

1961—62

Best Single Show: *Victoria Regina* (*Hallmark Hall of Fame*) (NBC)
Best Comedy Show: *The Bob Newhart Show* (NBC)
Best Dramatic Show: *The Defenders* (CBS)
Best Variety Show: *The Garry Moore Show* (CBS)
Best Actor: E. G. Marshall, *The Defenders* (CBS)
Best Actress: Shirley Booth, *Hazel* (NBC)
Best Performance in a Variety or Musical Show: Carol Burnett, *The Garry Moore Show* (CBS)

1962—63

Best Single Show: *The Tunnel* (NBC)
Best Comedy Show: *The Dick Van Dyke Show* (CBS)
Best Dramatic Show: *The Defenders* (CBS)
Best Musical Show: *Julie and Carol at Carnegie Hall* (CBS)
Best Variety Show: *The Andy Williams Show* (NBC)
Best Actor: E. G. Marshall, *The Defenders* (CBS)
Best Actress: Shirley Booth, *Hazel* (NBC)
Best Performance in a Variety or Musical Show: Carol Burnett, *Julie and Carol at Carnegie Hall* (CBS) and *Carol & Company* (CBS)

1963—64

Best Single Show: *The Making of the President 1960* (ABC)
Best Comedy Show: *The Dick Van Dyke Show* (CBS)
Best Dramatic Show: *The Defenders* (CBS)
Best Variety Show: *The Danny Kaye Show* (CBS)
Best Actor: Dick Van Dyke, *The Dick Van Dyke Show* (CBS)
Best Actress: Mary Tyler Moore, *The Dick Van Dyke Show* (CBS)
Best Performance in a Variety or Musical Show: Danny Kaye, *The Danny Kaye Show* (CBS)

1964—65

Outstanding Achievement in Entertainment: *The Dick Van Dyke Show* (CBS); *The Magnificent Yankee* (*Hallmark Hall of Fame*) (NBC); *My Name Is Barbra* (CBS)
Outstanding Individual Achievement in Entertainment: Lynn Fontanne, *The Magnificent Yankee* (*Hallmark Hall of Fame*) (NBC); Barbra Streisand, *My Name Is Barbra* (CBS); Dick Van Dyke, *The Dick Van Dyke Show* (CBS)

1965—66

Best Comedy Show: *The Dick Van Dyke Show* (CBS)
Best Variety Show: *The Andy Williams Show* (NBC)
Best Dramatic Show: *The Fugitive* (ABC)
Best Actor (Dramatic): Bill Cosby, *I Spy* (NBC)
Best Actress (Dramatic): Barbara Stanwyck, *The Big Valley* (ABC)
Best Actor (Comedy): Dick Van Dyke, *The Dick Van Dyke Show* (CBS)
Best Actress (Comedy): Mary Tyler Moore, *The Dick Van Dyke Show* (CBS)

1966—67

Best Comedy Show: *The Monkees* (NBC)
Best Variety Show: *The Andy Williams Show* (NBC)
Best Dramatic Show: *Mission: Impossible* (CBS)
Best Actor (Dramatic): Bill Cosby, *I Spy* (NBC)
Best Actress (Dramatic): Barbara Bain, *Mission: Impossible* (CBS)

Best Actor (Comedy): Don Adams, *Get Smart* (NBC)
Best Actress (Comedy): Lucille Ball, *The Lucy Show* (CBS)

1967—68

Best Comedy Show: *Get Smart* (NBC)
Best Dramatic Show: *Mission: Impossible* (CBS)
Best Actor (Dramatic): Bill Cosby, *I Spy* (NBC)
Best Actress (Dramatic): Barbara Bain, *Mission: Impossible* (CBS)
Best Actor (Comedy): Don Adams, *Get Smart* (NBC)
Best Actress (Comedy): Lucille Ball, *The Lucy Show* (CBS)

1968—69

Best Comedy Show: *Get Smart* (NBC)
Best Dramatic Show: *NET Playhouse* (NET)
Best Musical or Variety Show: *Rowan and Martin's Laugh-in* (NBC)
Best Actor (Dramatic): Carl Betz, *Judd for the Defense* (ABC)
Best Actress (Dramatic): Barbara Bain, *Mission: Impossible* (CBS)
Best Actor (Comedy): Don Adams, *Get Smart* (NBC)
Best Actress (Comedy): Hope Lange, *The Ghost and Mrs. Muir* (NBC)

1969—70

Best Comedy Show: *My World and Welcome to It* (NBC)
Best Dramatic Show: *Marcus Welby, M.D.* (ABC)
Best Variety or Musical Show: *The David Frost Show* (syndicated)
Best Actor (Dramatic): Robert Young, *Marcus Welby, M.D.* (ABC)
Best Actress (Dramatic): Susan Hampshire, *The Forsyte Saga* (NET)
Best Actor (Comedy): William Windom, *My World and Welcome to It* (NBC)
Best Actress (Comedy): Hope Lange, *The Ghost and Mrs. Muir* (ABC)

The Envelope, Please . . .

The show that has won best series the most times is . . .
ABC's Wide World of Sports (15)
(*Sesame Street* is second with 12)

Shows that won best series four years in a row are . . .
The Dick Van Dyke Show
All in the Family
Hill Street Blues

The soap opera that won best daytime series three times in a row is . . .
Santa Barbara

The soap opera that won best daytime series the most times is . . .
The Young and the Restless (4)

The series that have won the most Emmys are . . .
The Mary Tyler Moore Show (29)
Cheers (26)
Hill Street Blues (26)

The series that won the most Emmys in a single year is . . .
Hill Street Blues (8)

The series that received the most nominations is . . .
Cheers (101)

The series that received the most nominations in one season is . . .
NYPD Blue (26)

The person who won the most Emmys is . . .
producer/director Dwight Hemion (16) for

Frank Sinatra: A Man and His Music, Barbra Streisand . . . and Other Musical Instruments, The Kennedy Center Honors, etc.

The person who was nominated for an Emmy the most times is . . .
producer/director Dwight Hemion (37)

The person who was nominated the most times without winning is . . .
Susan Lucci (12) for *All My Children*
(Second is Angela Lansbury, 11, for *Murder, She Wrote*)

Actors who have won five Emmys for playing the same part are . . .
Ed Asner (two best actor and three best supporting actor) for Lou Grant (*The Mary Tyler Moore Show* and *Lou Grant*)
Art Carney (five best supporting actor) for Ed Norton (*The Jackie Gleason Show* and *The Honeymooners*)
Don Knotts (best supporting actor) for Barney Fife on *The Andy Griffith Show*

Actors who have won three Emmys for best acting on soap operas are . . .
David Canary (Adam and Stuart Chandler on *All My Children*)
Helen Gallagher (Maeve Ryan on *Ryan's Hope*)
Kim Zimmer (Reva Shayne on *Guiding Light*)

Actors who have won best actor in both comedy and drama are . . .
Robert Young (*Father Knows Best* and *Marcus Welby, M.D.*)
Carroll O'Connor (*All in the Family* and *In the Heat of the Night*)

The star who has won Emmys for acting, writing, and directing is . . .
Alan Alda (*M*A*S*H*)

The director who won an Emmy, a Tony, and
an Oscar in the same year is . . .
Bob Fosse (*Liza with a "Z," Pippin, Cabaret*)

Husbands and wives who have both won Emmys
are . . .
George C. Scott and Colleen Dewhurst
Hume Cronyn and Jessica Tandy
William Daniels and Bonnie Bartlett
Danny DeVito and Rhea Perlman
Phil Donahue and Marlo Thomas
Alfred Lunt and Lynn Fontanne

The husband and wife who won Emmys for play-
ing husband and wife on a TV series are . . .
William Daniels and Bonnie Bartlett (*St.
Elsewhere*)

1970—71

Best Comedy Show: *All in the Family* (CBS)
Best Dramatic Show: *The Senator* (NBC)
Best Musical Show: *The Flip Wilson Show* (NBC)
Best Actor (Dramatic): Hal Holbrook, *The Senator* (NBC)
Best Actress (Dramatic): Susan Hampshire, *The First Churchills* (*Masterpiece Theatre*) (PBS)
Best Actor (Comedy): Jack Klugman, *The Odd Couple* (CBS)
Best Actress (Comedy): Jean Stapleton, *All in the Family* (CBS)

1971—72

Best Comedy Show: *All in the Family* (CBS)
Best Dramatic Show: *Elizabeth R* (*Masterpiece Theatre*) (PBS)
Best Musical Show: *The Carol Burnett Show* (CBS)
Best Talk Show: *The Dick Cavett Show* (ABC)
Best Actor (Dramatic): Peter Falk, *Columbo* (NBC)
Best Actor (Comedy): Carroll O'Connor, *All in the Family* (CBS)

Best Actress (Comedy): Jean Stapleton, *All in the Family* (CBS)

1972–73

Best Comedy Show: *All in the Family* (CBS)
Best Dramatic Show: *The Waltons* (CBS)
Best Variety Musical Show: *The Julie Andrews Hour* (ABC)
Best Actor (Dramatic): Richard Thomas, *The Waltons* (CBS)
Best Actress (Dramatic): Michael Learned, *The Waltons* (CBS)
Best Actor (Comedy): Jack Klugman, *The Odd Couple* (ABC)
Best Actress (Comedy): Mary Tyler Moore, *The Mary Tyler Moore Show* (CBS)

Ethel Waters was the first black performer to be nominated for an Emmy Award in drama. The distinguished actress was nominated in 1962 for her work on an episode for the series *Route 66*. The first black woman to win an Emmy Award was Gail Fisher, who played the part of Joe Mannix's girl-Friday on the private eye series *Mannix*.

1973–74

Best Comedy Show: *M*A*S*H* (CBS)
Best Dramatic Show: *Upstairs, Downstairs* (*Masterpiece Theatre*) (PBS)
Best Variety Musical Show: *The Carol Burnett Show* (CBS)
Best Actor (Comedy): Alan Alda, *M*A*S*H* (CBS)
Best Actor (Dramatic): Telly Savalas, *Kojak* (CBS)
Best Actress (Comedy): Mary Tyler Moore, *The Mary Tyler Moore Show* (CBS)
Best Actress (Dramatic): Michael Learned, *The Waltons* (CBS)

1974–75

Best Comedy Show: *The Mary Tyler Moore Show* (CBS)
Best Dramatic Show: *Upstairs, Downstairs* (*Masterpiece Theatre*) (PBS)

Best Comedy, Variety, or Musical Show: *The Carol Burnett Show* (CBS)

Best Actor (Comedy): Tony Randall, *The Odd Couple* (ABC)

Best Actor (Dramatic): Robert Blake, *Baretta* (ABC)

Best Actress (Comedy): Valerie Harper, *Rhoda* (CBS)

Best Actress (Dramatic): Jean Marsh, *Upstairs, Downstairs* (*Masterpiece Theatre*) (PBS)

1975–76

Best Comedy Series: *The Mary Tyler Moore Show* (CBS)

Best Dramatic Show: *Police Story* (NBC)

Best Comedy, Variety, or Musical Show: *NBC's Saturday Night* (NBC)

Best Actor (Comedy): Jack Albertson, *Chico and the Man* (NBC)

Best Actor (Dramatic): Peter Falk, *Columbo* (NBC)

Best Actress (Comedy): Mary Tyler Moore, *The Mary Tyler Moore Show* (CBS)

Best Actress (Dramatic): Michael Learned, *The Waltons* (CBS)

1976–77

Best Comedy Show: *The Mary Tyler Moore Show* (CBS)

Best Dramatic Show: *Upstairs, Downstairs* (*Masterpiece Theatre*) (PBS)

Best Comedy, Variety, or Musical Show: *Van Dyke and Company* (NBC)

Best Actor (Comedy): Carroll O'Connor, *All in the Family* (CBS)

Best Actor (Dramatic): James Garner, *The Rockford Files* (NBC)

Best Actress (Comedy): Beatrice Arthur, *Maude* (CBS)

Best Actress (Dramatic): Lindsay Wagner, *The Bionic Woman* (ABC)

1977–78

Best Comedy Show: *All in the Family* (CBS)

Best Dramatic Show: *The Rockford Files* (NBC)

Best Comedy, Variety, or Musical Show: *The Muppet Show* (syndicated)

Best Actor (Comedy): Carroll O'Connor, *All in the Family* (CBS)

Best Actor (Dramatic): Ed Asner, *Lou Grant* (CBS)

Best Actress (Comedy): Jean Stapleton, *All in the Family* (CBS)

Best Actress (Dramatic): Sada Thompson, *Family* (ABC)

1978–79

Best Comedy Show: *Taxi* (ABC)

Best Dramatic Show: *Lou Grant* (CBS)

Best Comedy, Variety, or Musical Show: *Steve & Eydie Celebrate Irving Berlin* (NBC)

Best Actor (Comedy): Carroll O'Connor, *All in the Family* (CBS)

Best Actor (Dramatic): Ron Leibman, *Kaz* (CBS)

Best Actress (Comedy): Ruth Gordon, *Taxi* ("Sugar Mama") (ABC)

Best Actress (Dramatic): Mariette Hartley, *The Incredible Hulk* ("Married") (CBS)

1979–80

Best Comedy Show: *Taxi* (ABC)

Best Dramatic Show: *Lou Grant* (CBS)

Best Variety or Musical Show: *Baryshnikov on Broadway* (ABC)

Best Actor (Comedy): Richard Mulligan, *Soap* (ABC)

Best Actor (Dramatic): Ed Asner, *Lou Grant* (CBS)

Best Actress (Comedy): Cathryn Damon, *Soap* (ABC)

Best Actress (Dramatic): Barbara Bel Geddes, *Dallas* (CBS)

1980–81

Best Comedy Show: *Taxi* (ABC)

Best Dramatic Show: *Hill Street Blues* (NBC)

Best Variety, Musical, or Comedy Show: *Lily: Sold Out* (CBS)

Best Actor (Dramatic): Daniel J. Travanti, *Hill Street Blues* (NBC)

Best Actor (Comedy): Judd Hirsch, *Taxi* (ABC)

Best Actress (Dramatic): Barbara Babcock, *Hill Street Blues* (NBC)

Best Actress (Comedy): Isabel Sanford, *The Jeffersons* (CBS)

1981–82

Best Comedy Show: *Barney Miller* (ABC)

Best Dramatic Show: *Hill Street Blues* (NBC)

Best Variety, Musical, or Comedy Show: *Night of 100 Stars* (ABC)

Best Actor (Dramatic): Daniel J. Travanti, *Hill Street Blues* (NBC)

Best Actor (Comedy): Alan Alda, *M*A*S*H* (CBS)

Best Actress (Dramatic): Michael Learned, *Nurse* (CBS)

Best Actress (Comedy): Carol Kane, *Taxi* ("Simka Returns") (ABC)

1982–83

Best Comedy Show: *Cheers* (NBC)

Best Dramatic Show: *Hill Street Blues* (NBC)

Best Variety, Musical, or Comedy Show: *Motown 25: Yesterday, Today, Forever* (NBC)

Best Actor (Dramatic): Ed Flanders, *St. Elsewhere* (NBC)

Best Actor (Comedy): Judd Hirsch, *Taxi* (ABC)

Best Actress (Dramatic): Tyne Daly, *Cagney & Lacey* (CBS)

Best Actress (Comedy): Shelley Long, *Cheers* (NBC)

1983–84

Best Comedy Show: *Cheers* (NBC)

Best Dramatic Show: *Hill Street Blues* (NBC)

Best Variety, Musical, or Comedy Show: *The 6th Annual Kennedy Center Honors: A Celebration of the Performing Arts* (CBS)

Best Actor (Dramatic): Tom Selleck, *Magnum, P.I.* (CBS)

Best Actor (Comedy): John Ritter, *Three's Company* (ABC)

Best Actress (Dramatic): Tyne Daly, *Cagney & Lacey* (CBS)

Best Actress (Comedy): Jane Curtain, *Kate & Allie* (CBS)

1984—85

Best Comedy Show: *The Cosby Show* (NBC)

Best Dramatic Show: *Cagney & Lacey* (CBS)

Best Variety, Musical, or Comedy Show: *Motown Returns to the Apollo* (NBC)

Best Actor (Dramatic): William Daniels, *St. Elsewhere* (NBC)

Best Actor (Comedy): Robert Guillaume, *Benson* (ABC)

Best Actress (Dramatic): Tyne Daly, *Cagney & Lacey* (CBS)

Best Actress (Comedy): Jane Curtin, *Kate & Allie* (CBS)

1985—86

Best Comedy Show: *The Golden Girls* (NBC)

Best Dramatic Show: *Cagney & Lacey* (CBS)

Best Variety, Musical, or Comedy Show: *The Kennedy Center Honors: A Celebration of the Performing Arts* (CBS)

Best Actor (Dramatic): William Daniels, *St. Elsewhere* (NBC)

Best Actor (Comedy): Michael J. Fox, *Family Ties* (NBC)

Best Actress (Dramatic): Sharon Gless, *Cagney & Lacey* (CBS)

Best Actress (Comedy): Betty White, *The Golden Girls* (NBC)

1986—87

Best Comedy Show: *The Golden Girls* (NBC)

Best Dramatic Show: *L.A. Law* (NBC)

Best Variety, Musical, or Comedy Show: *The 1987 Tony Awards* (CBS)

Best Actor (Dramatic): Bruce Willis, *Moonlighting* (ABC)

Best Actor (Comedy): Michael J. Fox, *Family Ties* (NBC)

Best Actress (Dramatic): Sharon Gless, *Cagney & Lacey* (CBS)

Best Actress (Comedy): Rue McClanahan, *The Golden Girls* (NBC)

1987—88

Best Comedy Show: *The Wonder Years* (ABC)

Best Dramatic Show: *thirtysomething* (ABC)

Best Variety, Musical, or Comedy Show: *Irving Berlin's 100th Birthday Celebration* (CBS)

Best Actor (Comedy): Michael J. Fox, *Family Ties* (NBC)

Best Actor (Dramatic): Richard Kiley, *A Year in the Life* (NBC)

Best Actress (Comedy): Beatrice Arthur, *The Golden Girls* (NBC)

Best Actress (Dramatic): Tyne Daly, *Cagney & Lacey* (CBS)

1988—89

Best Comedy Show: *Cheers* (NBC)

Best Dramatic Show: *L.A. Law* (NBC)

Best Variety, Musical, or Comedy Show: *The Tracey Ullman Show* (Fox)

Best Actor (Comedy): Richard Mulligan, *Empty Nest* (NBC)

Best Actor (Dramatic): Carroll O'Connor, *In the Heat of the Night* (NBC)

Best Actress (Comedy): Candice Bergen, *Murphy Brown* (CBS)

Best Actress (Dramatic): Dana Delany, *China Beach* (ABC)

1989—90

Best Comedy Show: *Murphy Brown* (CBS)

Best Dramatic Show: *L.A. Law* (NBC)

Best Variety, Musical, or Comedy Show: *In Living Color* (Fox)

Best Actor (Comedy): Ted Danson, *Cheers* (NBC)

Best Actor (Dramatic): Peter Falk, *Columbo* (ABC)

Best Actress (Comedy): Candice Bergen, *Murphy Brown* (CBS)

Best Actress (Dramatic): Patricia Wettig, *thirtysomething* (ABC)

1990—91

Best Comedy Show: *Cheers* (NBC)

Best Dramatic Show: *L.A. Law* (NBC)

Best Variety, Musical, or Comedy Show: *The 63rd Annual Academy Awards* (ABC)

Best Actor (Comedy): Burt Reynolds, *Evening Shade* (CBS)

Best Actor (Dramatic): James Earl Jones, *Gabriel's Fire* (ABC)

Best Actress (Comedy): Kirstie Alley, *Cheers* (NBC)

Best Actress (Dramatic): Patricia Wettig, *thirtysomething* (ABC)

1991—92

Best Comedy Show: *Murphy Brown* (CBS)

Best Dramatic Show: *Northern Exposure* (CBS)

Best Variety, Musical, or Comedy Show: *The Tonight Show Starring Johnny Carson* (NBC)

Best Actor (Comedy): Craig T. Nelson, *Coach* (ABC)

Best Actor (Dramatic): Christopher Lloyd, *Avonlea* (Disney Channel)

Best Actress (Comedy): Candice Bergen, *Murphy Brown* (CBS)

Best Actress (Dramatic): Dana Delany, *China Beach* (ABC)

1992—93

Best Comedy Show: *Seinfeld* (NBC)

Best Dramatic Show: *Picket Fences* (CBS)

Best Variety, Musical, or Comedy Show: *Saturday Night Live* (NBC)

Best Actor (Comedy): Ted Danson, *Cheers* (NBC)

Best Actor (Dramatic): Tom Skerritt, *Picket Fences* (CBS)

Best Actress (Comedy): Roseanne Arnold, *Roseanne* (ABC)

Best Actress (Dramatic): Kathy Baker, *Picket Fences* (CBS)

1993—94

Best Comedy Show: *Frasier* (NBC)

Best Dramatic Show: *Picket Fences* (CBS)

Best Variety, Musical, or Comedy Show: *The Late Show with David Letterman* (CBS)

Best Actor (Comedy): Kelsey Grammer, *Frasier* (NBC)

Best Actor (Dramatic): Dennis Franz, *NYPD Blue* (ABC)

Best Actress (Comedy): Candice Bergen, *Murphy Brown* (CBS)

Best Actress (Dramatic): Sela Ward, *Sisters* (NBC)

Peabody Awards

*T*he George Foster Peabody Broadcasting Awards were first given out to radio programming in 1940 by the Henry W. Grady School of Journalism at the University of Georgia. In 1948, Peabody Awards also began to honor achievements in television. That year only two Peabodys were presented. (*Actor's Studio* won for Outstanding Contribution to the Art of Television; *Howdy Doody* won for Outstanding Children's Program.) In 1971, there were 10 winners in categories of entertainment, news, youth or children's programs, public service, promotion of international understanding, and special awards. From 1972 to the present day (with the exception of 1973), awards have not been given in specific categories.

TV Guide's awards for the dumbest achievements were once named after J. Fred Muggs, the chimp who was a regular on the *Today* show back in Dave Garroway's day. *TV Guide* has gotten up to the speed of the channel changers and nowadays they are known as the Zap Awards.

The Golden Globes

Best Actor in a Comedy or Musical Series

Year	Actor	Show
1993	John Goodman	*Roseanne*
1992	Burt Reynolds	*Evening Shade*
1991	Ted Danson	*Cheers*
1990	Ted Danson	*Cheers*

Year	Actor	Show
1989	Michael J. Fox	*Family Ties*
	Judd Hirsch	*Dear John*
	Richard Mulligan	*Empty Nest*
1988	Dabney Coleman	*The Slap Maxwell Story*
1987	Bruce Willis	*Moonlighting*
1986	Bill Cosby	*The Cosby Show*
1985	Bill Cosby	*The Cosby Show*
1984	John Ritter	*Three's Company*
1983	Alan Alda	*M*A*S*H*
1982	Alan Alda	*M*A*S*H*
1981	Alan Alda	*M*A*S*H*
1980	Alan Alda	*M*A*S*H*
1979	Robin Williams	*Mork and Mindy*
1978	Henry Winkler	*Happy Days*
1977	Henry Winkler	*Happy Days*
1976	Alan Alda	*M*A*S*H*
1975	Alan Alda	*M*A*S*H*
1974	Jack Klugman	*The Odd Couple*
1973	Redd Foxx	*Sanford and Son*
1972	Carroll O'Connor	*All in the Family*
1971	Flip Wilson	*The Flip Wilson Show*
1970	Dan Dailey	*The Governor and J. J.*

Best Actress in a Comedy or Musical Series

Year	Actress	Show
1993	Roseanne Arnold	*Roseanne*
1992	Candice Bergen	*Murphy Brown*
1991	Kirstie Alley	*Cheers*
1990	Jamie Lee Curtis	*Anything but Love*
1989	Candice Bergen	*Murphy Brown*
1988	Tracey Ullman	*The Tracey Ullman Show*
1987	Cybill Shepherd	*Moonlighting*

Year	Actress	Show
1986	Estelle Getty	*The Golden Girls*
	Cybill Shepherd	*Moonlighting*
1985	Shelley Long	*Cheers*
1984	Joanna Cassidy	*Buffalo Bill*
1983	Debbie Allen	*Fame*
1982	Eileen Brennan	*Private Benjamin*
1981	Katherine Helmond	*Soap*
1980	Linda Lavin	*Alice*
1979	Linda Lavin	*Alice*
1978	Carol Burnett	*The Carol Burnett Show*
1977	Carol Burnett	*The Carol Burnett Show*
1976	Cloris Leachman	*Phyllis*
1975	Valerie Harper	*Rhoda*
1974	Jean Stapleton	*All in The Family*
	Cher	*The Sonny and Cher Comedy Hour*
1973	Jean Stapleton	*All in the Family*
1972	Carol Burnett	*The Carol Burnett Show*
1971	Mary Tyler Moore	*The Mary Tyler Moore Show*
1970	Carol Burnett	*The Carol Burnett Show*

Best Actor in a Dramatic Series

Year	Actor	Show
1993	Sam Waterston	*I'll Fly Away*
1992	Scott Bakula	*Quantum Leap*
1991	Kyle MacLachlan	*Twin Peaks*
1990	Ken Wahl	*Wiseguy*
1989	Ron Perlman	*Beauty and the Best*
1988	Richard Kiley	*A Year in the Life*
1987	Edward Woodward	*The Equalizer*
1986	Don Johnson	*Miami Vice*
1985	Tom Selleck	*Magnum, P.I.*

Year	Actor	Show
1984	John Forsythe	*Dynasty*
1983	John Forsythe	*Dynasty*
1982	Daniel J. Travanti	*Hill Street Blues*
1981	Richard Chamberlain	*Shogun*
1980	Ed Asner	*Lou Grant*
1979	Michael Moriarty	*Holocaust*
1978	Ed Asner	*Lou Grant*
1977	Richard Jordan	*Captains and the Kings*
1976	Robert Blake	*Baretta*
	Telly Savalas	*Kojak*
1975	Telly Savalas	*Kojak*
1974	James Stewart	*Hawkins*
1973	Peter Falk	*Columbo*
1972	Robert Young	*Marcus Welby, M.D.*
1971	Peter Graves	*Mission: Impossible*
1970	Mike Connors	*Mannix*

Best Actress in a Dramatic Series

Year	Actress	Show
1993	Regina Taylor	*I'll Fly Away*
1992	Angela Lansbury	*Murder, She Wrote*
1991	Sharon Gless	*The Trials of Rosie O'Neill*
	Patricia Wettig	*thirtysomething*
1990	Angela Lansbury	*Murder, She Wrote*
1989	Jill Eikenberry	*L.A. Law*
1988	Susan Dey	*L.A. Law*
1987	Angela Lansbury	*Murder, She Wrote*
1986	Sharon Gless	*Cagney & Lacey*
1985	Angela Lansbury	*Murder, She Wrote*
1984	Jane Wyman	*Falcon Crest*
1983	Joan Collins	*Dynasty*

Year	Actress	Show
1982	Barbara Bel Geddes	*Dallas*
	Linda Evans	*Dynasty*
1981	Yoko Shimada	*Shogun*
1980	Natalie Wood	*From Here to Eternity*
1979	Rosemary Harris	*Holocaust*
1978	Lesley Ann Warren	*79 Park Avenue*
1977	Susan Blakely	*Rich Man, Poor Man (Book 1)*
1976	Lee Remick	*Jennie*
1975	Angie Dickinson	*Police Woman*
1974	Lee Remick	*The Blue Knight*
1973	Gail Fisher	*Mannix*
1972	Patricia Neal	*The Homecoming*
1971	Peggy Lipton	*The Mod Squad*
1970	Linda Cristal	*High Chapparel*

A TV Who's Who

TV Title Roles

Famous Characters and the Actors Who Played Them

Alice:	Linda Lavin (Alice Hyatt)
Angie:	Donna Pescow (Angie Falco)
Archer:	Brian Keith (Lew Archer)
Arnie:	Herschel Bernardi (Arnie Nuvo)
Banacek:	George Peppard (Thomas Banacek)
Baretta:	Robert Blake (Tony Baretta)
Barnaby Jones:	Buddy Ebsen
Barney Miller:	Hal Linden
Bat Masterson:	Gene Barry
Batman:	Adam West
Beauty and the Beast:	Linda Hamilton (Catherine Chandler), Ron Perlman (Vincent, the Beast)
Ben Casey:	Vince Edwards
Benson:	Robert Guillaume (Benson DuBois)
Beverly Hills Buntz:	Dennis Franz (Norman Buntz)
The Bionic Woman:	Lindsay Wagner (Jaime Sommers)
Blondie:	Pamela Britton
Blossom:	Mayim Bialik (Blossom Russo)
Booker:	Richard Grieco (Dennis Booker)
Boston Blackie:	Kent Taylor
Bridget Loves Bernie:	Meredith Baxter (Bridget Fitzgerald Steinberg), David Birney (Bernie Steinberg)
Bronco:	Ty Hardin (Bronco Layne)

Bronk:	Jack Palance (Alex Bronkov)
Buck Rogers in the 25th Century:	Gil Gerard
Cagney & Lacey:	Sharon Gless (Chris Cagney), Tyne Daly (Mary Beth Lacey)
Cannon:	William Conrad (Frank Cannon)
Charles in Charge:	Scott Baio
Chico and the Man:	Freddie Prinze (Chico Rodriguez), Jack Albertson (Ed Brown)
Cisco Kid, The:	Duncan Renaldo
Coach:	Craig T. Nelson (Hayden Fox)
Columbo:	Peter Falk (Lieutenant Columbo)
Commish, The:	Michael Chiklis (Tony Scali)
Dan August:	Burt Reynolds
Daniel Boone:	Fess Parker
Days and Nights of Molly Dodd, The:	Blair Brown
Dear John:	Judd Hirsch (John Lacey)
Dennis the Menace:	Jay North (Dennis Mitchell)
Dr. Kildare:	Richard Chamberlain (James Kildare)
Doogie Howser, M.D.:	Neil Patrick Harris (Douglas "Doogie" Howser)
Ensign O'Toole:	Dean Jones
Flo:	Polly Holliday (Florence Jean Castleberry)
Flying Nun, The:	Sally Field (Sister Bertrille)
Fresh Prince of Bel Air:	Will Smith (Will Smith)
The Fugitive:	David Janssen (Dr. Richard Kimble)
Get Smart:	Don Adams (Maxwell Smart, Agent 86), Barbara Feldon (Agent 99)
Ghost and Mrs. Muir, The:	Hope Lange (Carolyn Muir), Vincent Price (The Ghost)
Gidget:	Sally Field (Gidget [Francine] Lawrence)
Gilligan's Island:	Bob Denver (Gilligan)
Gomer Pyle, U.S.M.C.:	Jim Nabors
Greatest American Hero, The:	William Katt (Ralph Hinkley)

Hardy Boys Mysteries, The:	Shaun Cassidy (Joe Hardy), Parker Stevenson (Frank Hardy)
Harry-O:	David Janssen (Harry Orwell)
Hart to Hart:	Stefanie Powers (Jennifer Hart), Robert Wagner (Jonathan Hart)
Hazel:	Shirley Booth (Hazel Burke)
Hennessy:	Jackie Cooper ("Chick" [Charles J.] Hennessy)
Honey West:	Anne Francis (Honey West)
Hooperman:	John Ritter (Harry Hooperman)
Hopalong Cassidy:	William Boyd
Hunter:	Fred Dryer (Rick Hunter)
I Dream of Jeannie:	Barbara Eden (Jeannie)
I Love Lucy:	Lucille Ball (Lucy Ricardo)
I Married Joan:	Joan Davis (Joan Stevens)
Incredible Hulk, The:	Lou Ferrigno (The Incredible Hulk)
Ironside:	Raymond Burr (Robert Ironside)
Jake and the Fatman:	Joe Penny (Jake Styles), William Conrad (Jason Lochinvar McCabe)
James at 15:	Lance Kerwin (James Hunter)
Julia:	Diahann Carroll (Julia Baker)
Kate & Allie:	Susan Saint James (Kate McArdle), Jane Curtin (Allie Lowell)
Kaz:	Ron Leibman (Martin Kazinsky)
Knight Rider:	David Hasselhoff (Michael Knight)
Kojak:	Telly Savalas (Theo Kojak)
Kolchak: The Night Stalker:	Darren McGavin (Carl Kolchak)
Laverne & Shirley:	Penny Marshall (Laverne De Fazio), Cindy Williams (Shirley Feeney)
Leave It to Beaver:	Jerry Mathers (Beaver Cleaver)
Life and Legend of Wyatt Earp, The:	Hugh O'Brian
Life and Times of Grizzly Adams, The:	Dan Haggerty (James "Grizzly" Adams)
Life of Riley, The:	Jackie Gleason (Chester A. Riley)
Lobo:	Claude Akins (Sheriff Elroy P. Lobo)

Lone Ranger, The:	Clayton Moore
Lou Grant:	Ed Asner
MacGyver:	Richard Dean Anderson
Madigan:	Richard Widmark (Dan Madigan)
Magnum, P.I.:	Tom Selleck (Thomas Sullivan Magnum)
Major Dad:	Gerald McRaney (Major "Mac" [John D.] MacGillis)
Mama:	Peggy Wood (Marta Hansen)
Mancuso, F.B.I.:	Robert Loggia (Nick Mancuso)
Mannix:	Mike Connors (Joe Mannix)
Marcus Welby, M.D.:	Robert Young (Marcus Welby)
Mary Tyler Moore Show, The:	Mary Tyler Moore (Mary Richards)
Mary Hartman, Mary Hartman:	Louise Lasser
Matlock:	Andy Griffith (Benjamin L. Matlock)
Matt Houston:	Lee Horsley (Matlock Houston)
Maude:	Bea Arthur (Maude Findlay)
Maverick:	James Garner (Bret Maverick)
McCloud:	Dennis Weaver (Sam McCloud)
McMillan and Wife:	Rock Hudson (Stewart McMillan), Susan Saint James (Sally McMillan)
Michael Shayne:	Richard Denning
Mickey Spillane's Mike Hammer:	Darren McGavin (1957–59), Stacy Keach (1984–87)
Mr. & Mrs. North:	Richard Denning (Jerry North), Barbara Britton (Pamela North)
Mr. Novak:	James Franciscus (John Novak)
Mr. Peepers:	Wally Cox (Robinson Peepers)
Mork & Mindy:	Robin Williams (Mork), Pam Dawber (Mindy Beth McConnell)
My Friend Irma:	Marie Wilson (Irma Peterson)
My Little Margie:	Gale Storm (Margie Albright)
My Sister Sam:	Pam Dawber (Sam [Samantha] Russell)
Nancy Drew Mysteries, The:	Pamela Sue Martin

Nurse:	Michael Learned (Mary Benjamin)
Odd Couple, The:	Jack Klugman (Oscar Madison), Tony Randall (Felix Unger)
Our Miss Brooks:	Eve Arden (Connie Brooks)
Owen Marshall, Counselor at Law:	Arthur Hill
Parker Lewis Can't Lose:	Corky Nemec
Perry Mason:	Raymond Burr
Peter Gunn:	Craig Stevens
Petrocelli:	Barry Newman (Tony Petrocelli)
Police Woman:	Angie Dickinson ("Pepper" [Suzanne] Anderson)
Prisoner, The:	Patric McGoohan (Number Six)
Punky Brewster:	Soleil Moon Frye ("Punky" [Penelope] Brewster)
Quincy:	Jack Klugman (Dr. R. Quincy)
Range Rider, The:	Jock Mahoney (The Range Rider)
Remington Steele:	Pierce Brosnan
Richard Diamond, Private Detective:	David Janssen
Rifleman, The:	Chuck Connors (Lucas McCain)
Rockford Files, The:	James Garner (Jim Rockford)
Roseanne:	Roseanne Arnold (Roseanne Conner)
Saint, The:	Roger Moore (Simon Templar)
Sanford and Son:	Redd Foxx (Fred Sanford), Demond Wilson (Lamont Sanford)
Sara:	Geena Davis (Sara McKenna)
Scarecrow and Mrs. King:	Bruce Boxleitner (see "Scarecrow" Stetson), Kate Jackson (Amanda King)
Simon & Simon:	Gerald McRaney (Rick Simon), Jameson Parker (Andrew Jackson "A. J." Simon)
Six Million Dollar Man, The:	Lee Majors (Steve Austin)
Slap Maxwell Story, The:	Dabney Coleman (Slap Maxwell)
Sledge Hammer!:	David Rasche (Sledge Hammer)

Snoop Sisters, The:	Helen Hayes (Ernesta Snoop), Mildred Natwick (Gwen Snoop)
Spenser: For Hire:	Robert Urich
Starsky and Hutch:	Paul Michael Glaser (Dave Starsky), David Soul (Ken "Hutch" Hutchinson)
Superman:	George Reeves (Clark Kent)
T. J. Hooker:	William Shatner
Tarzan:	Ron Ely
That Girl:	Marlo Thomas (Ann Marie)
Thin Man, The:	Peter Lawford (Nick Charles)
Topper:	Leo G. Carroll (Cosmo Topper)
Trapper John, M.D.:	Pernell Roberts (John McIntyre)
Webster:	Emmanuel Lewis (Webster Long)
Welcome Back, Kotter:	Gabe Kaplan (Gabe Kotter)
Wiseguy:	Ken Wahl (Vinnie Terranova)
Wonder Woman:	Lynda Carter (Diana Prince)
Yancy Derringer:	Jock Mahoney

TV Celebrities A–Z

Adams, Don (1926–   ). He received his start in show business by winning an Arthur Godfrey talent scout contest. From there, he went on to working in nightclubs as an impressionist, making his television debut on *Perry Como's Kraft Music Hall*. It was the comedy spy show *Get Smart*, however, that lifted him to stardom and brought him three Emmy awards. His other television shows include: *The Partners, Don Adams' Screen Test, Inspector Gadget*, and *Check It Out*. He also made a movie based on *Get Smart—Get Smart Again!*

Albert, Eddie (1908–   ). Born Edward Albert Heimberger, he began in radio, and for a time on NBC he performed as a singer with Grace Bradt in an act known as The Honeymooners. His first appearance on television was on CBS in 1952 in a short-lived sitcom called *Leave It To Larry*. It was, however, his portrayal of Winston Smith in the Studio One production of George Orwell's *Nineteen Eighty-Four* that got his television career on track.

Eddie Albert remains best known for his role on Green Acres.

And what a career it has been! He has appeared in hundreds of television dramas, although he is probably best known to TV fans for his portrayal of Oliver Wendell Douglas on *Green Acres* and for playing the father of Elliot Weston on *thirtysomething*.

Alda, Alan (1936–   ). Born on January 28, 1936, in

New York City, Alan Alda is the son of stage and screen actor Robert Alda. Alan Alda achieved super TV stardom by playing Captain Benjamin Franklin ("Hawkeye") Pierce on one of the greatest series of all time—M*A*S*H. He got his start in television in 1964 when he appeared as a regular on "That Was the Week That Was," a program of political satire that had only a short life.

After appearing on Broadway in such plays as *The Owl and the Pussycat* and *The Apple Tree*, Alda landed the role of Jonathan Paige, a college professor convicted of manslaughter, in Truman Capote's television movie *The Glass House*. After landing the role of Hawkeye in M*A*S*H (Alda also wrote and directed numerous episodes on that series), he went into film production and directing. Alda is also very active in politics. He was the co-chairperson of the presidential subcommittee on the Equal Rights Amendment.

Allen, Steve (1921–   ).

Born in New York City, he was the son of vaudeville comedy performers, and so he took to performing comedy as naturally as a duck takes to water. He rose through the ranks of radio and television to become the original host of the *Tonight Show* and later he went head to head with Mr. Sunday night, Ed Sullivan, with *The Steve Allen Show*, which made stars of such comic performers as Don Knotts, Louis Nye, and Tom Poston.

A versatile performer and writer, Steve Allen has published books of poetry, short stories, mystery novels, and has written hundreds of popular songs. In addition, he wrote the lyrics and music to the title songs for such hit movies as *Picnic*, *On the Beach*, *Houseboat*, and *Bell, Book and Candle*.

For television, Allen also created *Meeting of the Minds*, in which actors portrayed famous persons from history engaged in exchanging ideas on a wide variety of subjects.

Arnaz, Desi (1917–1986).

Born Desiderio Alberto Arnaz y de Acha III in Santiago, Cuba, where Desi's father was the mayor. After a Cuban revolution in 1937, Arnaz and his mother fled to Miami. Arnaz played the guitar and was singing in a rhumba band in a Miami hotel when he was noticed by Xavier Cugat. He became a singer with Cugat's orchestra and from there he went on to appear in the movie *Too Many Girls*. It was while he was at RKO that he met Lucille Ball. They were married in 1940. A decade later, Desi and Lucy formed DesiLu Productions and achieved television immortality with their hit show *I Love Lucy*.

Ball, Lucille (1911–1989). After a 20-year career in movies and radio, Ball and her husband, Desi Arnaz, launched their own sitcom in 1951. Based on *My Favorite Husband*, a radio show that Ball had starred in for 3 years, *I Love Lucy* quickly catapulted to the top as the number-one comedy show on television. The popularity of the show—it was never lower than third in the ratings—was largely due to the antics of Lucy Ricardo, the wife of band leader Ricky Ricardo, and Ball proved, "a redheaded, uninhibited comedienne who takes pratfalls and pie-throwing in her stride, manages to add on an extra wriggle or a rubber-faced doubletake to each funny line." Lucy was annointed the first lady of TV comedy.

"You'd better be a little more careful today," comedian Lucille Ball would caution. "Your camera is getting older all the time."

Benny, Jack (1894–1974). Beginning his career as a violinist in vaudeville, Benny launched a career in radio that captured his every "W-e-e-l-l-l." Switching to TV in the 1950s, Benny had Sunday night shows every other week and then a regular half-hour show in the 1960s. His shows often included adverse reactions from the audience and guests to his violin playing and barbs about his fictitious stinginess. This performer, who never aged past 39, was a master of the silent look and the head-in-hand-sideways-glance that bespoke volumes. In the words of George Burns, Jack Benny was a "quiet laugh riot."

In the hearts of Americans Jack Benny will always be 39.

Movie Star's Beginnings on TV

Warren Beatty: *The Many Loves of Dobie Gillis*
Marlon Brando: *Actors Studio*
James Dean: *Campbell Sound Stage*
Clint Eastwood: *Rawhide*
Laurence Harvey: *The Alcoa Hour/Goodyear Playhouse*
Goldie Hawn: *Rowan and Martin's Laugh-In*
Grace Kelly: *The Web*
Michelle Pfeiffer: *B.A.D. C.A.T.S.*
Steve Martin: *The Sonny and Cher Comedy Hour*
Walter Matthau: *Philco TV Playhouse*
Paul Newman: *The Aldrich Family*
Nick Nolte: *Rich Man, Poor Man*
Denzel Washington: *St. Elsewhere*
Robin Williams: *Happy Days*
Bruce Willis: *Moonlighting*
Debra Winger: *Wonder Woman*

Berle, Milton (1908–). This slapstick comedian was the first superstar of fledgling television. Starting in 1948 with his *Texaco Star Theater*, Berle's popularity was so great that Tuesday night was a disaster for restaurants and theaters— everyone was home (or at someone else's home) watching the schtick of Mr. Television. NBC even signed him to a 30-year contract, not foreseeing the day when his popularity would wane. But that time came early: 1956. Still, Uncle Miltie has remained a nostalgic favorite ever since.

Milton Berle (as Superman) and Henny Youngman trade
quips on America's first hit TV show.

The TV Hall of Fame

In 1984, the Academy of Television Arts and Sciences, established the Television Hall of Fame to honor performers, writers, executives, and other people who have made lasting contributions to the medium. Each year only seven individuals are inducted.

The first seven people inducted into the Television Hall of Fame were

Milton Berle	Edward R. Murrow
Norman Lear	Lucille Ball
William S. Paley	David Sarnoff
Paddy Chayefsky	

Other people elected in subsequent years include

Gracie Allen	Joan Ganz Cooney
Steve Allen	Bill Cosby
Roone Arledge	Jacques Cousteau
Desi Arnaz	Walter Cronkite
Fred Astaire	Walt Disney
Jack Benny	Phil Donahue
Leonard Bernstein	James Garner
Carol Burnett	Jackie Gleason
David Brinkley	Leonard Goldenson
George Burns	Mark Goodson
Sid Caesar	Andy Griffith
John Chancellor	Joyce C. Hall (honored
Dick Clark	for sponsoring the
Fred Coe	*Hallmark Hall of Fame*)
Perry Como	Jim Henson

Don Hewitt	Dinah Shore
Bob Hope	Red Skelton
Chet Huntley	Frank Stanton
Ted Koppel	Ed Sullivan
Ernie Kovacs	David Susskind
Sheldon Leonard	Danny Thomas
Mary Tyler Moore	Ted Turner
Bob Newhart	Burr Tillstrom
Agnes Nixon*	Mike Wallace
Carroll O'Connor	Barbara Walters
Rod Serling	Jack Webb
Eric Sevareid	David Wolper

*Agnes Nixon is the only member of the soap opera fraternity to be in the Television Hall of Fame. She was the creator or cocreator of four daytime soap operas: *All My Children*, *One Life to Live*, *Loving*, and *As the World Turns*.

Blanc, Mel (1909–1989).

This master of more than 400 different voices—he supplied the voice of Barney Rubble in *The Flintstones* and Cosmo Spacely in *The Jetsons* as well as Bugs Bunny, Elmer Fudd, and other animated characters—was also Benny's violin teacher on *The Jack Benny Program*. In addition, he did the sputters and gasps of the old skinflint's Maxwell as it ran out of gas.

Booth, Shirley (1907–1992).

After winning both a Tony and an Oscar for *Come Back, Little Sheba*, Booth captured an Emmy for playing the housekeeper on *Hazel*, the popular cartoon character in *The Saturday Evening Post* who was featured in a TV serial (1961–66).

Brinkley, David (1920–   ).

Brinkley has been a fixture on TV with his wry analysis of the news since he was paired with Chet Huntley on *The Huntley-Brinkley Report* (1956–71). Since 1981, Brinkley has been the host of *This Week with David Brinkley*. Combined with Brinkley's own continued popularity and perspicacity, his long-running show has gained him the mantle of elder statesman of the news media business.

Brokaw, Tom (1940–). Like Johnny Carson, Brokaw started out in Omaha. After newscasting stints in Atlanta and Los Angeles, Brokaw broke into the national spotlight, reporting during the Watergate hearings. Next was the *Today* show and *NBC Weekend News*. Since 1982, he has been the anchor on the *NBC Nightly News*.

Burr, Raymond (1917–1993). Burr played Perry Mason, an L.A. defense lawyer on the show of the same name from 1957 to 1966, winning two Emmys along the way. Based on Erle Stanley Gardner mysteries, Perry Mason would pull off courtroom victories over prosecutor Hamilton Burger (William Talman) by catching witnesses off-guard on the stand with his sharp questioning and introducing surprise witnesses that his private investigator Paul Drake (William Hopper) had tracked down or using details that his secretary Della Street (Barbara Hale) had turned up. From 1967 to 1975, Burr played Robert Ironside in the police drama *Ironside*, a former San Francisco chief of detectives now confined to a wheelchair from where he fought criminals as a consultant. (For sci-fi and trivia buffs, Burr played a journalist named Steve Martin in the first Godzilla film, *Godzilla, King of the Monsters*, as well as in *Godzilla 1985*: "No matter what happens," intones Burr, "Godzilla will live.")

Buttons, Red (1919–). Schooled in the borscht belt of the Catskills, this king of slapstick (he got his name for his red hair and the fancy buttons on his costumes) was rewarded with his own variety show to host in 1952. By 1955, *The Red Buttons Show* seemed to collapse of its own weight.

Caesar, Sid (1922–). Born in Yonkers, New York, Sid Caesar originally studied to be a musician and, for a short time, he was employed as a saxaphonist in Shep Field's Orchestra. In 1942, he joined the Coast Guard and made his comedy debut in the Coast Guard musical *Tars and Spars*. It was in that production that he met the director Max Liebman, who would be so influential in Caesar's television career. In 1949, Liebman produced *The Admiral Broadway Revue*, an hourlong revue on NBC-TV. That show marked Caesar's first appearance on television. Imogene Coca was also a member of the cast.

With Imogene Coca, Caesar went on to *Your Show of Shows*—a program that is now considered one of the greatest and most innovative of television comedies. In *Look* magazine's first annual television awards, presented in 1950, Caesar was voted the "Best Comedian on TV." Caesar went on to win Emmys for 1952 and 1957.

Campanella, Joseph (1927–). This three-time Emmy nominee has had a long and varied career. In the 1960s Campanella appeared in *Combat, The Fugitive, Ironside, Mission: Impossible*, and *The Virginian*, and he was on *The Bold Ones* from 1969 to 1972. In the 1970s and 1980s he has been seen on *Night Gallery* and *Quincy* and has narrated numerous Jacques Cousteau and National Geographic specials.

Carson, Johnny (1925–). In 1962, Johnny Carson replaced Jack Paar as the host of the *Tonight Show*, and he did not step down from that role until 30 years later, when he chose comedian Jay Leno to take over. It was Carson who made the *Tonight Show* the greatest moneymaker in NBC history.

Born October 23, 1925, in Corning, Iowa, Johnny took up magic at age 12, and, as the Great Carsoni, made his first professional stage appearance at the Norfolk Rotary Club when he was 14. For that first appearance, he was paid all of $3. By the time he retired from hosting the *Tonight Show* he was earning considerably more than that.

Johnny had his first half-hour comedy show—*Carson's Cellar*—on station KNXT-TV in Los Angeles. He graduated from that show to become a script writer for Red Skelton. Then one day in August of 1954, Skelton injured himself

During his 40-year career, Joseph Campanella has appeared in over 1,000 productions in all media.

during a dress rehearsal. With only two hours' notice, Carson stepped in for Skelton and garnered such good attention that he was awarded his own prime time show—*The Johnny Carson Show*.

Actor-singer-songwriter David Cassidy, former star of The Partridge Family.

Carson later hosted the game show—*Who Do You Trust?* In 1977, he was named the Man of the Year by Harvard University's Hasty Pudding Club.

Cassidy, David (1950–   ).

Cassidy won enormous popularity from 1970 to 1974 as Keith Partridge on *The Partridge Family.* He also had a music career that garnered several gold records, beginning with "I Think I Love You" in 1970. In 1978 he was nominated for an Emmy Award for his portrayal of a detective on *Police Story*. Cassidy composed and sang the theme song for *The John Larroquette Show*.

Dick Clark, Dick Clark, Dick Clark, Dick Clark, Dick Clark, and Dick Clark

Dick Clark has had his name in the title of six series: *Dick Clark Presents the Rock and Roll Years, The Dick Clark Show, Dick Clark's Golden Greats, Dick Clark's Live Wednesday, Dick Clark's Nighttime*, and *Dick Clark's World of Talent*.

Chamberlain, Richard (1935–).

Born George Richard Chamberlain, "the king of the miniseries" once told the *Los Angeles Times* that "The fun of acting is playing different parts, being different people. If you're just going to play one part all your life, you might as well sell insurance." Chamberlain's first television role was a bit part in a *Gunsmoke* episode—but his big break came when he was cast to play James Kildare in the *Dr. Kildare* TV series. The part catapulted him to stardom. In 1963, for example, an audience survey by *TV Guide* voted him the favorite male performer of the year (that same year he also recorded an album of songs—*Richard Chamberlain Sings*). He went on to play *Hamlet*, both on stage (where he received fine reviews) and for a 1970 production by the Hallmark Hall of Fame. He has played the leads in numerous miniseries, including the role of Jack Blackthorne in *Shogun* and Father Ralph de Bricassart in *The Thorn Birds*.

Cosby, Bill (1938–).

The first black actor to co-star in a weekly dramatic series, *I Spy*, Cosby played Alex Scott, a CIA undercover agent. A *Fame* magazine poll in 1966 hailed him as "the most promising new male star," a promise that he more than fulfilled. His situation comedy shows have made him one of the most popular and highly paid entertainers in America. In 1993, he headed up a group that tried to buy NBC.

Daly, John (1914–1991). Daly had successful careers in both news and entertainment, serving as the news anchor of the *ABC Evening News* from 1953 to 1960 and the host of *What's My Line?* on CBS from 1950 to 1967. (At one time, news commentators were not taken quite so seriously: Walter Cronkite, Douglas Edwards, and Mike Wallace all enjoyed stints as game show hosts.) In 1954, Daly won an Emmy for best news reporter or commentator, and in 1955, he was nominated for Emmys in both news and entertainment categories.

Dana, Bill (1924–   ). Dana began as a writer on *The Steve Allen Show*, but he was discovered to be even funnier when he read his material ("My name is . . . Jose Jiminez"). The Jiminez character eventually developed into a bellhop and his own show, *The Bill Dana Show* (1963–65).

Danson, Ted (1947–   ). Struggling as a New York actor in the 1970s may have prepared Danson for his phenomenally popular role in the 1980s as Sam Malone, the womanizing, ex-ballplaying bartender on *Cheers*.

Denver, John (1935–   ). Denver worked his way up from Maynard G. Krebs, the unemployable beatnik, on *The Many Lives of Dobie Gillis* (1959–63) to Gilligan, the deckhand on the *Minnow* who should have been without a job on *Gilligan's Island* (1964–67). If the truth be told, Gilligan's first name (though never used) was to have been Willie.

DeVito, Danny (1944–   ). Before turning to a big-time movie career, the diminutive DeVito played Louie De Palma, the tyrannical dispatcher for the Sunshine Cab Company on *Taxi* (1978–83).

Disney, Walt (1901–1966). As host of *Disneyland*, *Walt Disney's Wonderful World of Color*, and *The Wonderful World of Disney*, this cartoonist-turned-producer personally raised the quality of children's programming. It was Disney, the first of the movie people to go into television, whose voice was used for the internationally famous Mickey Mouse.

Donahue, Phil (1935–). This eight-time Emmy Award winner for best host of a talk show prowls the set of *Donahue*, mike in hand, ready to pounce on the next comment from a member of the audience. The show's traditionally high ratings stem from the earnestness of its white-haired host and the guests who discuss the important topic of the day (all three major presidential candidates for the 1992 election appeared on the show) or the outrageous (cross-dressing for success).

Douglas, Mike (1925–). Starting out as a singer (he dubbed the songs for Prince Charming in *Cinderella*), Douglas became a popular talk show host (*The Mike Douglas Show*) during the 1970s.

Downs, Hugh (1921–). Downs has been on TV from its very beginnings (he was the announcer for *Kukla, Fran & Ollie*) to the latest episode of *20/20*. He served as the announcer of *Caesar's Hour* (1956–57) and *The Jack Paar Show* (1957–62), and was the host of the *Today* show (1962–71), *Concentration*, and *Over Easy* (a show about aging). Down's number of hours on TV has established his place in *The Guiness Book of World Records* and led to his autobiography, *On Camera: My Ten Thousand Hours on Television*.

Durante, Jimmy (1893–1980). The Schnozzola (his nickname for his proboscis, of course) was a long-time vaudeville performer who successfully made the transition to TV. The secret to his charm was lodged in his broken-bottle voice born in the Bronx and his collection of old jokes and songs like "Inka Dinka Do." Durante ended each appearance with "Goodnight, Mrs. Calabash, wherever you are." Toward the end of his career, Durante identified this mystery lady as his wife who had died in 1943; she was nicknamed after the owner of a rooming house in Chicago.

Fawcett, Farrah (1946–). It seems hard to believe that this actress was a regular on *Charlie's Angels* for only 1 year (1976–77) when you consider the cottage industry in dolls and posters that sprang up. "When the show was number three I figured it was our acting," she once said. "When we got to be number one I decided it could only be because none of us [Fawcett, Kate Jackson, and Jacklyn Smith] wears a bra." Since then, she has shown a flair for drama with *The Burning Bed* and comedy with *Good Sports*, a series that sputtered in 1991.

Ford, Tennessee Ernie (1919–1991). Catapulting to fame in 1955 with his ballad "Sixteen Tons," Ford starred in the daytime with *The Tennessee Ernie Ford Show* (1955–57) and at nighttime in *The Ford Show* (1956–61).

Friendly, Fred W. (1915–   ). Friendly and Edward R. Murrow worked together for 12 years, first producing radio's *Hear It Now*, then television's *See It Now*. After serving as president of CBS News and consultant to the Ford Foundation for public television, Friendly in recent years has originated a PBS series on media and society and been the Edward R. Murrow Professor at the Columbia University Graduate School of Journalism. His *Due to Circumstances Beyond Our Control* is not only a memoir but also a series of essays on broadcast journalism.

Frost, David (1939–   ). Frost's first appearance on American television was as host of the satirical *That Was the Week That Was*. After "TW3," Frost interviewed public personalities on *The David Frost Show* (1969–72) and *The David Frost Review* (1971–73). His biggest splash was pulling off 4 ninety-minute interviews with Richard Nixon in 1977, the first interviews since the former president's resignation.

Gleason, Jackie (1916–1987). Born in Brooklyn, New York, Herbert John "Jackie" Gleason appeared in numerous clubs and cabarets, and after working a brief stint as a disc jockey for radio station WAAT, Gleason went to Hollywood to appear in such movies as *Navy Blues* (1941) and *Springtime in the Rockies* (1942). His television career took off in 1949, when he played the part of Chester Riley on *The Life of Riley* series. From there he went on to *The Calvacade of Stars* for the old DuMont network. It was on

Nicknames of Television Personalities

The Singing Cowboy: Gene Autry
Jungle Jim: James T. Aubrey (CBS president)
The Smiling Cobra: James T. Aubrey (CBS president)
The Old Redhead: Arthur Godfrey
Canada's First Lady of Song: Gisele Mackenzie
King of the Cowboys: Roy Rogers
The Perfect Fool: Ed Wynn
Mr. Television: Milton Berle
The Great One: Jackie Gleason
The Man of a Thousand Voices: Mel Blanc
The Prince of Menace: Vincent Price
Queen of the Cowgirls: Dale Evans
Schnozzola: Jimmy Durante

that show that Gleason developed *The Honeymooners*, and the rest, as they say, is history. Among comic television characters created by "The Great One" were Ralph Kramden, the Poor Soul, Joe the Bartender, and the society playboy Reggie Van Gleason III. In addition to his acting and directing chores, The Great One (as Gleason liked to be known) also composed music for a number of best-selling records.

Griffin, Merv (1925–   ). Practically everything Griffin touches has turned to gold. Starting out as a singer, by 1948 he was featured with Freddy Martin, the top band in the land, and in 1951 he made his singing debut on TV. From 1959 to 1963, Griffin hosted the game shows *Keep Talking, Play Your Hunch*, and *Talent Scouts*. Moreover, Griffin also developed game shows—not just any game shows, but *Jeopardy!* in 1964 and *Wheel of Fortune* in 1975—two shows that are still popular. From 1965 to 1986, he hosted a talk show, *The Merv Griffin Show*. The guests were mainly showbiz types like Zsa Zsa Gabor, but at the zenith of his popularity in the early 1970s, Merv was on opposite Johnny Carson.

Griffith, Andy (1926–   ).
Griffith's first splash was with a popular recording of the monologue of a country bumpkin witnessing football for the first time, "What It Was Was Football," and on the flip side an incredulous retelling of "Mary Had a Little Lamb." From there it was on to a starring role in *No Time for Sergeants*, first on *The U.S. Steel Hour* in 1955, then on Broadway and finally on the silver screen. But it was with his portrayal of Andy Taylor, the easy-going sheriff of Mayberry, North Carolina, on *The Andy Griffith Show* that he hit the big time. The show was in the top ten for its entire run from 1960 to 1968, and was rated number one its final season. His next two TV series, *The Headmaster* and *The New Andy Griffith Show*, were less successful. It wasn't until *Matlock* in 1986 that Griffith hit his stride once again. This time he was Benjamin L. Matlock, a defense lawyer with the record of a Perry Mason type and a southern drawl to boot.

Hagman, Larry (1931–   ).
The son of actress Mary Martin, Hagman's first sitcom role was as an astronaut, air force Captain Tony Nelson, married to an other worldly Barbara Eden on *I Dream of Jeannie* (1965–70). His second was J. R., the merciless oil tycoon with the seductive smile on *Dallas* (1978–91). The show's popularity, due in large part to J. R., whose smile and morals would shame a snake oil salesman, peaked on November 21, 1980, when the "Who Shot J. R.?" episode became one of the highest-rated shows ever, beating out even the final episode of *Roots*. (By the way, it was Kristin, who was J. R.'s secretary, mistress, and sister-in-law.)

Hall, Monty (1923–   ).
Hall was the host of *Let's Make a Deal* (1963–76), a popular game show that featured crazily dressed contestants who traded money for known and unknown gifts (hidden in boxes and behind doors).

Halmi, Robert Sr. (1924–   ).
Television producer and founder of RHI Entertainment, which is the leading inde-

pendent producer of movies and miniseries for the U. S. television industry. His production company has won 27 Emmys and many other awards. His son, Robert Halmi Jr., is also a producer with the company. Recent productions by the Halmis include: *The Yearling, My Life: The Magic Johnson Story*, and *Scarlett*.

Henson, Jim (1936–1990). Henson was creator of the Muppets (a marriage between marionettes and puppets). Henson's Bert and Ernie, Cookie Monster, Grover, Kermit the Frog (he did the voice), and Oscar the Grouch helped make *Sesame Street* into the huge success it is today. This five-time Emmy Award winner also did the unthinkable by bringing *The Muppet Show* to prime-time TV from 1976 to 1981.

Herlihy, Ed (active 1947–1971). Herlihy was a familiar voice during the Golden Age of Television and later as the announcer of the *Kraft Television Theatre* (1947–55), *The Perry Como Show* (1959–61), *Kraft Music Hall* (1961–63; 1967–71), and for 1 year *The Tonight Show* (1962).

Hitchcock, Alfred (1899–1980). Host of *Alfred Hitchcock Presents* (1955–65), Hitchcock appeared at the beginning of each show lining up his own silhouette with a line drawing of his girth. After opening comments in a British accent that sounded half submerged in the Thames, it was off to episodes that relished trick endings and his own concluding comments suggesting that wrongs had been righted. When technicians recast his intros in color and hooked them up with new episodes, the master of the macabre returned in a Hitchcockian turn of the screw to host a new series five years after his death.

Hope, Bob (1903–   ). Born in England, Hope became the quintessential American who puts on Christmas shows for the troops each year as well as four or so other specials. His shows usually run along the same lines: an opening monologue followed by skits with his guests, musical numbers, and ending with Hope singing "Thanks for the Mem-

Ed Herlihy, the golden-voiced announcer for <u>Kraft Television Theatre</u> and other shows, now a humorist lecturer.

ories." In addition to these specials, Hope was also a regular host for the Academy Awards.

Ken Howard, veteran of stage and screen, has appeared in numerous television ventures, including The Thorn Birds, Dynasty, and The White Shadow.

Howard, Ken (1944–). Howard started out as a stage actor, winning a Tony Award in 1970 for *Child's Play*. Since then he has appeared on television in *Adam's Rib, The Manhunter, It's Not Easy, The Thorn Birds, Dynasty*, and *Dynasty II: The Colbys*. Perhaps he is best remembered for playing Ken Reeves from 1978 to 1981, a high school basketball coach on *The White Shadow*, a show Howard helped create.

Television and the Kennedy Center for the Performing Arts

/n 1978, the Kennedy Center for the Performing Arts created its Honors Awards. Each year the Kennedy Center recognizes the achievements of five distinguished persons who have contributed greatly to the performing arts in America. Television performers who have been selected for this honor are:

Bob Hope   George Burns

Lucille Ball   Johnny Carson

Perry Como

Howard, Ron (1954–   ). Howard did not grow up watching TV but appearing on it. From 1960 to 1968, he played Opie on *The Andy Griffith Show*; from 1974 to 1980, he was Richie Cunningham on *Happy Days*. In his 30s, Howard turned to producing and directing movies.

Huntley, Chet (1911–1974). Huntley was the co-anchor with David Brinkley on NBC's *Huntley-Brinkley Report* that ran from 1956 to 1970. As with most good teams, there were obvious differences between the two men. Huntley was the stolid one reporting from New York; Brinkley was the witty one reporting from Washington. The two became such a fixture in American culture that a 1965 poll showed them to rank higher in popularity than the Beatles.

James, Dennis (1917–   ). Starting out in radio, James made the transition to TV, becoming the first host of a game show, a sports show, and a variety show. But it was as a wrestling announcer that he cut his teeth, making his often emitted "Okay, Mother" a household phrase. (His variety show from 1948 to 1951 was called—you guessed it—*Okay, Mother*.) However, it is as the host of *The Price Is Right* that he will be remembered. Because he had been a premed student in college, Ed Sullivan asked him to help raise money for cerebral palsy. He also hosted the first telethon.

Jennings, Peter (1938–   ).

A high school drop-out, this newsman from Canada was the co-anchor on CTV (Canada's commercial station) when ABC brought him to New York to be the anchor of *ABC Evening News*. Jennings was often criticized for being too young (he was only 26 at the time), too good looking, and too inexperienced. After 3 years, he was dispatched on various assignments to get that experience, becoming the bureau chief in Beirut from 1969 to 1976 and later part of a three-reporter team on *ABC World News Tonight*. When Frank Reynolds died in 1983, Jennings returned to anchor the *ABC Evening News*. Jennings was no longer too young and too inexperienced, though many still consider him to be very good looking.

Kovacs, Ernie (1919–1962).

One of the first comedians to explore the unique visual capabilities of television humor, Kovacs was a pioneer in the use of trick photography and bizarre camera angles, foreshadowing ideas used today by David Letterman. He created such characters as the nasal sounding poet Percy Dovetonsils, a Chinese songwriter named Irving Wong, and a German disc jockey bearing the heavy moniker Wolfgang Sauerbraten. His career ended tragically when, in 1962, he was killed in a car accident.

Landon, Michael (1937–1991).

Landon appeared in hit shows half his life, from his role as Little Joe Cartwright on *Bonanza* (1959–73) to Charles Ingalls on *Little House on the Prairie* (1974–82) to Jonathan Smith on *Highway to Heaven* (1984–88). But he was not only an actor, he was also the creator, director, producer, and writer of his last two hit series. To some, Landon's work was corny, too steeped in traditional American values. But he was true to himself in both his work and his personal life.

Lansbury, Angela (1925–). This actress started off in Hollywood, then went to Broadway (where she won Tony Awards for *Mame, Dear World, Gypsy,* and *Sweeney Todd*), and wound up as a mystery writer turned amateur detective on *Murder, She Wrote,* where Lansbury has been playing the Jessica Beatrice Fletcher role since 1984. Though the show is highly rated, one of the few successes she has not achieved is in the Emmy Award department; she is still winless after 11 nominations.

Lasser, Louise (1939–). Daughter of tax maven S. Jay Lasser and former wife of Woody Allen (1966–70), Lasser played Mary Hartman, your typical spaced-out housewife living in Fernwood, Ohio, on *Mary Hartman, Mary Hartman.* (The show was called this because of the belief that everything on soap operas is said at least twice.) In this send-up of soap operas created by Norman Lear, Mary Hartman took to heart everything she heard on TV commercials as the unvarnished truth.

Leachman, Cloris (1926–). Although she had been a runner-up in the 1946 Miss America contest, it wasn't until 1970 and *The Mary Tyler Moore Show* that Leachman's career finally took off. (In 1971, she also won an Academy Award for *The Last Picture Show.*) Leachman played Phyllis Lindstrom on "MTM" from 1970 to 1975 and the same character on her own show, *Phyllis,* as well as parts in numerous TV movies. By the time the dust settled, she had won 6 Emmys.

Lear, Norman (1922–). The hottest producer of the 1970s started off the decade with *All in the Family* and followed that megahit with *Good Times, The Jeffersons, Maude,* and *Sanford and Son.* Lear's shows were marked by the courage to deal with the controversial subjects of the day, such as abortion, feminism, homosexuality, and racial prejudice. However, the Midas touch did abandon Lear from time to time as evidenced by his short-lived *All That Glitters, All's Fair, Apple Pie, The Dumplings, In the Beginning, Hot l Baltimore,* and *The Nancy Walker Show.* In re-

Cloris Leachman played Phyllis Lindstrom on *The Mary Tyler Moore Show* and its spinoff, *Phyllis*.

cent years, Lear has become more and more involved in social issues.

Lehrer, Jim (1934–   ). Smooth and sincere, this Washington-based co-anchor of *The MacNeil-Lehrer Newshour* (with Robert MacNeil in New York) has a knack of getting the people he is interviewing to feel comfortable. When he is off the air, Lehrer is a prolific writer of novels, nonfiction, and plays.

Leno, Jay (1951–   ). Leno was a stand-up comic, a TV

writer, and a talk-show guest (his first appearance on *The Tonight Show* was in 1977) before landing Johnny Carson's job in the spring of 1992. He's a hard worker, preferring to try out many of his jokes at a local club before airing them on TV.

Letterman, David (1947–). This five-time Emmy Award winner seemed to be a cinch for Johnny Carson's old job (he had pinch-hit for Carson 50 times before getting his own show) when the master of late night retired in 1992. In a surprise move, however, Letterman was passed over for Jay Leno. Then the fun started. Letterman left NBC and his *Late Night with David Letterman* for a hefty salary of $14 million a year to do *The Late Show with David Letterman* on CBS that would compete directly with *The Tonight Show*. And who was his very first guest? The same person who launched *Late Night* in 1982—Bill Murray.

Lewis, Jerry (1926–). For some reason this comedian is as famous in France as the Arc de Triomphe; however, back home in the United States his reception is at best mixed. Lewis's TV heyday was on *The Colgate Comedy Hour*, a show he hosted with Dean Martin from 1950 to 1955. Since they went their separate ways, neither one ever achieved the top billings they did as a team.

Lewis, Shari (1934–). Lewis and Lamb Chop have been doing their "knock-knock" jokes and entertaining kids for more than 40 years. Her own show—*The Shari Lewis Show*—was on NBC from 1960 to 1963, and she has appeared as a guest on hundreds of other telecasts.

Liberace (1919–1987). Using only his last name (his given names were Wladiu Valentino), Liberace carved a niche for himself on TV in the 1950s with his broad toothy smile, lispy speech, lace cuffs, velvet jackets, and candelabra burning on the piano as he played semiclassical pieces. On *The Liberace Show*, it seemed he introduced the same violinist every week ("I'd like you to meet my brother, George"). In answer to harsh criticism, Liberace once replied that he cried all the way to the bank.

The one and only Liberace.

Linkletter, Art (1912–   ). Host of radio shows that made the transfer to TV as *Life with Linkletter* (1950–52) and *People Are Funny* (1954–61), the man from Moose Jaw, Saskachawan, was at his best with children. One of a series of spin-off books from the TV show was called *Kids Say the Darndest Things*.

Moore, Mary Tyler (1936–   ). MTM's first appearance on TV was as Happy Hotpoint, an elf in a commercial. Then she had several guest shots until she landed her first big part on *The Dick Van Dyke Show*. From 1961 to 1966 she picked up two Emmys as Laura Petrie, Dick Van Dyke's perky wife. Afterwards there was a forgettable Broadway musical and a couple of movies, *Thoroughly Modern Millie* with Julie Andrews and *Change of Habit* with Elvis Presley. However, it was her role as Mary Richards, an assistant producer of a TV news show in Minneapolis, that she had the part she was born to play. From 1970 to 1977 people often stayed home on Saturday night just to watch *The Mary Tyler Moore Show*. Her looks, brains, and humor won her four Emmys and the hearts of millions of viewers. She won another Emmy in 1978 for *First You Cry,* a Tony for *Whose Life Is It Anyway?* in 1980, and critical acclaim the same year for *Ordinary People.*

Murrow, Edward R. (1908–1965). Edward R. Murrow was TV's first influential newscaster. After helping to form CBS news in 1935, Murrow hosted two shows that made their imprint on the history of broadcast journalism. The first was *See It Now*, a public affairs program that was on from 1952 to 1955; the second was *Person to Person*, a visit via television to the houses of famous people that aired from 1953 to 1959. Another noteworthy program was *Harvest of Shame*, a 1960 documentary about how the migrant workers of America, the very people who pick our food, go hungry. Most likely Murrow's most profound contribution was his taking on Senator Joseph McCarthy on *See It Now* and exposing the Wisconsin senator for the kind of person he was. At the end of this remarkable series of programs, Murrow said in his inimitable style: "When the record is finally written, as it will be one day, it will answer the question, who has helped the Communist cause and who has served his country better, Senator McCarthy or I. I would like to be remembered by the answer to that question." The answer is as certain as was his closing line: "Good night . . . and good luck."

Nabors, Jim (1932–   ). Although he came off like a country bumpkin as a gas station attendant on *The Andy Griffith Show* and a private in the marine corps on *Gomer Pyle,*

Television Stars and the Presidential Medal of Freedom

*T*he Presidential Medal of Freedom (established in 1963 by President John F. Kennedy) is the highest civilian award granted in the United States. Here are some television personalities who have been so honored.

Edward R. Murrow (1964)
Walter Cronkite (1981)
Tennessee Ernie Ford (1984)
Frank Reynolds (1985)
Frank Sinatra (1985)
Lucille Ball (1989)

U.S.M.C., Nabors had a fine singing voice. He recorded a dozen albums in the late 1960s and early 1970s that hit the top of the charts.

Nelson, Ozzie (1906–1975). Nelson seemed like an easygoing father, but in truth he was a very ambitious and driven man. After becoming an Eagle Scout at 13, a star football player at Rutgers, and a band leader touring with his band, Nelson produced and directed *The Adventures of Ozzie & Harriet*, a low-budget show that lasted from 1952 to 1966. It was, in fact, the longest-running sitcom in history and became synonymous with middle-class white America. One of the ways that Ozzie kept the budget low was by including his family members on the show, his wife and sons, David and Ricky. Also, when Ricky turned out to have musical ability, Nelson helped fashion his son's musical career. All the exposure on the show led to enormous record sales.

Newhart, Bob (1929–   ). If Newhart looks like an accountant, it's because he once was. But his mind found too many things funny to stick to figures, so he became a stand-up comic and then a variety show host. However, it's as the main character on sitcoms that he found his métier, first as a psychologist on *The Bob Newhart Show* (1972–78), then as a Vermont innkeeper on *Newhart* (1982–90), and then as a cartoonist on *Bob*.

Nimoy, Leonard (1931–).
In 1964, Nimoy was in a TV show produced by Gene Roddenberry, who later created *Star Trek*. "Someday I'm going to put ears on you and star you in a science fiction series," Roddenberry told him. And that is just what happened as Nimoy became Mr. Spock, half-human and half-Vulcan. Although in recent years Nimoy has turned to directing, he will forever be identified with the role of Mr. Spock on *Star Trek*. The title of his autobiography, written in 1975, is the plaintive *I Am Not Spock*.

O'Connor, Carroll (1922–).
O'Connor was a character actor in small parts until he broke through in Norman Lear's *All in the Family* in 1971. Playing the archetype of the prejudiced man, Archie Bunker, O'Connor won four Emmy Awards and helped rewrite what could be presented on television. Over the long run of this character—*All in the Family* (1971–79) and *Archie Bunker's Place* (1979–83)—O'Connor made Bunker a major part of pop culture.

Paar, Jack (1918–).
Paar broke in with radio and later entered TV as a game show and talk show host. In 1957, Paar hit the jackpot with *The Tonight Show*. (Steve Allen had been the first host from 1954 to 1957.) It was soon his show, and even renamed *The Jack Paar Tonight Show*. Paar talked into the night with the likes of Cliff Arquette who appeared as Charley Weaver, Joey Bishop, Peggy Cass, Hans Conried, singer Genevieve, comedian Dodi Goodman, Hermione Gingold, storyteller Alexander King, Elsa Maxwell, pianist Jose Melis, and Betty White. Some of Paar's highlights during his 5-year stint were trying to trade tractors for prisoners of the Bay of Pigs, broadcasting

For Star Trek Fans:
10 Other TV Shows in Which
Leonard Nimoy Appeared

Series	Show	Date of First Episode Broadcast
M. Squad	"Badge for a Coward"	May 24, 1960
Twilight Zone	"A Quality of Mercy"	December 29, 1961
Gunsmoke	"A Man a Day"	December 30, 1961
Perry Mason	"The Case of the Shoplifter's Shoe"	January 3, 1963
Combat	"The Wounded Don't Cry"	October 22, 1963
Kraft Suspense Theater	"The World I Want"	October 22, 1963
Man From U.N.C.L.E.	"The Project Strigos Affair"	November 24, 1964
Outer Limits	"I Robot"	November 14, 1965
Gunsmoke	"The Treasure of John Walking Fox"	April 16, 1966
Columbo	"A Stitch in Time"	February 11, 1973

from the Berlin Wall, walking out for a month when NBC censors cut a joke of his about water closets, and talking with Nixon and Kennedy on the show (one at a time) before the 1960 election. Paar did the show until 1962. The next year he hosted *The Jack Paar Program*, a variety show that lasted for 3 years.

Parks, Bert (1914–   ).
Parks was the emcee of no fewer than 13 quiz shows—from *Party Line* in 1947 to *Strike It Rich* in 1973. Nevertheless, it is as the host of the Miss America Pageant that he will be long remembered. From 1955 to 1980 Parks serenaded the winner with his throaty warbling of "There she is . . ."

Parker, Fess (1925–   ).
Parker was Davy Crockett on a miniseries during the 1955–56 season on *Disneyland*. Judging by the number of coonskin caps donned across the United States, Parker could have played Crockett for the rest of his career. However, when Crockett died at the Alamo in the fifth episode, so did Parker's acting credits until another frontiersman came along to revive it. From 1964 to 1970 Parker latched onto the title role on *Daniel Boone*.

Perkins, Marlin (1905–1986).
Perkins started out showing animals from the Lincoln Park Zoo on a local station in Chicago. From there he graduated to *Zoo Parade* (1951–57) and *Mutual of Omaha's Wild Kingdom* (1968–85). Johnny Carson once had an ongoing skit showing the gray-haired zoologist waxing eloquent while his hapless assistant (Jim Fowler in real life) was left to wrestle with the beast.

Price, Vincent (1911–1993).
Known as "The Prince of Menace," he appeared in numerous Hollywood horror films, such as *The Raven* and the 3-D thriller *House of Wax*. Television fans know him primarily for his appearance on *The $64,000 Question*, on which he displayed his considerable knowledge of art (he had studied art history at Yale and was a collector of paintings) and for acting as the suave and sophisticated host of PBS's *Mystery* series.

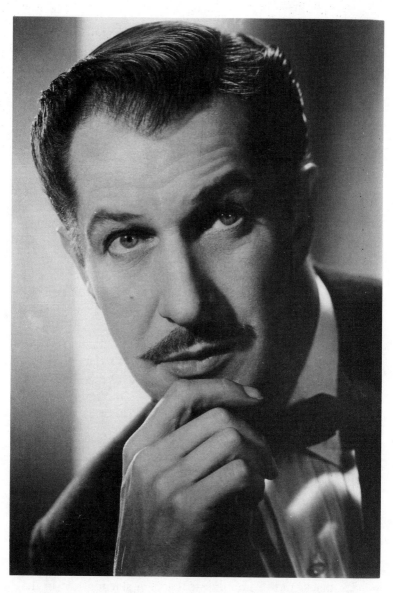

The movie star Vincent Price became the host of TV's
Mystery. Known for his roles in horror films, Vincent
Price was also an authority on art.

Rather, Dan (1931–). Rather rose to prominence reporting Hurricane Carla in 1961, President Kennedy's assassination in 1963, and his feisty questioning of Richard Nixon during the Watergate period. After *CBS Weekend News* and *60 Minutes* in the 1970s, Rather's next stop was to the top: taking over for Walter Cronkite in 1981 as anchor of the *CBS Evening News*. In 1993, Connie Chung joined as co-anchor in an attempt to raise CBS out of the ratings doldrums.

Reasoner, Harry (1923–1991). An anchorman on *ABC Evening News* (1970–78), Reasoner came off as everybody's favorite uncle, "Harry Reasonable." (This was tested his last 2 years when Barbara Walters was brought in to be his co-anchor.) Reasoner returned to CBS and *60 Minutes* to be a correspondent on the show that he and Mike Wallace had started back in 1968.

Reed, Donna (1921–1986). After winning an Oscar in 1953 for playing a prostitute in *From Here to Eternity*, Reed starred as the all-American mom on *The Donna Reed Show* from 1958 to 1966. She was so good as the representative of the mom–apple pie–American flag trinity that she was sometimes referred to as Madonna Reed.

Reynolds, Burt (1936–). Maybe if Reynolds had had his druthers, he would have been a back in pro football. However, an auto accident shelved that ambition, so he set his sights on acting. After guest roles on *General Electric Theater, Schlitz Playhouse, Alfred Hitchcock Presents, Route 66,* and *The Twilight Zone*, Reynolds lassoed the part of Quint Asper on *Gunsmoke* and played the part of Native American blacksmith from 1962 to 1965. A starring role in the movie *Deliverance*, many guest appearances on *The Tonight Show*, and a centerfold layout in *Cosmopolitan* skyrocketed him into the upper stratosphere of superstardom. In recent years Reynolds has completed the cycle by returning to TV and winning an Emmy as Wood Newton, a high school football coach, on the popular sitcom *Evening Shade*.

Rogers, Roy (1911–). Rogers, "The King of the Cowboys"; his wife, Dale Evans, "The Queen of the West"; Roy's sidekick Pat Brady; and Roy's wonder horse, Trigger, battled for the side of good on *The Roy Rogers Show* (1951–57). Also, in residence around the Double R Bar Ranch were Dale's horse, Buttermilk; the German shepherd, Bullet; and Brady's jeep, Nellybelle. Rounding out the half-hour show popular with the tots sitting on the floor around the TV were The Sons of the Pioneers to sing their specialty, "Happy Trails to You."

Sales, Soupy (1926–1994).

This comedian, born Milton Hines, starred on *The Soupy Sales Show*, which was widely syndicated in the 1960s. In 1955, ABC chose him as the network summer replacement for *Kukla, Fran & Ollie*. In 1959, he hosted a Saturday morning program for children called *Lunch with Soupy Sales*. David Newman and Robert Benton, who later went on to achieve fame as Hollywood scriptwriters, said of Soupy Sales: "Soupy is television. Put him in another medium and he'd vanish. He belongs on that little screen, live, trading one-liners with the puppets and the cameramen as if there were no difference between them."

Savalas, Telly (1924–1993).

Savalas breaks the stereotype of a news director because that is just what he once was for ABC. But then in his thirties the acting bug bit. *Armstrong Circle Theatre, The Untouchables, The Fugitive*—the telly roles began to pile up, but they all led to one: Detective Kojak. It was as Kojak on the show of the same name that Telly Savalas will be remembered. He will always be thought of as the bearish, bald-headed, lollipop sucking. tough-as-nails cop on the streets of New York, muttering his immortal: "Who loves ya, baby?"

Seymour, Jane (1951–   ).

Seymour began her theatrical career as a dancer with the Royal Festival Ballet. Then she was an actress in movies and on TV in England. In the 1970s she came to the U.S. for her first of many roles as the beautiful, somewhat aloof femme fatale. After *Captains and the Kings, Seventh Avenue, East of Eden*, and *War and*

Television Performers Born on Christmas Day

John Ashley	Barbara Mandrell
Earl Brown	Tony Martin
Dean Cameron	Mike Mazurki
Frank Ferguson	Irish McCalla
Fred Hillebrand	Robert L. Ripley
Mabel King	Gary Sandy
Barton MacLane	Rod Serling

Remembrance, she was bestowed with the title "Queen of the Miniseries."

Shatner, William (1931–). This Canadian actor appeared on *Studio One*, *Omnibus*, *Naked City*, *The Twilight Zone*, and the *Outer Limits* and was a regular on *For the People* and *The Barbary Coast* (1975–76). He was Sergeant Hooker on *T. J. Hooker* (1982–86) and is the host of *Rescue 911* (1989–). However, it will be his Captain James T. Kirk on *Star Trek* (1966–69) for which he will always be remembered. Shatner plays Kirk in the classic mold of the American hero, never losing his cool even when the U.S.S. *Enterprise* runs into trouble as it goes "where no man has gone before."

Shore, Dinah (1917–1994). Few people realize that this popular singer and daytime talk show host actually first appeared on television as early as 1939, when she was seen in a special broadcast shown at the New York World Fair. In 1951, she appeared twice a day on a 15-minute show sponsored by Chevrolet—*Chevy Show*. When it became an hour-long show, the slogan as sung by Shore— "see the U.S.A. in your Chevrolet"—entered into the national vocabulary.

William Shatner, of Star Trek fame, and Greg Evigan, from Tek War.

Selleck, Tom (1945–   ). Selleck's first break on TV was *Lancer: Yesterday's Vengeance* in 1969. Next he was someone tall, dark, and handsome on *The Young and the Restless* (1974–75) until he landed the Thomas Magnum role on the show *Magnum P.I.* that made him a poster boy on many an office worker's wall. In recent years Selleck has turned to feature films such as *Three Men and a Baby* and *Mr. Baseball.*

Tom Selleck was frequently hailed as America's sexiest TV actor.

Silvers, Phil (1912–1985). Silvers worked his way up through vaudeville to two hits on Broadway, *High Button Shoes* in 1947 and *Top Banana* in 1951. But it was all a prelude to his portrayal of Sergeant Ernie Bilko on *The Phil Silvers Show* from 1955 to 1959. (The show was originally titled *You'll Never Get Rich*, but it became obvious after a couple of months that it was merely a star vehicle for Silvers.) Bilko was the con man extraordinaire. His aversion to work was as strong as his attraction to wealth, not an easy duo to pull off when you're in the employ of the U.S. Army. But Bilko did it by good humoredly bilking those around him with a silver tongue. After winning two Emmys in 1955, Silvers never achieved such fame again, as he spells out in his autobiography, *The Laugh's on Me.*

Skelton, Red (1910–   ).
The Red Skelton Show was a mainstay on Tuesday night—placing in the top 20 TV shows 16 times from 1951 to 1971. The son of a clown, Red followed in the footsteps of a father he never knew. He went from being a circus clown to radio comedy in the 1930s and finally to TV in the 1950s. Skelton created such wonderful characters as Sheriff Deadeye, Clem Kadiddlehopper, Freddy the Freeloader, Willie Lump Lump, Cauliflower McPugg, and San Fernando Red. It is not hard to guess which one was the sharpshooter, the mooch, the drunk, the boxer, or the con artist. The sketch that stays with many was the night Skelton played a politician who mistakenly picks up his youngster's homework. By the time he reached his "And in conclusion . . . *W, X, Y,* and *Z,*" the audience was in tears. Skelton's 20-year run surpasses by far all other TV comedians.

Smothers Brothers—Tom Smothers (1937–   ) and Dick Smothers (1930–   ).
Starting out as singers on the coffeehouse circuit (Tom played guitar and Dick the bass), these brothers were chosen to host a variety show in 1967. Although it may have helped the careers of Glen Campbell, Mac Davis, and Joan Baez, that is not why are remembered. There was a young, disenchanted, anti–Vietnam War audience that responded to the irreverence of the Smothers Brothers. Everything was fair game for Tom and Dick as well as some of their guests. Pat Paulson ran a mock campaign for president and may have lost real votes for Hubert Humphrey and cost him the presidency. David Steinberg delivered a mock sermon that enraged many ministers across the country. The Smothers Brothers were told to tone it down by the brass at CBS; however, neither

camp budged. But that turns out to be an uneven battle as the network simply cancelled the series. Tom and Dick Smothers were glimpsed from time to time on TV after that, but their day in the sun was over. And when compared to what *Saturday Night Live* presented a few years later, it now all seems rather tame.

Sullivan, Ed (1901–1974).
Sullivan started out as a sports reporter. From there he went to a column about show business called "Little Old New York" for the *New York Daily News*. In 1948 he began his variety show originally called *Toast of the Town*. Sullivan was an improbable host. Labeled "The Great Stone Face," he seemed ill at ease in his body and uncomfortable to be on center stage. Besides, he talked funny, saying things like "a really big shew." (For years it was de rigueur for impressionists to do him.) But Sullivan had an eye for talent and seemed to know what the public wanted to see. When *The Ed Sullivan Show* finally went off the air in 1971, a special Emmy was presented to Ed Sullivan "for his showmanship, taste and personal commitment in entertaining a nation for 23 years."

Thomas, Danny (1914–1991).
Thomas starred as a stand-up comic and family man on *Make Room for Daddy*, which after the first year was renamed *The Danny Thomas Show* (1953–64). Later Thomas formed a production company with Sheldon Leonard that came out with the *The Andy Griffith Show*, *The Dick Van Dyke Show*, *Gomer Pyle, U.S.M.C.*, and *The Mod Squad*. Not bad for someone who originally labeled TV as something "only for idiots."

Van Dyke, Dick (1925–   ).
Van Dyke rose to fame with the role of Rob Petrie on *The Dick Van Dyke Show* (1961–66). Although he won three Emmys, he quit at the height of the show's popularity to concentrate on films. After making *Bye, Bye Birdie*, *Chitty, Chitty, Bang, Bang*, and *Mary Poppins*, Van Dyke returned to TV for *The New Dick Van Dyke Show* (1971–74). Instead of being a head comedy writer (as on the first show), Van Dyke now played a TV show host. Since then he has been in a few made-for-TV movies.

Wagner, Robert (1930–　). After playing a heartthrob in such 1950s movies as *Prince Valiant* and *With a Song in My Heart*, Wagner turned to TV and played the suave lead in several series: Alexander Mundy in *It Takes a Thief* (1968–70), Jonathan Hart in *Hart to Hart* (1979–84), Pete Ryan in *Switch* (1975–78), and James Greyson Culver in *Lime Street* (1985).

Wallace, Mike (1918–　). Wallace started out in Chicago as the narrator for radio's *The Lone Ranger* and *The Green Hornet*. And in the 1950s he was the emcee of six quiz shows on TV. But it was as a CBS News correspondent and on *Mike Wallace Interviews*, a show that ran from 1957 to 1958, that his challenging interviewing style was established. Ten years later he began as a co-editor of *60 Minutes* and has been there ever since. Although he has won numerous Emmys on *60 Minutes*, one of his most famous shows was "The Uncounted Enemy—A Vietnam Deception" for *CBS Reports*. General William Westmoreland sued CBS for Wallace's assertion that the U.S. Army lied about enemy troop strength. CBS eventually won the lawsuit.

Walters, Barbara (1931–　). Walters had a meteoric rise on *The Today Show*: from staff writer to onscreen regular in 1964 to the cohost spot with Jim Hartz in 1974. Beginning in 1971 Walters was also the host of *Not for Women Only*. But it was the bidding war in 1976 between ABC and NBC for her services that brought Walters to national consciousness. She chose ABC's million-dollar-a-year offer because she would be the coanchor with Harry Reasoner of the *ABC Evening News*—the first woman coanchor of a major network news program. Since 1984, Barbara Walters has been the cohost of *20/20* with Hugh Downs and has had her own *Barbara Walters Specials*—interviews with subjects ranging from chiefs of state to popular personalities.

Quite a bit of material has been written about television stars, but what about their fans? Some fans go to numerous sacrifice to see their favorite stars. In his book about his adventures in the wonderful wacky world of TV—*Hi-Ho Steverino* (1992)—Allen tells us about some of his die-hard followers, including Dorothy Miller and "Lillian Lillian." Allen says Dorothy Miller followed him from Hollywood to New York: "Incredibly, she came to our show every night by train from Philadelphia where she worked as a clerk-typist for the U.S. Army Quartermaster Corps." As for the woman known as "Lillian Lillian," "The oddest thing about Lillian was that wherever we went, she showed up. When we did the *Tonight* show once at Niagara Falls, there she was, smiling from the front row. And she followed our circus to Havana, to Hollywood, and to Fort Worth, Texas. I never knew how she got her tickets, how she managed to get a front-row seat, or where she stayed in the various cities to which she followed us."

Young, Robert (1907–   ). Young was on the radio with *Father Knows Best* before its TV run from 1954 to 1960. In his role as Jim Anderson, Robert Young won an Emmy as your basic Mr. Nice Guy who sells insurance and still has plenty of quality time for his family. After that Young played Cameron Garrett Brooks, a writer, on *Window on Main Street* from 1961 to 1962. Young made a TV movie about a doctor that became the long-running (1969–76) series *Marcus Welby, M.D.* Young won another Emmy for playing the archetype of the family doctor—the kind of doctor that no one seems to have.

Robert Young proved that Father really did know best.

Zimbalist, Efrem Jr. (1918–   ). This son of classical music stars, violinist Efrem Zimbalist and opera diva Alma Gluck, first won fame playing a private eye. From 1958 to 1964 he was Stuart Bailey, a button-downed, pipe-smoking Ph.D. on *77 Sunset Strip*. His other major TV success was as Inspector Lewis Erskine on *The F.B.I.*

The Fans

Fan Clubs

Andy Griffith Show, The

The Andy Griffith Rerun
   Watcher's Club
27 Music Square
Suite 146
Nashville, TN 37203

The Andy Griffith
   Appreciation Society
John Meroney
P.O. Box 330
Clemmons, NC 27012

Avengers, The

On Target, The Avengers
c/o Dave Rogers
114 Dartmouith Street
Burslem, Stoke-on-Trent,
Staffs ST6 IHE UK

Battlestar Galactica

Charlie Clint
7716 North Fessenden
   Street
Portland, OR 97203

Bewitched

I Put a Spell on You
The Bewitched Fan Club
1551 Eaton Avenue
San Carlos, CA 94070

Blake's 7

The Blake's 7 Information
   Network
c/o Heather Nachman
1305 Maywood Road.
Richmond, VA 23229

Dark Shadows

The World of Dark
    Shadows
c/o Kathleen Resch
P.O. Box 2262
Mission Station
Santa Clara, CA 95055

Jim Pierson
P.O. Box 92
Maplewood, NJ 07040

Dr. Who

Companions of Dr. Who
Charles L. Duval
P.O. Box 56764
New Orleans, LA 70156

The Dr. Who Fan Club of
    America
P.O. Box 6026
Denver, CO 80206

Dr. Who Information
    Network
Geoffrey Toop
P.O. Box 912
Station F
Toronto, Ont. M4Y 2N9
    Canada

Hitchhiker's Guide to the Galaxy

Galactic Hitchhiker's Guild
3039 NE 181st
Portland, OR 97230

Honeymooners, The

The Honeymooners Fan
    Club
RALPH
c/o C. W. Post Center
Greenvale, NY 11543

Howdy Doody

Jeff Judson
12 Everitts Hill Road
Flemington, NJ 08822

The Howdy Doody Times
12 Everitts Hill Road
Flemington, NJ 08822

I Love Lucy

We Love Lucy
Box 480216
Los Angeles, CA 90048

Laramie

Marcia Studley
2108 Lorenzo Lane
Sacramento, CA 95864

Lost in Space

International Irwin Allen
    Fan Club
c/o Joel Eisner
1671 16th Street #129
Brooklyn, NY 11229

Some Board Games Inspired by Television Shows and What They Might Be Selling for Today If You Can Find Them

Game	Year	Manufacturer	Price
Have Gun Will Travel	1959	Parker Brothers	$35
Gomer Pyle	1964	Transogram Board Game	$25
Patty Duke	1963	Milton Bradley	$20
Get Smart: Exploding Time Bomb Game			$65
I Dream of Jeannie	1965	Milton Bradley	$30
Barnabus Collins "Dark Shadows"			$40
Colombo Detective	1973	Milton Bradley	$15
Dukes of Hazzard	1981	Ideal Co.	$10
6 Million Dollar Man	1975	Parker Brothers	$10
Ben Casey, M.D.	1961	Transogram	$30
Let's Make a Deal	1970	Ideal	$20
Flying Nun	1968	Milton Bradley	$25
My Favorite Martian Game	1960s		$75

Individuals seeking information about purchasing television collectibles might read issues of *Toy Shop: Toys for Sale,* "the nation's only indexed toy publication." It is published at 700 East State Street, Iola, WI 54990. Single copies sell for $3.50.

Lost in Space Fannish
   Alliance
c/o Flint Mitchell
7331 Terri Robyn Drive
St. Louis, MO 63129

Man from U.N.C.L.E., The

U.N.C.L.E. HQ
Lynda Mendoza
P.O. Box 165
Downer's Grove, IL 60515

Mission: Impossible and Space: 1999

Barbara Bain/Martin
   Landau Fan Club
c/o Terry S. Bowers
603 North Clark Street
River Falls, WI 54022

Mister Ed

The Mister Ed Fan Club
P.O. Box 1009
Cedar Hill, TX 75104

Monkees, The

Monkee Business Fanzine
Maggie McManus
2770 South Broad Street
Trenton, NJ 08610

Prisoner, The

Six of One
Bruce Clark
871 Clover Drive
North Wales, PA 19454

Once Upon a Time
David Lawrence
515 Ravenel Circle
Seneca, SC 29678

Rockford Files, The

The Cannell Files (Stephen
   Cannell shows)
c/o Debbie Okoniewski
4951 Cherry Avenue #83
San Jose, CA 95118

Starsky and Hutch

Between Friends
c/o Carol Huffman
1804 Barron Lane
Forth Worth, TX 76112

Star Trek

Star Trek Welcommittee
(guide to all Star Trek
   groups)
P.O. Box 12
Saranac, MI 48881

Starfleet (82 chapters)
Starfleet HQ
P.O. Box 1470
San Antonio, TX 76112

Star Trek: The Official Fan
  Club
Dan Madsen
P.O. Box 111000
Aurora, CO 80011

Star Trekkers/All Channels
  Open
Vicky Walters
c/o J. A. Siefert
P.O. Box 286
Wildwood, FL 34785

Westerns

Western Heroes
  Appreciation Society
743 Harvard
St. Louis, MO 63130

Westerns & Serials Fan Club

Norman Kietzer
Route 1, Box 103
Vernon Center, MN 56090

Wild Wild West

Romance on the Rails
c/o Lori Beatty
5233 Elkhorn
Greenwell Springs, LA
  70739

More Complete Listings of Fan Clubs Are Available From:

The Fan Club Directory
2730 Baltimore Avenue
Pueblo, CO 18003

Fandom Directory
Harry A. Hopkins
Fandata Publications
7761 Asterella Court
Springfield, VA 22152

The Fandom Directory
P.O. Box 4278
San Bernardino, CA 92409

The National Association
  of Fan Clubs
Blanche Trinajstick
2730 Baltimore Avenue
Pueblo, CO 81003

Pop Stand Express
4951 Cherry Avenue #83
San Jose, CA 95118
(fan magazines &
  newsletters)

Some More TV Collectibles and (Approximately) What You Would Pay for Them If You Could Find Them

Cosmopolitan Magazine for January 1953 with Lucille Ball on the cover: $75

Hogan's Heroes WWII jeep model kit: $85
Complete set of 1979 Fleer *Gong Show* trading cards (52 different images): $20

November 1958 *TV Guide* with Jack Paar on the cover: $15

Howdy Doody lunchbox: $175

Gunsmoke lunchbox: $85

Paperback of *Rod Serling's Night Gallery*: $12

1966 *The Munsters* Paper Dolls (published by Whitman): $30

1963 Milton Bradley Beverly Hills Card Game: $25

1976 *Howdy Doody* paint-by-numbers kit: $25

Dennis the Menace hand puppet: $28

Farah Fawcett *Charlie's Angels* doll (by Hasbro): $25

TV Museums

The Museum of Television and Radio (MT&R), located in New York City, has scheduled screenings every day (except Monday) in its two theaters and screening rooms. In addition, MT&R has a library of 50,000 radio and television programs for review in special listening and console rooms. There is also a gallery that features special exhibits about radio and television as well as a museum shop.
The Museum of Television and Radio
25 West 52 Street
New York, NY 10019-6101 (212)621-6800.

Cable TV has its own museum. The National Cable Television Center and Museum is located at Pennsylvania State University, Sparks Building (Level B), University Park, PA 16802. The phone number is (814) 865-1875. The fax is (814) 863-7808.

Famous Sign-offs

"So long for now, and spaceman's luck to all of you."
  —*Tom Corbett,* Space Cadet

"The story you have just seen is true. The names have been changed to protect the innocent."
  —*Announcer George Fenneman at the conclusion of each* Dragnet *episode.*

"There are eight million stories in the naked city; this has been one of them."
  —*Naked City*

"Peace."
  —*Dave Garroway* (Wide Wide World)

"Good night . . . and good luck."
  —*Edward R. Murrow* (Person to Person)

"Goodbye, kids."
  —*Clarabell at the end of the final episode of* The Howdy Doody Show *on September 24, 1960. (Lew Anderson, in continuing the tradition of this clown, had never spoken on camera before.)*

"Next week, the Beatles and the Pieta."
  —*Ed Sullivan* (Toast of the Town)

"Good night, David."
"Good night, Chet."
> —*David Brinkley and Chet Huntley* (NBC News)

"[Perhaps] there will be better and happier news, one day, if we work at it."
> —*Chet Huntley on his last broadcast of* NBC Nightly News *on July 31, 1970*

"Good health, good life, and may God bless. Goodnight."
> —*Red Skelton on his farewell show after 18 years on network TV on August 29, 1971*

"Na Nu, Na Nu."
> —*Mork* (Mork & Mindy)

"We now return control of your television set to you until next week at this same time, when the Control Voice will take you to . . . the Outer Limits."
> —*The Outer Limits*

Index